A Life of George Westinghouse

Biography of the Engineering Pioneer – his Electrical Inventions, Railway Air Brake and Successes in Business

By Henry G. Prout

PANTIANOS
CLASSICS

Published by Pantianos Classics

ISBN-13: 978-1-78987-267-5

First published in 1921

George Westinghouse

Contents

Preface .... *v*

Chapter One - Introductory 7

Chapter Two - The Air Brake 19

Chapter Three - Friction Draft Gear 50

Chapter Four - General Sketch of Electric Activities 56

Chapter Five - The Induction Motor and Meter 76

Chapter Six - The Rotary Converter 81

Chapter Seven - The Chicago World's Fair 83

Chapter Eight - Niagara Falls 87

Chapter Nine - Electric Traction 96

Chapter Ten - Steam and Gas Engines 107

Chapter Eleven - The Turbo-Generator 121

Chapter Twelve - Signaling and Interlocking 128

Chapter Thirteen - Natural Gas 135

Chapter Fourteen - Various Interests and Activities 139

Chapter Fifteen - European Enterprises 155

Chapter Sixteen - Financial Methods, Reorganization, Equitable-Life Episode 162

Chapter Seventeen - The Personality of George Westinghouse ... 169

Chapter Eighteen - The Meaning of George Westinghouse 187

    Appendix A - Patents 194

    Appendix B - *Group Lists Comments on Selected Patents* 206

"The history of the world is the biography of great men." - *Carlyle*

Preface

MANY officers and members of The American Society of Mechanical Engineers have thought that the Society ought to publish the lives of some of its great men. In 1912 it published a special edition of the "Autobiography of John Fritz, Honorary Member and Past President." This life of George Westinghouse, Honorary Member and Past President, is the second in what may be a series of such biographies.

The activities of George Westinghouse were many and varied, and many different activities went on simultaneously. He dealt in the same week, and often in the same day, with organization, financial and executive affairs, commercial affairs, and the engineering details of half a dozen companies in two hemispheres. They were as far apart in kind as the air brake and natural gas, and as far apart in geography as San Francisco and St. Petersburg. That being so, it seemed that a chronological narrative would of necessity lead to some confusion, not to say fatigue, for the reader. It was decided to treat each topic by itself without regard to what might be going on at the same time in other fields, with a short preliminary chapter to which the reader might return to orient himself should he care, for instance, to know what other serious things were in hand at a critical moment in the history of the air brake. It was hoped that by this treatment a certain continuity of impression might be kept in each story told by itself.

Another reason for the segregation of topics is their technicality. By their nature they cannot be easy reading, even for all engineers, and segregation makes skipping easy. Finally, from the first chapter and the last two, a reader who is quite impervious to engineering of any kind (if such a being exists) can get a notion of Westinghouse and of what he meant to mankind.

The variety in Westinghouse's life seemed to dictate the form that a biography should take. Other conditions seemed to indicate the best way of preparing it. He left no written record except in the files of his numerous companies. He wrote almost no private letters. He kept no journals or even notebooks. He made but few addresses and wrote few papers. Some record of his work might be made after a laborious search of office files, so far as the files of forty-eight years still exist, but the result would be formal and without color. It would not be a life, and George Westinghouse was a very human being. Furthermore no one man has the range of knowledge and the comprehensive judgment of the relative importance of the things done to fit him to write an adequate life of George Westinghouse. Lord Rosebery said that it would take a syndicate to write the life of Gladstone; perhaps this is quite as true of a life of Westinghouse.

Fortunately, there are many men still living and working who were close to Westinghouse, some of them almost from the beginning of his active life, and those men have contributed liberally from the stores of their memories and impressions. The editor's duty has been to digest these contributions, to coordinate them, and to keep a reasonable perspective. In this he has been aided by the Committee of The American Society of Mechanical Engineers appointed for that purpose. Sometimes the language of the writers has been used with little change. This is particularly the case with the descriptive parts of the air brake chapter, although even there large liberties have been taken. [1] Generally the contributions sent in have been freely rewritten, as was expected by those who wrote them. Such a method, while very ancient, has its difficulties, but the outcome in this case may serve to give the reader a fairly just conception of the man of whom Lord Kelvin said: "George Westinghouse is in character and achievements one of the great men of our time."

The purpose has been to write a life of George Westinghouse. For clearness and accuracy, and to give authority for statements made, it has seemed well to mention the names of some of those who helped him, but there has been no attempt to make systematic or approximately complete mention of the many men to whose cooperation he owed a great deal; one would not know where to stop. By those qualities of mind and heart which this book will make known to the reader, Westinghouse attached to himself a large group of able, loyal, and even devoted assistants. Amongst them were many brilliant and constructive minds organizers, administrators, executives, and engineers. The committee and the editor regret that it is not practicable to enter upon the delicate task of telling what these men did in the work here chronicled.

For the material in this book the reader is much indebted to Henry Herman Westinghouse, Charles A. Terry, John F. Miller, Benjamin G. Lamme, Paul D. Cravath, Herbert T. Herr, and Lewis B. Stillwell. Important passages and suggestions have been supplied by Edwin M. Herr, Loyall A. Osborne, Charles F. Scott, Reginald Belfield, Calvert Townley, Frank H. Shepard, Hubert C. Tener, Albert Kapteyn, T. U. Parsons, J. H. Luke, Albert Chinn, and J. J. Elmer.

The committee in charge of the work were: Charles A. Terry, chairman; Paul D. Cravath, Alexander C. Humphreys, James H. McGraw, Charles F. Scott, Lewis B. Stillwell, Ambrose Swasey, with Henry Herman Westinghouse always in consultation.

[1] The editor is particularly grateful to Mr. John F. Miller, who put into the air brake chapter labor, knowledge, taste, and judgment.

The advance of mankind has everywhere depended on the production of men of genius. - *Huxley*.

Chapter One - Introductory

GEORGE WESTINGHOUSE was born in the little village of Central Bridge, New York, October 6, 1846. He came of Westphalian stock. His great-grandfather, John Hendrik Westinghouse, came to America with his mother, a widow, in 1755, John being then fifteen years old. They settled in that part of New Hampshire Grants which later became Vermont, at Pownal, Bennington County. It was a good place to settle. It was one of the little foci of the free colonial spirit. It was named for Thomas Pownal (or Pownall), who became Governor of Massachusetts in 1757, and was a friend of Franklin, of the colonists, and of intercolonial union. Carlyle says that he reported to Pitt his fear that "the French will eat America from us in spite of our teeth." In Pownal the Westinghouses acquired land and built a log cabin, and here John cleared the land, raised a large family, and died in 1802. From him his great-grandson inherited stature, for John stood six feet four inches high, and inherited mechanical knack, for John made for his mother an inlaid wooden work-box while they were on the ocean. This box is still possessed by a member of the family.

John's son, John Ferdinand, passed his life in Pownal. He had twelve children, the fifth of whom was George, born in 1809 and died in 1884. This George married Emaline Vedder and they had ten children, the eighth having been the George of whom we write. Three generations in the flanks of the Vermont mountains could hardly evolve as complete a Yankee as six generations, but in this case the product was reasonably satisfactory. In simplicity and energy, in standards of conduct and habit of thought and in idiom of speech the two Georges could not be distinguished from their neighbors six or seven generations out of Devonshire.

A laborious investigator of the family history, a certain Doctor Carl Alexander von Wistinghausen, writes that "Members of the family have repeatedly won for themselves and their heirs patents of nobility by service rendered to the state." Very likely so; at any rate, there was energy in the blood. One George was a captain in the Russian navy and distinguished himself greatly in battle in command of a frigate, and several of the family were ennobled in the Russian service. Our George Westinghouse had but mild and casual interest in the annals of the family and we find only a few fragments concerning the Wistinghausens or the Westinghouses.

His mother was of Dutch-English stock and was kin to Elihu Vedder, an American artist of considerable repute. Both parents came of generations of farmers and mechanics, neither rich nor poor, self-respecting, self-reliant, and competent, the sort of people who make the bulk and strength of the nation. One has but to study the portrait of the father to see where George Westinghouse got his character. It shows power, courage, dignity, and kindness, and the lofty head indicates not only mental capacity, but imagination. The mother, too, is said to have had imagination, taste, and fancy and a real altruism of spirit. The photographs that we have are not so informing as those of the father, for they were made after she had borne ten children and had endured much sorrow from the death of her husband and sons. Doctor Fisher, a minister who knew the family intimately for many years, writes: "From his mother he gained vivacity, alertness, and a cheerful spirit. She was a woman of clear and definite religious faith and of thoughtful views on great questions. I feel sure she gave to her son reverence and faithfulness." These qualities George had in eminent degree, and he and his wife gave to this mother loving and tender care through the declining years that she spent in their home.

Three of the sons, John, Albert, and George, served in the Union army and navy in the Civil War and won commissions. Albert was a youth of distinct gifts of mind and character. The tradition is that he was the most promising of the sons. He was captured at the battle of Gaines's Mill, was in Libby Prison a short time, was exchanged, and received a commission as second lieutenant in the 2d New York Veteran Volunteer Cavalry. With a comrade he swam a bayou under fire and brought back a bateau which was used to ferry over the command. This deed was mentioned in reports. Albert was killed leading a cavalry charge late in December 1864.

George Westinghouse, Senior.

John served as an engineer officer in the navy. After the war he returned to his father's business in Schenectady. Here he established a night school and mission, and he gave time, money, and work to helping the unfortunate. One of those whom he had befriended, writing in 1913, says: "That man did a great work for hundreds of poor little boys and girls, picking them up out of the streets and helping them to start in a new life. I have accidentally met three men who are holding good positions and claim they owe all that they are to John Westinghouse."

This excellent man died comparatively young, and the writer remembers hearing George Westinghouse say that the first night in his life that he lay awake was the night after John died. George was forty-four years old when John died and for twenty-five years he had led a life that might have hardened a man's sensibilities.

George, too, had war experience which had its effect upon his character, for it was his privilege to live through a great historical period and to take an active part in it. He was in the middle of his fifteenth year when the Civil War broke out and he promptly ran away to enlist. With like promptness his father nipped his military career then, but two years later, when he was about sixteen and a half, he was permitted to go to the war as an enlisted man. After a little service in the infantry and cavalry he became an engineer officer in the navy. A boy so young, going into a veteran army, had little chance for distinction, although boys but little older, who entered service even later, did sometimes get to be field officers. The chief interest in this episode is that it was characteristic of the individual and the nation. The lads of those days rushed to the colors with beautiful spirit. Gaily they tramped the weary marches. Firmly they endured and fought. Gladly they volunteered for desperate deeds. The records of the War Department show that 41.4 per cent of the enrolments in the Union army were boys of eighteen and under, and 77.7 per cent were twenty-one and under. [1]

Amongst these gallant and ardent youths were the Westinghouse brothers. The boys did not realize then what a great thing they were doing. Their historical imagination was undeveloped. They had little capacity for analysis or expression. They did their work at the front and then went home, to college or work, and their war book was closed and they thought little about it and talked less. They did not suspect that they were heroes. It was quite the fashion to think of serving one's country as an adventure and a privilege and duty. The hero talk of the platform and the newspapers was a later development. The boys of the sixties did not know it, but in mind and character they were lifted up and strengthened by contact with the deeds and sacrifices of war. They became the leaders of a nation, which was enriched and strengthened beyond estimate by their war training. All of this Westinghouse came to understand, as the years went on, but he seldom talked of his war experiences. In an address delivered a little more than two years before his death he said: "My early greatest capital was the experience and skill acquired from the opportunity given me, when I was young, to work with all kinds of machinery, coupled later with lessons in that discipline to which a soldier is required to submit, and the acquirement of a spirit of readiness to carry out the instructions of superiors."

Of the important place that the youngest brother, Henry Herman Westinghouse, has taken in the world, we may not speak here. Many of those who read this volume know it well.

Briefly, George Westinghouse had an inheritance of good blood and sound tradition. He was born and reared in an environment of work, thrift, and responsibility. He did not happen; he was a logical product, and ran true to form. An eminent engineer who has been in the Westinghouse service since 1888, writing of his early impressions of Westinghouse, says: "He did not appeal to me, even then, as being a wizard, but he seemed to be a plain human being with lots of initiative, with nerve to attempt difficult things, and money enough to see them through to success or failure. He met my ideas of what an engineer should be. I do not think that my earliest impressions were changed much in later years. I acquired further ideas of him as I learned more about him, but these were additions rather than modifications."

His father had much mechanical skill and ingenuity. Seven patents for his inventions are now before us and there are said to be one or two more. These all have the fundamental qualities of the inventions of his son. Not one of the son's patents is a flash out of the blue sky or a vision on the horizon. Every one is calculated to meet a situation that he has seen in his own practice. Every one is for something to be made in his own shops and no one of them was invented to sell or as a speculation. Every one is worked out with such completeness of detail that a competent shop foreman could take the Patent Office drawings and specifications and build an operative machine. In each one we see the engineer and the trained mechanic. This is true of practically every one of some four hundred inventions patented by him. The father's inventions were for comparatively simple mechanisms but they had the same underlying qualities of practical use and of thoroughness in mechanical design. They were for horsepowers, winnowers, thrashing machines, and a sawing machine, all of which were the standard product of the Westinghouse shop at Schenectady. The latest of these patents was issued in 1865, the year in which the son returned from his service in the navy, and three months before the issue of his own first patent.

In 1856 George Westinghouse, Sr., established in Schenectady a shop for making agricultural machinery, mill machinery, and small steam engines. This shop, bearing the sign "G. Westinghouse & Co.," long stood at the very gate of the great works of the General Electric Company. Here George Westinghouse, Jr., passed a happy and busy boyhood. This shop was his real academy and college; his university was the world. In 1865 he was mustered out, a veteran of the Civil War, an officer, not yet nineteen years old. In September he entered Union College, Schenectady, as a sophomore and three months later he went back to the shop. This was the end of his college career. His father was able and willing to send him through college, but George preferred active work. There is an old "Hands Book" of G. Westinghouse & Company now existing. We find that George began work in the shop at fifty cents a day in May 1860. He was then thirteen and a half. He worked into September, and in the next March began work again at seventy-five cents a day and kept at it till near the end of September. In March 1862, he began again at seventy-five cents a day, which was raised in April to eighty-seven and one-half cents, and at this rate he worked till the end of February, when he was promoted to a dollar a day. At the end of April he was raised to one dollar twelve and one-half cents till the end of September 1863, when the record stops, to be taken up again in July 1865. In the meantime Uncle Sam had paid him his modest wages. From this little record we can deduce quite a number of interesting things, amongst them the conclusion that after George Westinghouse was thirteen years old he had about a year and a half in school and college. It is not a deduction from this, but it is a fact, that he spoke and wrote uncommonly good English.

With the return of George Westinghouse to his father's shop the systematic work of his life began, not to be interrupted until his death forty-nine years later. The first patent issued to him, so far as we find, was October 31, 1865, for a rotary steam engine. His work on this invention had begun two or three years before, and he continued to invent unceasingly as long as he lived. In his last illness he designed a wheel chair to be operated by a little electric motor. The rotary engine was a favorite plaything for many years, and the writer remembers seeing Westinghouse, when he was forty-five years old, wearing a frock coat, working over a rotary engine in his shop in an interval between a board meeting and a reception. It was the equivalent of a rubber of bridge, or a game of golf. It is hardly necessary to say that the rotary engine never served any other purpose except that it may have affected his line of thought when he took up the steam turbine, as will be told in the chapter on steam engines. Westinghouse would not have said that this is exactly true. He used to relate that a small boy who had made a picture of a minister and found it unsatisfactory added a tail and called it a dog. Encouraged by this, Westinghouse turned his rotary engine around and made an excellent water meter of it, and established another industry.

Patents for a car replacer (for re-railing a car or engine), and for a railroad frog followed in 1867, 1868, and 1869, and these inventions were the foundation of a little business which seemed to a courageous young man to justify his marriage, which took place August 8, 1867, that is before he was twenty-one. His courtship was as impetuous as that of Lord Randolph Churchill, who was engaged to Miss Jerome three days after he first saw her. Westinghouse met Marguerite Erskine Walker by chance on a railroad train. That evening he told his father and mother that he had met the woman he was going to marry. The wedding soon followed. Mrs. Westinghouse was a devoted wife and survived her husband but three months. For nearly forty-seven years they lived together, and through these years affection, faith, and trust never flagged. When they were on the same continent there was daily communication by telephone, after the long-distance telephone was developed. When they were separated by the Atlantic there was a daily cable message. They died respectively in March and June 1914, and are buried in the National Cemetery at Arlington. Their only child is George Westinghouse, 3d.

Their first home was "Solitude," in the Homewood district of Pittsburgh. Here a substantial old house was added to and changed until it became a commodious dwelling, and handsome lawns and gardens grew with fortune. This home was always in commission, however long or far they might wander. It was the seat of a large and handsome hospitality. There were few houses in the land in which one would meet such a number and variety of interesting people as passed through that simple and comfortable home. In course of time they established another home at Lenox, Massachusetts, which was, in later years, the favorite residence of Mrs. Westinghouse. For a few years they maintained a house in Washington during the season, but it never became one of their homes.

The foundation of the fame and fortune of George Westinghouse was the air brake. His first brake patent was issued April 13, 1869, he being then twenty-two and a half years old, and still resident at Schenectady. It was reissued July 29, 1873, the inventor being then resident in Pittsburgh. In the years between he had taken out twenty or more other patents on details of brake apparatus. His attorneys were Bakewell, Christy & Kerr. All of these gentlemen (now dead) became eminent in patent law, but they had no greater professional pleasure and distinction than this of having helped at the birth of the air brake. The twenty-odd air brake patents issued in the four years to the middle of 1873 by no means exhausted the fountains of invention in that art. They continued to flow copiously for years; the particulars will be related in other chapters.

In a system of traffic control the relations of brakes and signals are close, and it was natural that the attention of Westinghouse should have been engaged by experiments, inventions, and practice that he saw developing in England and at home. As early as 1880 he acquired the American rights for English patents for interlocking switches and signals, and about the same time he bought certain American patents for the control of signals by track circuits. This was the foundation of another great industry which will be described in a later chapter. In this field Westinghouse made radical and highly important inventions, taking out numerous patents; but so many interests crowded upon him that, although his productive activity in signaling and interlocking was intense for a few years, the period was comparatively short. In one year, 1881, for instance, we find six patents in signaling and interlocking, one of them fundamental and revolutionary. In the same year we find ten brake patents, one for a telephone switch and four in other arts twenty-one patents in one year.

The eleven years 1880-1890 inclusive brought many great things and were a period of prodigious activity. In those years the Westinghouse Brake Company, Limited (British) was started; the Union Switch & Signal Company was launched; the natural-gas episode began, and the Philadelphia Company was formed; the Westinghouse Machine Company, the Westinghouse Electric Company, and the Westinghouse Electric Company, Limited (British) were started; the quick-action brake was produced, and thus the one great crisis in the history of the air brake was met and triumphantly passed; and, perhaps most important of all, Westinghouse revolutionized the electric art by his vision of the possibilities of the alternating current. The particulars of all these deeds will be set forth in their proper places. Here we only ask attention to the capacity for work, the boldness of conception, and the marvellous activity of creative imagination shown by Westinghouse from the beginning of his thirty-fourth year to the end of his forty-fourth. He did many things and great things in the twenty-four years that followed, but it is not an unreasonable suggestion that those eleven years were the years of his greatest creative power. In those years he took out 134 patents, an average of over one patent a month, and he stimulated and directed the work of many other inventors. Meanwhile he began and carried forward the financial and administrative organization of several companies, each one of which might have absorbed the energies of an ordinary man. His commercial and technical activities were felt in England and on the continent of Europe, and he established personal relations with philosophers, as well as with financial and business men, in many countries, and he was not yet forty-five. Bacon says: "A man that is Young in Yeares may be old in Houres, if he have lost no Time. But that happeneth rarely. Generally, youth is like the first Cogitations, not so Wise as the Second. For there is a youth in thoughts as well as in Ages. And yet the Invention of Young Men is more lively than that of Old: And Imaginations streame into their mindes better and, as it were more divinely." It would be hard to say when imaginations streamed most divinely into the mind of Westinghouse.

We have no yardstick by which to measure them. They are only partly revealed in his inventions; and inventions, in the narrow sense of the word, were not by any means the greatest of his imaginations. We shall see, as we go on, conceptions and visions which have affected mankind far more than anything that he invented. But the number of his patented inventions gives us a quick notion of his fertility. We have seen that in an amazing eleven years he took out more than a patent a month; but for forty-eight years he took out a patent every month and a half.

A quick and comprehensive view of the extent of his work in organizing companies is given in the table of Westinghouse companies inserted here. The table includes a very few companies which Westinghouse did not establish, and in which he personally or through his other companies never owned a majority of the stock. In those companies he did have investments of more or less importance, and he did, during their formative years, exercise great and even controlling influence. He served them as president and director, or perhaps with no office but with money or credit. He was never an idle passenger in any enterprise. A picture of his life would not be complete without a glimpse of such companies, but it does not seem wise to take the reader's time or to divert his attention by circumstantial accounts of them. One of the more important of these companies of temporary interest to him is the Standard Underground Cable Company, of which Westinghouse was president ten years, 1886-1896, and which is now the largest maker of electric wires and cables in the United States, with an annual gross business of about

WESTINGHOUSE ASSOCIATED COMPANIES
CHRONOLOGICALLY ARRANGED

WESTINGHOUSE AIR BRAKE CO.
WESTINGHOUSE EUROPEAN BRAKE CO.
COMPAGNIE DES FREINS WESTINGHOUSE
AMERICAN BRAKE CO.
WESTINGHOUSE BRAKE CO., LTD.
WESTINGHOUSE MACHINE CO.
WESTINGHOUSE FOUNDRY CO.
UNION SWITCH & SIGNAL CO.
WESTINGHOUSE CO. (SCHENECTADY)
PHILADELPHIA COMPANY
WESTINGHOUSE BREMSEN GESELLSCHAFT
WESTINGHOUSE, CHURCH, KERR & CO.
SAWYER-MAN ELECTRIC CO.
WESTINGHOUSE ELECTRIC CO.
CONSOLIDATED ELECTRIC LIGHT CO.
UNITED ELECTRIC LIGHT & POWER CO.
FUEL GAS AND ELECTRICAL ENG'R'G CO.
EAST PITTSBURGH IMPROVEMENT CO.
WESTINGHOUSE ELECTRIC & MANUFACTURING CO.
WESTINGHOUSE ELECTRIC CO., LTD. (LONDON)
BRYANT ELECTRIC COMPANY
PITTSBURGH METER CO.
WATERHOUSE ELECTRIC CO.
PERKINS ELECTRIC SWITCH MANUFACTURING CO.
STANDARD UNDERGROUND CABLE CO.
STANDARD CAR HEATING & VENTILATING CO.
R. D. NUTTALL CO.
WESTINGHOUSE GLASS CO.
WORLD'S FAIR EQUIPMENT CO.
ELECTRO-MAGNETIC TRACTION CO.
SECURITY INVESTMENT CO.
EMERY PNEUMATIC LUBRICATOR CO.
FRENCH WESTINGHOUSE ELECTRIC CO.
MANHATTAN GENERAL CONSTRUCTION CO.
WALKER ELECTRIC CO.
SOCIÉTÉ ANONYME WESTINGHOUSE (RUSSIA)
BRITISH WESTINGHOUSE ELECTRIC & MFG. CO.
WESTINGHOUSE PATENT BUREAU (LONDON)
NERNST LAMP CO.
CLYDE VALLEY ELECTRIC POWER CO., LTD.
TRACTION & POWER SECURITIES CO.
WESTINGHOUSE AUTOMATIC AIR & STEAM COUPLER CO.
SOCIÉTÉ ANONYME WESTINGHOUSE (FRANCE)
WESTINGHOUSE ELEKTRICITAETS-GESELLSCHAFT, m. b. H.
WESTINGHOUSE TRACTION BRAKE CO.
COOPER HEWITT ELECTRIC CO.
TRAFFORD WATER CO.
WESTINGHOUSE INTERWORKS RAILWAY CO.
McCANDLESS LAMP CO.
CANADIAN WESTINGHOUSE CO., LTD.
LAURENTIDE MICA CO., LTD.
COMPAGNIA ITALIANA WESTINGHOUSE DEI FRENI

WESTINGHOUSE ASSOCIATED COMPANIES
CHRONOLOGICALLY ARRANGED

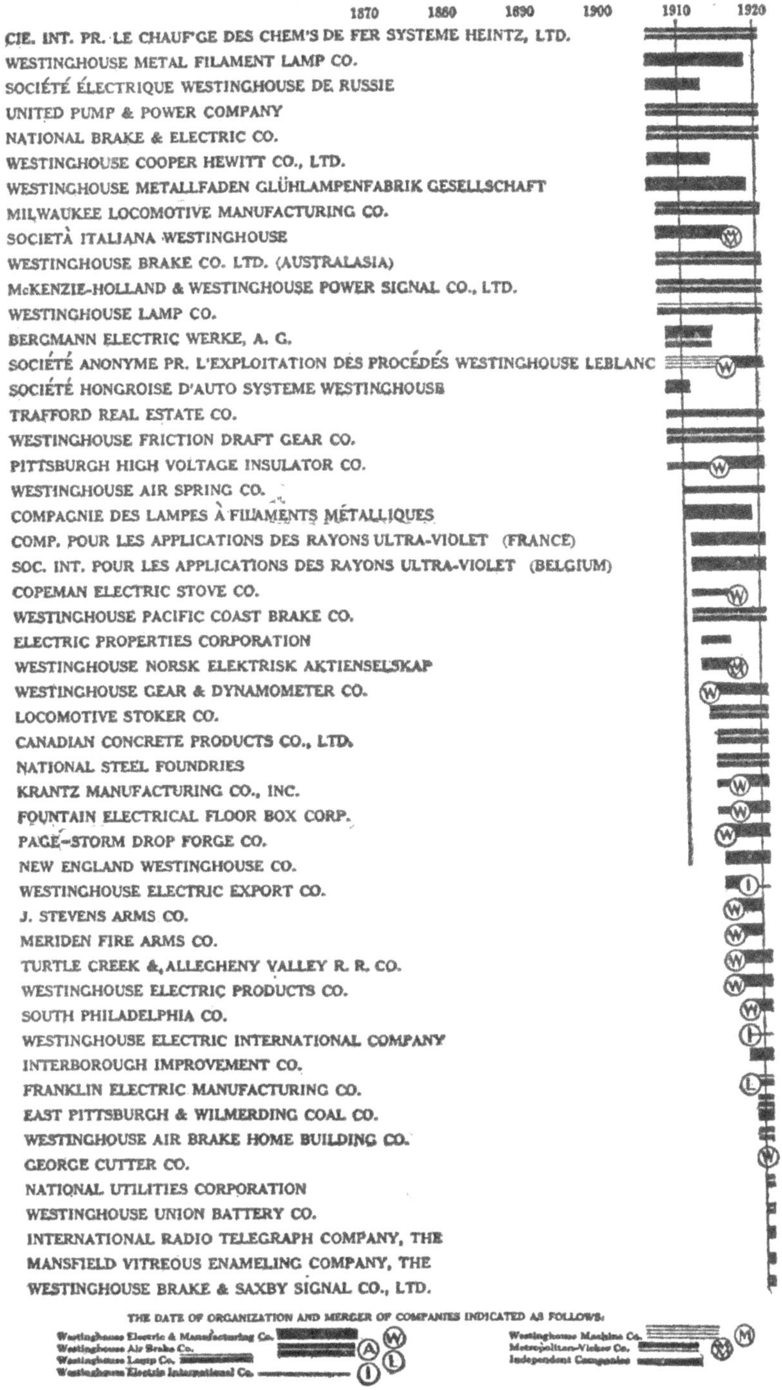

1870　　　1880　　　1890　　　1900　　　1910　　　1920

CIE. INT. PR. LE CHAUF'GE DES CHEM'S DE FER SYSTEME HEINTZ, LTD.
WESTINGHOUSE METAL FILAMENT LAMP CO.
SOCIÉTÉ ÉLECTRIQUE WESTINGHOUSE DE RUSSIE
UNITED PUMP & POWER COMPANY
NATIONAL BRAKE & ELECTRIC CO.
WESTINGHOUSE COOPER HEWITT CO., LTD.
WESTINGHOUSE METALLFADEN GLÜHLAMPENFABRIK GESELLSCHAFT
MILWAUKEE LOCOMOTIVE MANUFACTURING CO.
SOCIETÀ ITALIANA WESTINGHOUSE
WESTINGHOUSE BRAKE CO. LTD. (AUSTRALASIA)
McKENZIE-HOLLAND & WESTINGHOUSE POWER SIGNAL CO., LTD.
WESTINGHOUSE LAMP CO.
BERGMANN ELECTRIC WERKE, A. G.
SOCIÉTÉ ANONYME PR. L'EXPLOITATION DES PROCÉDÉS WESTINGHOUSE LEBLANC
SOCIÉTÉ HONGROISE D'AUTO SYSTEME WESTINGHOUSE
TRAFFORD REAL ESTATE CO.
WESTINGHOUSE FRICTION DRAFT GEAR CO.
PITTSBURGH HIGH VOLTAGE INSULATOR CO.
WESTINGHOUSE AIR SPRING CO.
COMPAGNIE DES LAMPES À FILAMENTS MÉTALLIQUES
COMP. POUR LES APPLICATIONS DES RAYONS ULTRA-VIOLET (FRANCE)
SOC. INT. POUR LES APPLICATIONS DES RAYONS ULTRA-VIOLET (BELGIUM)
COPEMAN ELECTRIC STOVE CO.
WESTINGHOUSE PACIFIC COAST BRAKE CO.
ELECTRIC PROPERTIES CORPORATION
WESTINGHOUSE NORSK ELEKTRISK AKTIENSELSKAP
WESTINGHOUSE GEAR & DYNAMOMETER CO.
LOCOMOTIVE STOKER CO.
CANADIAN CONCRETE PRODUCTS CO., LTD.
NATIONAL STEEL FOUNDRIES
KRANTZ MANUFACTURING CO., INC.
FOUNTAIN ELECTRICAL FLOOR BOX CORP.
PAGE-STORM DROP FORGE CO.
NEW ENGLAND WESTINGHOUSE CO.
WESTINGHOUSE ELECTRIC EXPORT CO.
J. STEVENS ARMS CO.
MERIDEN FIRE ARMS CO.
TURTLE CREEK & ALLEGHENY VALLEY R. R. CO.
WESTINGHOUSE ELECTRIC PRODUCTS CO.
SOUTH PHILADELPHIA CO.
WESTINGHOUSE ELECTRIC INTERNATIONAL COMPANY
INTERBOROUGH IMPROVEMENT CO.
FRANKLIN ELECTRIC MANUFACTURING CO.
EAST PITTSBURGH & WILMERDING COAL CO.
WESTINGHOUSE AIR BRAKE HOME BUILDING CO.
GEORGE CUTTER CO.
NATIONAL UTILITIES CORPORATION
WESTINGHOUSE UNION BATTERY CO.
INTERNATIONAL RADIO TELEGRAPH COMPANY, THE
MANSFIELD VITREOUS ENAMELING COMPANY, THE
WESTINGHOUSE BRAKE & SAXBY SIGNAL CO., LTD.

THE DATE OF ORGANIZATION AND MERGER OF COMPANIES INDICATED AS FOLLOWS:

Westinghouse Electric & Manufacturing Co. — (A) (W)　　Westinghouse Machine Co. — (M)
Westinghouse Air Brake Co.　　　　　　　　　　　　　　Metropolitan-Vickers Co.
Westinghouse Lamp Co. — (L)　　　　　　　　　　　　　Independent Companies
Westinghouse Electric International Co. — (I)

15

$35,000,000. The present president, Mr. Joseph W. Marsh; says: "The value of Mr. Westinghouse's connection with the company soon made itself felt in increased business and the changing of annual losses into profits. Although his official connection with the company terminated in 1896 he always manifested a friendly and helpful interest in its progress during the remainder of his life, and such interest on his part never failed to translate itself in tangible and practical ways that were of great value."

As soon as the air brake was fairly under way in America Westinghouse took it to England, and within ten years, that is, before he was thirty-five, he had organized companies and established shops in England, France, and Russia. He was famous and had a fortune sufficient for his moderate needs. We have taken the years 1880 and 1890 as possibly the period of Westinghouse's greatest creative power; but from what has just been said it is seen that the earlier decade ending with 1880 was rich in accomplishment, but it was confined mostly to the brake.

After 1890 the years were crowded with great events. The crisis of 1893 almost swamped the Electric Company, but it emerged safely. The company secured the contract for lighting the Columbian Exposition of 1893 at Chicago and made a brilliant technical success. This encouraged the development of the company's incandescent lamp industry, and, what was much more important, it had a great influence on the direction and progress of the broader activities of Westinghouse and his engineers in the electrical field. It affected his thought and it strengthened his position in the fierce struggle just opening up. In October 1893, the company took the contract for the first electric generators at Niagara Falls. This was a revolutionary event in the development of the electric art romantic in conception and dramatic in execution. Many eminent men of various nations took part in the preliminary studies, and the foundations of some great reputations in electrical engineering were laid there. The world-meaning of the episode was that the question of the distribution and use of power through the agency of the alternating electric current was settled for all time. For Westinghouse this was a personal victory; some estimate of its meaning to mankind will be attempted later in this volume.

We may now turn back a few years. Late in 1883 Westinghouse became interested in the production and distribution of natural gas, and in 1884 the Philadelphia Company was formed to carry on that industry. In a few years he took out thirty-eight gas patents, mostly for means of distribution and control, and he practically created a new art. These were amongst the 134 patents taken out in the years 1880-1890.

It was a logical consequence of the natural-gas episode that Westinghouse should become interested in gas engines and in the manufacture of fuel gas. The Westinghouse Machine Company, founded by a younger brother, Henry Herman Westinghouse, and later taken over by George, developed and built gas engines of great size and in large numbers. They also built gas producers with some success, but the producer-gas enterprise was disappointing.

About 1895 Westinghouse became interested in the steam turbine and this was an absorbing interest till his death. He continued incessantly to study, invent, and design, and his work profoundly influenced the development of the art. Eventually building turbines became much the largest part of the work of the Westinghouse Machine Company, and, working with the Electric Company, they built many turbo-generator units for power houses, some of them of immense size. The marine side of the industry developed more slowly but it is now very important. The efficient speed of a propeller is low; the efficient speed of a turbine is high; consequently, great efficiency cannot be got from a direct-connected unit. Two possibilities were obvious, to modify the propeller or to interpose between the turbine and u the propeller a reduction gear. Westinghouse made many ingenious, interesting, and costly propeller experiments which so far have been of no practical value. He took up simultaneously (about 1909) a reduction gear invented by Admiral Melville, U. S. N., and Mr. MacAlpine a novel and highly interesting conception. This gear is now much used in turbine-driven ships of the navy.

In 1905 came the explosion in the Equitable Life Assurance Society, which led to the purchase of the stock by Mr. Ryan and the appointment of three trustees to control the reorganization and management of that great concern of international importance. The trustees chosen were Grover Cleveland, Morgan J. O'Brien, and George Westinghouse. As a tribute to character this was one of the greatest honors that Westinghouse ever received, although he had been recognized in many ways. He was a Doctor of Philosophy, Union College; Doctor of Engineering, Koenigliche Technische Hochschule, Berlin; decorated with the Legion of Honor, the Order of the Crown of Italy, and the Order of Leopold, Belgium. He received the Grashof medal, perhaps the highest engineering honor in Germany, and the John Fritz medal, a great engineering honor in America, and the Edison medal of the American Institute of Electrical Engineers. He was one of the two honorary members of the American Association for the Advancement of Science and was an honorary member and served a term as president of The American Society of Mechanical Engineers. He declined honorary degrees from several colleges in America. One only heard of these honors by accident; Westinghouse shrank instinctively from titles. "George Westinghouse" was distinction enough for him. There was unconscious recognition of this distinction in a press cable to Europe giving the names of the trustees chosen for the Equitable Life: "Grover Cleveland, ex-President of the United States; Morgan J. O'Brien, Justice of the Supreme Court of New York, and George Westinghouse."

In the years from 1893 to 1907 the business of the numerous Westinghouse companies grew enormously. It is estimated that 50,000 people were employed in production and distribution. The Westinghouse shops were scattered from San Francisco to St. Petersburg. In all these activities Westinghouse had a constant part in executive conduct as well as in planning and administration perhaps apart too close and constant for the best results. He was a prolific inventor, a bold and resourceful financier, a man of capacious imagination and foresight as to things to be done, and a powerful executive; tut perhaps he was not a great administrator. Lord Fisher, paradoxical "Jackey," said that "no great commander is ever a good administrator." One may guess that he had in mind the thought that a "good" administrator is too much bound by the formulas of seniority and precedence, for he also said: "Some day the Empire will go down because it is Buggins's turn," and at another time he said: "Favoritism is the secret of efficiency." Doubtless Lord Fisher would have called Westinghouse a great commander. Whether or not he was a great administrator is debated amongst those who knew him best and appreciated him most. At any rate, sometimes the administrative machinery absorbed more of his time and thought than it ought. But in spite of an overburden of administrative care, his teeming mind went on through these later years inventing, contriving, and organizing.

In 1907 came the tragedy of Westinghouse's life. The great panic caused the failure and receivership of the Electric Company, the Machine Company, and some minor companies, but did not affect the Air Brake Company or the Union Switch & Signal Company. A reorganization was eventually brought about, based upon a brilliant project devised by Westinghouse, but the actual control of the Electric Company passed out of his hands, and in less than four years he ceased to have any official relations with the company. It was a terrific blow. The writer remembers passing, one night, the great works at East Pittsburgh brilliantly lit up. As we came in sight of the electric sign "Westinghouse Electric & Manufacturing Company," Westinghouse turned his face toward the bleak hills on the other side of the way with an expression so pathetic, so tragic, as to wring one's heart. Not a word was spoken for a long time.

At lunch one day either Mr. Charles Terry or the writer told Westinghouse that some one said he never knew when he was beaten. Perhaps he took this as some reflection on his intelligence. He flashed up: "I should know if I were beaten but I never was beaten." And he never was. The game might be lost, but the indomitable spirit was not beaten. The short years of his life that remained after the tragedy were filled with the same unceasing activity and the same undying hope. The affairs of the Machine Company, the development of the steam turbine and of the reduction gear, the invention and development of an air spring for automobiles, and various minor interests completely filled the busy hours of the long days.

Late in 1913 the magnificent structure gave way. An organic disease of the heart developed. The quizzical humor still lived, the inventive spirit still was active, but the body slowly faded away, and on March 12, 1914, he died.

[1] Authority of Lieutenant-General S. B. M. Young, USA.

Chapter Two - The Air Brake

WE do not go far in the life of Westinghouse before we realize that he made two fundamental contributions to civilization:

First, he advanced the art of transportation by the invention and development of the air brake.

Second, he advanced the manufacture of power by the development of the use of the alternating current in the distributing and applying power by electricity.

Just what we mean by "manufacture of power" will be discussed later; of course we do not mean creation of power. The improvement of transportation and the manufacture of power have been amongst the major elements in human progress. Of that, too, more will be said later. It is enough to say here that Westinghouse helped the evolution of transportation by an early set of activities and he helped the manufacture of power by a later set of activities. We shall now consider the air brake as the first and most important of the activities in the field of transportation.

The life of George Westinghouse illustrates and confirms the statement that the faculties of observation and reflection necessarily precede invention. Keen observation and intense reflection are the stepping-stones by which the inventive mind rises into creative effort. Westinghouse was a close observer, and the results of his observations, stored in a powerful memory, were the mental grist that his active mind worked over, sometimes for years, until it came forth in some form to contribute to the safety, happiness, and support of his fellow men.

Westinghouse's earlier inventions were important in setting the current of his career and developing his characteristic tendencies, and he came to be one of the most prolific of inventors. In forty-eight years he took out some 400 patents in many arts; that is to say a patent every month and a half of his working life. He developed the use of natural gas and took out thirty-eight patents in that art. He did important work in power signaling and interlocking. He made many inventions in steam engineering. When we look over his life we discover that his labors for the advancement of the electric science and art may have done quite as much for the progress of civilization as the development of the air brake, but he is best known to mankind by the brake. It is by this that the people know him, and this is always first mentioned in his recognitions and honors from governments and learned societies. As we proceed, some effort will be made to point out the absolute and relative place in history of his various doings, but at the moment we are concerned only with the story of the brake.

We have said elsewhere that each of the inventions of Westinghouse was made to meet some need that he saw. The occurrence that led to the invention of the air brake was the mischief that followed a head-on collision which might have been avoided had means for the prompt and powerful application of brakes been available. This incident happened on the railway between Schenectady and Troy in 1866.

The first form of power brake that occurred to Westinghouse was a buffer brake, the brakes on each individual car being automatically applied by impact when the brakes were set on the locomotive. After some shop experiments, this idea was abandoned for a design that contemplated a coupled chain running through the length of the train, by which the car brakes could be applied through the manipulation of some power device on the locomotive. Visiting Chicago with this in mind, he found a chain brake installed on the Aurora Accommodation of the Chicago, Burlington & Quincy Railroad which, in a large measure, anticipated his own idea and at the same time demonstrated its inherent weakness. This brake, patented in 1862, was the invention of Augustine I. Ambler, of Milwaukee. His Chicago experience led Westinghouse to design a chain brake in which a steam cylinder under the locomotive displaced Ambler's clumsy friction-drive windlass for tightening the brake chain.

This idea was superseded by a more practical one, through the thought that, in order to avoid excessive slack, each car must have its independent brake cylinder, supplied with steam from the locomotive by a continuous pipe with the necessary flexible couplings between the cars. At this stage of his study, when he was wrestling with the problem of condensation, occurred the interesting and almost romantic incident of the magazine subscription which he made while at work in the Westinghouse shop at Schenectady at the solicitation of a young woman, evidently for personal reasons and not because of any particular interest in the magazine. As it happened, this purchase turned out to be one of the most important he ever made, although he never saw the fair agent again. The first or second number of the magazine received brought to his eager attention an illustrated article on the Mont Cenis tunnel, then under construction. Both headings of this tunnel, then 3000 or more feet from the entrances, were being driven by rock drills worked by compressed air. This gave him his cue in a flash, and thereafter his efforts were centered on brake designs in which the operating force was compressed air as the medium for transmitting power from the locomotive to the brake mechanism on each car., Acting with his usual promptness, he embodied his new ideas in a set of drawings, and at once began to look for financial help to defray the cost of making the apparatus needed for a practical demonstration. As he travelled about the country soliciting orders for his railway frog, he had opportunities to present the matter of his air brake to many railway officials whom he endeavored to interest in his invention, and whose cooperation he sought for its development. As he himself says: "None of those approached appeared to have faith in the idea, though I afterward found that the acquaintances made and the many discussions I had had with railway people were of great advantage later in the introduction of the air brake on the railways with which they were connected."

Meanwhile, on July 10, 1868, he filed a caveat in the Patent Office which marked the beginning of a long series of patents relating to the air brake art, totalling 103 between the year 1869 and the year 1907, when he filed his last air brake patent. In this first caveat Westinghouse describes himself as George Westinghouse, Junior, of Schenectady, New York, but the affidavit accompanying it was made before Alderman Nicholson at Pittsburgh on June 24, 1868, and the specifications are attested by A. S. Nicholson and George H. Christy, the last mentioned of whom was from that time forward until his death in 1909 one of Westinghouse's patent counsel. Earlier in 1868, Westinghouse had spent considerable time in Pittsburgh, where his railway frog was being manufactured by Anderson & Cook, and had made an arrangement with Mr. Ralph Baggaley of that city to bear the cost of making the first brake apparatus.

WHO INVENTED THE AIR BRAKE?

As we take up a description of the apparatus and an account of its introduction, let us note that the first air brake patent of George Westinghouse was 88,929, dated April 13, 1869. This patent was reissued July 29, 1873, as 5504. It is in the proceedings and decision of the U. S. Circuit Court of Appeals for the Northern District of New York in the suit brought by George Westinghouse, Jr., against the Gardner & Ransom Air Brake Company, based principally on this reissued patent, that the whole question of Westinghouse's claim to be the original inventor of the first form of air brake is thoroughly thrashed out and judicially determined. Voluminous testimony was taken from April to November 1874. The case was tried at Cleveland, Ohio, before Justice Swayne and Judge Walker, and from the court's decision, handed down June 16, 1875, the following excerpts are taken:

The case was argued exhaustively, and at great length, by able and eminent counsel. The importance of the case, and the large interests involved, as well as the value of the invention itself to the patentee and to the public at large, fully justified the elaborate discussion which the case received, and rendered necessary the careful consideration which we have given to it. The printed record covers about 750 pages; and nearly thirty patents and provisional specifications offered in evidence by the defendant on the issue of novelty and priority of invention, and not included in the printed record, were discussed at the hearing.

The issue of novelty was most vigorously contested.

As already stated, nearly thirty United States and English patents, and English provisional specifications, were offered in evidence on part of the defendant and voluminous expert testimony was taken with reference thereto.

As to all of these in their bearings on the claims last above referred to, our opinion is the same as above stated. They go to show that Westinghouse was not the first to conceive the idea of operating railway brakes by air pressure, and that he was not the inventor of the larger part of the devices employed for such purposes. But such fact does not detract at all from his merit or rights as a successful inventor. The organisms covered by the fourth and fifth claims of his patent reissue 5504, seem to have been entirely new with him, and the incorporation of these elements, together with that of graduating the air pressure in the brake cylinders also shown to be new and of the highest importance and utility in claims 1, 2, 3, and 6, with other substantial and material differences not necessary to enumerate, fully substantiate his pretensions as an original and meritorious inventor, and entitle him as such to the amplest protection of the law.

Suggestive as these prior patents and provisional specifications may have been, they do not any of them embody that which Westinghouse has invented and claimed, and a prior description of a part cannot invalidate a patent for the whole.

So far as appears from the testimony in this case, none of the alleged prior inventions of air brake apparatus have ever successfully been applied to practical use, and when we consider the immense importance of the introduction of the air brake on railroads, and the incalculable benefit which it has conferred on the public in the readiness and certainty with which trains can thereby be controlled, and the comparative immunity from accidents thus secured, and also the number of devices which have been patented for this purpose, in connection with the fact that Westinghouse was the first, so far as appears in the record and proofs, to put an air brake into successful actual use such considerations only strengthen and confirm the soundness of the conclusions to which a careful examination of these prior patents has led us that there are substantial and essential differences between these prior patents and the Westinghouse apparatus, and that to these differences we may justly attribute the successful and extensive introduction of the Westinghouse air brake.

All of this goes to show that there is very little new under the sun in the sense of complete and unanticipated inventions, as every student of the history of patents knows. A famous inventor says that "our ancestors were very dishonest. They stole all our best inventions." In 1868 Westinghouse was only twenty-two years old. His experience in taking out patents was limited, and his knowledge of the prior art of power braking was confined to the steam brake of Goodale and the mechanical brakes of Ambler and Loughridge. Therefore, he was an independent but not original discoverer of the fundamental idea of applying brakes to the wheels of all the vehicles in a train through the instrumentality of air, compressed by an independent, steam-driven air pump, stored in a tank or reservoir and conveyed at will by pipes to brake cylinders under the cars. From 1852 onward, various patentees in England and the United States filed applications disclosing this general purpose, and partly or wholly providing for and describing in more or less detail the principal devices necessary to accomplish it. None of these patents, however, nor all of them together, covered a complete and workable combination, as did Westinghouse's original patent which, in addition to all the essential devices enumerated and described in the previous patents, provided at least two additional novel devices equally important in actual operation. The first of these was the three-way cock which served as the first form of engineer's brake valve, and the other was the hose coupling for connecting the air pipes between the cars. These couplings contained automatic valves so arranged that when the couplings were parted the valves closed and retained any existing air pressure in the brake pipes and the cylinders. In case of a break in two; this feature permitted the continued use of the brakes on the portion of the train attached to the locomotive and was most important, since otherwise air would have passed through and out of the train pipe and the operation of the brakes would have been entirely destroyed.

These two mechanical elements, original with Westinghouse, in combination with the other devices, some of which were already known, formed the basis of his first air brake invention; but the immediate and later success of the Westinghouse brake was not due so much to the ingenuity of the inventor in providing the missing links and working out this particular combination as to other factors. It was not the ideas described in his patent and embodied in the apparatus built and shown in a machine shop in Pittsburgh in 1868 that were principally responsible for the amazing train of events which followed so fast. It was the man behind the idea, with his vision, his will, his courage, and his commercial instinct. As mere invention, Westinghouse's subsequent contributions to the air brake art were far more novel and brilliant than his original conception, and likewise of much greater importance, both mechanically and commercially. The great underlying thing to understand and to remember is that he created a new art and a beautiful art. The magnitude of that art, its complexity, and the time, the skill, and the patience that went to its building, we shall try to show.

THE FIRST AIR-BRAKED TRAINS

The first step toward the successful use of compressed air in braking railway trains had to be taken in the long trail that leads from the crude and simple straight-air brake of 1868 to the complicated and powerful automatic apparatus now in use, and that first step was taken by George Westinghouse on a momentous day in September 1868, when the Steubenville Accommodation on the Panhandle Railroad, equipped with brake apparatus designed by him and built, not only under his supervision, but partly with his own hands, began its initial trip from the Union Station in Pittsburgh.

The essential parts of the air brake as first assembled were:

An air pump driven by a steam engine receiving its supply from the boiler of the locomotive; A main reservoir on the locomotive into which air was compressed to about sixty or seventy pounds per square inch; A pipe leading from the reservoir to a valve mechanism convenient to the engineer; Brake cylinders for the tender and each car; A line of pipe from the engineer's brake valve passing under the tender and all of the cars, with a connection to each brake cylinder. Flexible hose connections between the cars provided with couplings having valves which were automatically opened when the two parts of the couplings were joined and automatically closed when the couplings were separated.

The piston of each cylinder was attached to the ordinary hand-brake gear, and when the piston was thrust outward by the admission of compressed air, the brakes were applied. When the engineer had occasion to stop his train, he admitted the air from the reservoir on the locomotive into the brake cylinders through the train pipe. The pistons of all cylinders were, it was then supposed, simultaneously moved to set all of the brakes with a force depending upon the amount of air admitted through the valve under the control of the engineer. To release the brakes the handle of the brake valve was moved so as to cut off communication with the reservoir, and then to open a passage from the brake pipe to the atmosphere, permitting the air which had been admitted to the pipes and cylinders to escape. This primitive but useful and successful brake came to be known as the straight-air brake, as distinguished from the automatic brake which displaced it entirely in a few years we shall see why. The vital difference is that in the straight air brake increase of pressure in the train pipe applies the brakes. In the automatic brake decrease of pressure applies the brakes. That is why it is automatic. If the train is torn in two or if a hose connection between two cars bursts the brakes go on; with the straight-air brake they would go out of action.

The success of the apparatus on the first train was followed by the equipment of a train of six cars on the Pennsylvania Railroad, and in September 1869, this train was placed at the disposal of the Association of Master Mechanics, representing many railways, then in session at Pittsburgh. The train was run to Altoona and the air brakes alone were used to control the speed of the train on the eastern slope of the Alleghanies, and special stops were made at the steepest places on the line in such unprecedentedly short distances as to establish in the minds of all present the fact that trains could be efficiently and successfully controlled by brakes operated by compressed air.

The next event of importance was to put brakes (in November 1869) on a train of ten cars on the Pennsylvania Railroad, which was taken to Philadelphia to demonstrate to the directors of that railroad the success of the apparatus, and this was followed by similar demonstrations at Chicago and Indianapolis. The outcome of these demonstrations was immediate orders for equipment from the Michigan Central and the Chicago & North Western Railways, and shortly thereafter for the Union Pacific, in the West, and for the Old Colony and Boston & Providence in the East.

With this auspicious start, the progress of the new device was so rapid that by April 1, 1874 (that is, five years and a half after the first trial train was run), 2281 locomotives and 7254 cars had been equipped with the straight-air brake, including 148 locomotive and 724 car equipments shipped to foreign countries. These equipments were manufactured and supplied by the Westinghouse Air Brake Company, a corporation of Pennsylvania, which was chartered September 28, 1869, and began operations in leased premises at the corner of Liberty Avenue and 25th Street, Pittsburgh, early in 1870.

From the very commencement of the brake business, Westinghouse insisted on the great importance of uniformity of design and manufacture. Standards were adopted and adhered to, in all parts of the brake apparatus requiring uniformity to insure interchange of the rolling stock so fitted upon various roads. It would be difficult to overstate the value of this policy to the railroads of the United States in terms of safety, time, or money. If the brake equipment installed upon 71,500 locomotives, 63,000 passenger-service cars, and 2,800,000 freight cars in the United States now so equipped, involved a bare half-dozen standards instead of a single one, the increased cost and delay in handling the transportation of the country would be beyond estimate. In fact, this instinct for standardizing was a fundamental thing in the nature of Westinghouse. It appears all through the years, in his practice and in his teaching.

THE COMING OF THE AUTOMATIC BRAKE

The transition from the straight-air brake to the automatic brake will be described presently. This involved a change in the principle of operation, and demanded important additions to the devices. The change was radical and it was vital. But all the later forms of Westinghouse brake apparatus, ranging from the plain automatic brake of 1874 through various types of quick-action automatic brakes to the standard form of today, show the desirability, if not the necessity, of having each succeeding type of brake interchange and operate harmoniously with its predecessors, and this point has never been lost sight of. This very practical consideration as a limiting condition has been one of the most difficult factors in the development of brake apparatus of sufficient flexibility and power to meet the ever-changing demand incident to the introduction of heavier tonnage cars, more powerful locomotives, higher speeds, and increased length of trains.

Before passing to the development of the automatic brake, it is interesting to note the extent to which the straight-air brake came to be used in the brief time which covered the active life of that type of apparatus and to record its creditable performance.

In 1876 there were in use in the United States 15,569 locomotives and 14,055 passenger cars, of which 2645 locomotives and 8508 passenger cars, or 37.7 per cent of the whole, were equipped with Westinghouse straight-air brakes.

At this time the Pennsylvania Railroad operated trains consisting of a locomotive, one express car, one baggage car, three coaches and six Pullmans. The average weight of a passenger locomotive and tender with fuel and water was fifty tons; baggage and express cars, ten tons; passenger coaches, sixteen tons, and Pullman coaches, twenty-seven tons. On that basis, the Pennsylvania trains above described would weigh 580,000 pounds. With the straight-air brake the average length of stop from thirty miles an hour was 500 feet. In the good old days of the hand brake, which trainmen afterward affectionately called the "Armstrong brake," stops from thirty miles an hour were seldom made under 1600 feet. The straight-air brake was a great step forward, but to Westinghouse its defects and limitations were soon manifest. At what early date after its introduction he began the study of how to remedy its defects, is not definitely known.

In July 1871, he made his first trip to Europe for the purpose of introducing his invention, and remained abroad until August of the next year. Despite his ability to show how fast American railroads were equipping their trains with his straight-air brake, he found it exceedingly difficult to make any impression on the railway managers of Great Britain. In his efforts to get favorable attention, he sought the assistance of the editors of *Engineering,* then and now a famous journal. After several interviews, Mr. Dredge, one of the editors, handed Westinghouse a draft of an editorial that he proposed to publish on the general subject of air brakes. This editorial was an argument for better brakes on British railways, and in it the editor named the qualities that he considered essential to the satisfactory operation of continuous brakes. Several of his specifications were fully met by the Westinghouse straight-air brake, but at least two of them were not: "If a part of the train breaks loose from the rest, the brakes must come automatically into play; the failure of the brake apparatus on one or more carriages must not interfere with the action of the brakes on the rest of the train." The precise statement of these two requirements may have suggested new ideas to Westinghouse or may have crystallized ideas already in his mind. At any rate it was not very long thereafter that evidence of his serious study along these lines appeared in his patents. The first public disclosure of the result of this study is found in United States patents 124,404 and 124,405, both filed December 6, 1871, and issued March 5, 1872. The specification of 124,404 reads in part as follows:

In the air brake apparatus heretofore in use a single line of pipe conveys the compressed air from the main reservoir on the locomotive to each brake cylinder. If this pipe becomes accidentally broken at any point it is, of course, useless for braking purposes from that point to the rear end of the train. For this and other reasons I have devised an apparatus consisting in part of a double line of brake pipes, which may be cooperative or independently operative in braking, at the pleasure of engineer...

The improvement herein described consists in the features of construction and combination by which, first, an air reservoir, auxiliary to or independent of the main reservoir, is combined on each car with the brake cylinder; second, by means of a cock or cocks, such additional reservoir, when used as an auxiliary reservoir, is charged with compressed air from one brake pipe, and the brake cylinder from the other, such pipes in such use being interchangeable or not, at pleasure; third, and by means of a single cock, either brake pipe may be used for charging the reservoir and the other for operating the brakes; fourth, when a car becomes disconnected from the train by accident or otherwise, a port or ports will thereby be opened in a communicating pipe or pipes, by which the air from such auxiliary reservoir will be admitted freely to the brake cylinder, so as automatically to apply the brakes; and, fifth, the conductor and engineer may communicate signals or orders to each other by the use of the brake pipes and the compressed air.

Later the specification, referring to the "receiver or reservoir," as shown on the drawings, says:

It may be used as a reservoir auxiliary to the main reservoir, or as an independent reservoir, one on each car, for storing up the air necessary to apply the brakes. In this latter use I combine with it any known device for compressing air, such as an air pump, fan blower, steam injector, &c.; and if an air pump it may be worked by an eccentric on one of the car axles or in other known way.

Four things mentioned for the first time in this patent are significant: the double line of pipe, the installation of separate or auxiliary reservoirs on each car, the employment of the brake system as a means of communication by signals, and the installation of independent compressing apparatus on each vehicle, including the suggestion of axle-driven compressors. Priority of invention is claimed for the first three.

The method of operation described in this patent covered the usual and familiar straight-air system, using either one of the brake pipes for that purpose. The brake pipe not so employed provided a connection between the main reservoir and the auxiliary reservoirs and, together with the auxiliaries remained at all times charged with a predetermined pressure. By means of cross pipes at the end of each car, communication was established between the "operating pipe" and the storage or "reservoir pipe" through three-way valves that were operated automatically to charge the brake cylinder with auxiliary reservoir air in case of a break in two or in the event of a car leaving the rails. The various devices provided to accomplish this purpose are crude and their availability in actual service somewhat questionable, but as the first step in the development of an automatic brake, the idea disclosed by this patent is interesting.

The signals referred to were operated by admitting air from the charged reservoir pipe into the operating pipe. Air gages were installed in each car and in the engineer's cab. The face of each gage showed eight points distinctly marked at equal distances around the complete circle, and each point, when indicated by the index finger of the gage, conveyed a distinct order or message, as "flag station," "stop for orders," "stop," and so forth. The position of the index finger was determined by the amount of pressure admitted into the operating pipe through the controlling valve on each car as manipulated by the operator. The attention of the engineer was directed to the gage by an alarm whistle likewise installed in the cab. This idea developed into the well-known and simple air signal, now and for years past in universal use, which will be discussed later.

It will be noted that the automatic action of the brake described in patent 124,404 was an independent emergency feature, and not in any way under the control of the engineer; in other words, it was not possible for the engineer to use the air stored in the auxiliary reservoirs under the cars for the application or release of the brakes. That this feature could be made "cooperative," or "independently operated," that is to say, both independent of and dependent upon the will of the engineer, is indicated in the above quotation from the specification of patent 124,404. The devices necessary to render it "cooperative" are covered by patent 124,405 issued concurrently. The specification of this patent so well describes the functions of an automatic brake controlled by the engineer through the fluctuation of air pressure in the brake pipes that it is here reproduced in part:

I now propose further to improve this system of railway brakes by bringing this continuous reservoir pipe into communication with the brake cylinders at pleasure, through the agency of compressed air admitted from the main reservoir into the other brake pipe; by such construction and arrangement of intermediate devices that, by simply discharging compressed air from this continuous reservoir pipe, a communication will be opened from the auxiliary reservoir to the brake cylinder, whereby the brakes will be applied; by a system of valves and ports which shall effectuate all these results by their automatic action, except as their action is governed by the engineer at the main reservoir.

By the italics, attention is directed to the elements that differentiate this patent from the previous one and mark it as the pioneer patent in automatic braking so far as the fundamental idea is concerned. The "intermediate devices" and the "system of valves and ports" used to accomplish the functions described, underwent many changes, and by the exercise of great ingenuity were eventually reduced to the simple and beautiful plain triple valve in its final form, as covered by patent 220,556, but so far as providing means whereby the discharge of air from the "reservoir pipe" by the engineer *at will*, or by the rupture of brake pipe, would apply the brakes in emergency, the triple valve of 1879 is the legitimate, although more richly endowed, successor of the strange congeries of valves embodied in the structure covered by patent 124,405. This structure was made and successfully tested on the rack, but was never put into practice because it was soon superseded by a succession of much simplified devices to be described later. For this reason and because of its complicated construction, no detailed description of its operation is attempted, but if the student of the air brake art will examine the specification of this notable patent, he will get a new conception of the mechanical ability of the man who worked out this combination, and a still higher appreciation of the later developments by which even more remarkable results were obtained.

Much complexity was due to the fact that during the transition period Westinghouse used two brake pipes, the "operating pipe" and the "reservoir pipe." If these pipes had been used invariably for the purpose designated by their respective names, the valves, ports, and passages required would have been greatly reduced in number; but in the earliest stages of this development, Westinghouse evidently considered it essential that *either* pipe could be used as an "operating pipe," and to accomplish this purpose the number of independent valve devices was doubled, if not trebled.

Before dismissing the apparatus covered by patent 124,405, it is interesting to note that the term "triple valve" is not found in its specification or in that of the succeeding patent, but in patent 138,827, filed February 1, 1873, in which it does appear for the first time, a reference is made to these earlier devices as such. The term "triple valve" has become fundamental in air brake language. It was coined to express the threefold function of the device, viz., to apply the brakes, to release them, and to charge the auxiliary reservoirs. Since the devices described in the previous patents were not designed automatically to release the brakes when automatically applied, the structures they cover can scarcely be called "triple valves" in the strict use of that term.

In patent 138,827, issued May 13, 1873, the triple valve first assumed the general form maintained for many years. It was a true triple valve in that it automatically performed the three functions and was thus in reality the first of the long series of triple valves. In this valve and its immediate successors the pressures in brake pipe and auxiliary reservoir were separated by a rubber diaphragm or "flexible annulus," as it is termed in the patent specification, whereby all or nearly all the friction encountered in previous valve devices was avoided and an absolutely air-tight joint secured.

Perhaps it should be explained here that there are two kinds of stops - the service stop, as at stations, and the emergency stop. In the service stop the brakes are slowly applied and not with the full power. In the emergency stop the full power is brought into effect as quickly as that can be done without sliding the wheels. Installed as supplemental to the straight-air brake as before, but now on a separate line of pipe with no connection between the two lines, the automatic brake was still essentially an emergency brake, since with the first diaphragm valve it was impracticable to apply the automatic brake except with maximum pressure. However, when thus applied on the comparatively short passenger trains of that day, it was decidedly quicker than the straight-air brake and resulted in shorter stops.

After the usual service tests of this valve and before it was released for manufacture, the third and final form of "diaphragm triple valve" was brought out, embodying several improvements in construction described in patent 149,901, issued April 21, 1874. This valve was used quite extensively in the earliest commercial installations of automatic brakes. It formed part of the automatic equipment installed on the train placed at the disposal of the committee on Science and the Arts of the Franklin Institute by the Pennsylvania Railroad for test purposes, which tests resulted in the award to Westinghouse of the Scott medal. The train consisted of an engine, tender, and seven passenger cars. The weight is not given, but it presumably approximated 325,000 pounds. The trial runs for which this train was furnished were made on the Pennsylvania Railroad fifteen miles from Philadelphia on May 20, 1873. A number of tests were made and while scientific accuracy was not possible, due to the lack of timing and other special apparatus used in later tests, the following figures for three of the runs are fairly indicative of the actual results obtained. A critical student of the art will discover shorter and more consistent stops in other records of about the same time. In answer to signal, the train stopped in 547 feet from 30 miles an hour on an up-grade of 29.6 feet to the mile. On application of brakes from the train, the stop was in 15 seconds in 553 feet, from a speed of 32 or 33 miles an hour on a down-grade of 31.7 feet per mile. With engine detached, the train stopped in 10J^ seconds in 323 feet, from 40 miles an hour on a down-grade of 28.2 feet per mile. The report concluded as follows:

The committee say that these experiments have demonstrated to them the extraordinary efficiency of this apparatus, and they especially call attention to the value and importance of the arrangement which secures the instant automatic application of the brakes on the engine and on each car of the train independently of the train hand, in certain contingencies which are of common occurrence and are the cause of frequently disastrous accidents.

The committee believes that by contriving and introducing this apparatus, Mr. Westinghouse has become a great public benefactor and deserves the gratitude of the travelling public at least. They believe that his inventions are worthy of and should receive the award of the Scott Legacy Medal.

Accordingly, the committee proposed the adoption of the following resolution:

Resolved, that this Committee (of Science and Arts) recommend to the Board of Managers of the Institute that they make the award of the John Scott's Legacy Premium and Medal to George Westinghouse, Jr., of Pittsburgh, for his improvements in air brakes for railway trains.

FUNDAMENTALS OF THE AUTOMATIC BRAKE

At the time of this trial the automatic brake had become finally differentiated from the straight-air brake. It may be well, therefore, to give here a short description of its principal features before taking up the further development of the triple valve and other automatic-brake devices. The plain automatic brake and also the straight-air brake, included an air compressor and main reservoir on the locomotive, a valve in the cab, known as the engineer's brake valve, brake cylinders under the tender and each car, a line of pipe and flexible hose connections, to form a continuous air conduit from the main reservoir to the rear of the train. These features were common to the automatic and the straight-air brakes.

In the straight-air brake, compressed air was carried from the main reservoir on the engine through the engineer's brake valve and through the brake pipe to the brake cylinders, thus applying the brakes. The brakes were released by so manipulating the engineer's valve as, through it, to discharge to the atmosphere the compressed air from the brake pipe and likewise from all the brake cylinders with which it was directly connected. Normally, therefore, in the straight-air brake system, the air in the brake pipe was at atmospheric pressure when the train was running and charged with air at any desired pressure less than the main reservoir pressure when the brakes were being applied.

In the automatic brake system, this normal operation was completely reversed. When running, the brake pipe was fully charged with air at a predetermined pressure and the brakes were applied through a *reduction* of brake pipe pressure by the manipulation of the engineer's valve, so opening a special valve on each car, or by the accidental separation of the car, or by any rupture in the brake pipe or the hose connections. This automatic action was secured by two important features installed on each car, in addition to those used in common with the straight-air brake, viz., an auxiliary or supplemental reservoir and the triple valve interposed between the main brake pipe, auxiliary reservoir, and brake cylinder. Through the triple valve, when air under pressure was admitted to the brake pipe, the auxiliary reservoir was charged to brake-pipe pressure. At the same time, a port was opened from the brake cylinder to the atmosphere. This was the normal or running position with the brakes fully released. A reduction of brake-pipe pressure caused the piston of the triple valve to shift its position, closing the port between the brake cylinder and the atmosphere and also the port between the brake pipe and the auxiliary reservoir. At the same time, and by the same movement, communication was established between the auxiliary reservoir and the brake cylinder, and thus the brakes were automatically applied." The restoration of brake-pipe pressure reversed this operation, released the brakes, and recharged the auxiliary reservoir. It will be observed that now only one line of brake pipe was used. The simple, automatic and effective performance of all these functions was through that marvel of ingenuity, the triple valve.

DEVELOPMENT OF THE TRIPLE VALVE

In its perfected state, the flexible diaphragm triple valve was a sensitive and highly efficient device, but the use of poppet valves with their liability to leakage, the normally closed exhaust port, and the perishable nature of the rubber diaphragm, soon led to the invention of the "piston-and-slide-valve" type of triple valve, the experimental form of which was covered by patent 168,359, dated October 5, 1875. This form was quickly followed by the first commercial valve of this type described in patent 172,064, dated January 11, 1876, which embodied in its structure a most important improvement, the feature of lost motion in the slide valve. The utilization of this feature effected the opening and closing of the feed port in response to slight variations of pressure, thus greatly increasing the sensitiveness of the triple by obviating the necessity of raising the pressure sufficiently to overcome friction of the slide valve. This triple was standard from 1876 to 1879. The next and last step in the development of the plain triple valve was the invention of the graduating valve, which made possible a still finer graduation of the brakes, both in application and release. The triple valve in which this refinement was embodied is covered by patent 220,556, dated October 14, 1879. With slight modifications, this is the form of plain triple that remained standard for passenger-car equipment until the invention of the quick-action triple valve in 1887, and for locomotives and tenders until the introduction of the ET equipment in 1908.

We have seen that Westinghouse filed in the patent office his first caveat for the air brake in July 1868, that is, three months before he was twenty-two, and this patent was issued the next April. We have traced for ten years the course of the main stream of invention which led to the perfection of what is known as the plain triple valve and to the solid establishment of the automatic system. Presently, we shall take up the greatest invention in the air brake art, the quick-action, automatic triple, and shall relate something of the story of the brake as it is today; but first we will glance at a few smaller but essential details which go to make up a system.

SUNDRY ACCESSORIES

In 1870 Westinghouse patented a steam-driven air pump, to compress air for braking, which has persisted in type to this day improved, of course, in detail. It is doubted if any other steam-driven engine has been made which has equalled in reliable service this air pump, under working conditions so severe.

The engineer's operating valve of 1870 was improved in 1879, by what was called the "excess-pressure" valve which was designed to hold in the main reservoir a pressure greater than the standard brake-pipe pressure. This was important in providing for emergencies and permitting prompt release of the brakes and quick recharge of the auxiliary reservoirs. This seems to have met the requirements of passenger service, but when, in the course of years, the air brake came to be applied to very long freight trains the need of further improvement was disclosed by an interesting experience. An experimental train of fifty stock cars fitted with automatic brakes was being run over the Pittsburgh Division of the Pennsylvania Railroad. In those days, very few engineers had handled so long a train with the air brake. The Pennsylvania Railroad engineer on this train was a good air brake man in passenger service, but he had no experimental knowledge, or theoretical either, of the difference between braking a ten-car and a fifty-car train. When he came to let his train down the eastern slope of the Alleghanies, he got into trouble. The grade is long and often well over 100 feet to the mile, and there are sharp curves, the famous "Horseshoe Curve" amongst them.

As he started down the grade, the engineer did what he would have done with the trains he was used to; he put on brakes and quickly "lapped" his brake valve that is, he put it in the proper position for running with brakes set. The result was to set the brakes on the leading cars and to cause a surge of air from the rear cars that at once released them. This operation was repeated three or four times; air pressure was getting low, and it looked as if there must be a call for hand brakes or a runaway down a bad grade and through the curves. Westinghouse was in the cab, and it was suggested that he should take the brakes, a suggestion promptly and gratefully accepted by the engineer. By delicate handling, Westinghouse let the train smoothly down the grade, and at the same time built up the air pressure. From this experience quickly came the invention of the engineer's equalizing valve - a most important improvement in air brake equipment.

The equalizing valve was designed so to control the discharge of air as to equalize the pressure through the whole length of the brake pipe, and secure uniform application of the brakes. This prevents the things that happened on the Altoona grade setting brakes on the head cars, failure to set them on the rear cars, and the release of the forward brakes by a surge of air from the rear. Probably no man could have reasoned out such conduct by compressed air; it had to be developed and discovered by experiment. The history of the art is full of such situations. This valve was the joint invention of George Westinghouse and his nephew, Frank Moore. [1] In its first form it was used in the classical Burlington brake trials of 1886 and 1887. It was improved in 1889, and then no important change was made in it for twenty years.

Everybody knows that in 1833 Robert Stephenson invented a steam driver brake for locomotives. Forty years later George Westinghouse followed him. Westinghouse knew the desirability of power brakes on the locomotive as the most important single factor in braking trains, because of the greater comparative weight of the locomotive. At the outset the use of driver brakes met with strong opposition, which persisted for many years, due to the notion that the increased brake power would not compensate for the increased wear of driver tires. Now the supreme importance of braking locomotives to the limit is universally recognized. If man is a reasoning animal, he is sometimes perverse. The writer remembers in the early seventies, hearing officers of the old army, men of Civil War experience, argue stubbornly against breech-loading rifles. "The men would fire away their ammunition too fast. It would be impossible to keep the firing-line supplied."

The first driver brake invented by Westinghouse was patented in 1873. Vertical brake cylinders are installed on the engine frame and brake shoes are applied to the driving wheels by means of a steam- or air-actuated piston operating through a system of hangers and levers. In a later form, usually called a "cam brake," patented in 1876, the segmental levers or cams are so hung that "during the beginning of their stroke the touching point of their operative faces shall be below the line joining the centers of curvature." By this arrangement, the segmental levers give to the brake shoes a quick motion, or throw, to the surfaces of the wheels, thus rapidly taking up the shoe clearance before the application of full brake pressure. Piston travel was thus substantially reduced, speed of application increased, and valuable space utilized to the best advantage. That cam brakes are now seldom seen is largely due to change in number and arrangement of driving wheels in modern locomotives.

Westinghouse was an early inventor in the brake-beam field, and his contributions to this element of the art of power braking were very valuable. The lack of strength and rigidity in the brake rigging in general use in America and the much more substantial and mechanical methods employed in England for transmitting brake pressure to the wheels led Westinghouse to design the pioneer metallic brake beam patented in 1873. This was soon followed by a wooden beam supported by metallic tension rods, giving greater strength and rigidity than the ordinary wooden beam, with less weight. Both of these came into general use and contributed much to the efficiency of the brakes in reducing the length of train stops.

The earliest form of hose coupling invented by Westinghouse was one of the elements of novelty that contributed largely to the successful issue of the patent suit against the Gardner & Ransom Brake Company mentioned earlier. The special feature that distinguished this from any ordinary coupling was the valve mechanism that closed automatically when the connection was separated and the fact that separation under any unusual strain was accomplished without rupture. These fundamental features were retained in the later and improved forms of hose couplings covered by half a dozen patents and the type is in use today. It is hard to exaggerate the importance of this seemingly unimportant device among the various units that constitute a complete car-brake equipment. The fact that it has persisted for more than forty-six years shows how well it has performed its function and played its part in advancing the art of power braking.

Adjustment of slack caused by the wear and replacement of brake-shoes, has always been and will always be one of the difficulties in power braking. The desirability of taking up slack automatically, not only to save labor but to insure greater uniformity in brake applications was seen early by Westinghouse, and in 1872 he secured a pioneer patent on a device designed to accomplish this purpose. The mechanism described in this and later patents included all the essential elements requisite to fulfil the function for which they were designed. They had, however, the drawback of taking up false piston travel when used in connection with the wooden brake beams and weak levers and brake rods common to the equipment when the invention was made. For this reason, the use of automatic slack adjusters was discontinued until the general adoption of strong and rigid brake gear and brake beams.

Another interesting invention originally included in complete sets of automatic brake equipment for passenger cars, and subsequently abandoned, was a trip device for automatically setting the brakes in case of derailment. To accomplish this object, a valve controlling the discharge of air from the brake pipe was actuated by a stem extending downward near the track; carrying a cross bar in such proximity to the rail that if the truck were derailed the cross bar would strike the track, lift the valve from its seat, and, by discharging air from the brake pipe, apply the brakes. Experience showed that brakes were sometimes set by loose objects on the right-of-way and an emergency stop was made under inconvenient or even dangerous conditions. There is a tradition that on the Long Island Railroad a hen, scuttling across, tripped the brakes and stopped a train. A variant makes it a prairie-chicken on the Wabash. Whatever the facts may have been, the story belongs to the important class of truths that might be true. At any rate the use of the trip was discontinued. Numerous variations have been patented but the objection has never been overcome.

The fact has been told that as early as March 1872, Westinghouse conceived the idea of employing brake-pipe air pressure as a means for communicating between the vehicles in the train and the engineer by visible and audible signals. In working out this idea, audible signals alone were found to meet every practical requirement, and the index gages described in the original patent were abandoned. A patent issued in 1876 covers the various devices later designed by Westinghouse to constitute a complete train air-signal equipment, and described their application and use. In this patent the statement is made that the same mode of operation may be employed in connection with a separate line of pipe leading to the escape valves, but it is preferable to employ the volume of air in the brake pipe for the purpose. Later on, in actual service it was found that under certain conditions brake operations interfered with the simultaneous transmission of signals. For a time, therefore, it was thought improbable that railway companies would consider the train air signal of sufficient value to justify the installation of an entirely separate line of pipe for that purpose, including special hose and couplings, but the prompt adoption of the separate train air-signal system by the Pennsylvania Railroad due in large part to the initiative of Mr. T. N. Ely, settled this question for all time, and it soon became standard on all passenger trains equipped with automatic brakes. Various minor changes and improvements were made subsequently in train air-signal apparatus, but it is today essentially the same as when first designed and put into service by Westinghouse in 1876.

This interlude of half a dozen minor things has seemed proper for two reasons: They are part of the system and they help to bring to our minds something of the versatility and industry of the man of whom we are reading. Now we shall resume the history of the air brake.

THE BURLINGTON BRAKE TRIALS

When we take up the story again, in its chronological order, we find ourselves facing the most stirring and critical series of events in the history of the air brake the Burlington Brake Trials, and their consequences. That incident, comparatively brief, was a fine example of victory snatched from defeat by the fortitude and the resource of the commander. And the commander was at the moment almost alone in the world in thinking that victory was possible.

In 1885 there was no kind of continuous brake in much use in freight service, but an important beginning had been made on the Denver & Rio Grande, the Central Pacific, the Northern Pacific, the Atchison, Topeka and Santa Fe, and the Union Pacific. There were special reasons why these roads should have led the movement. They had mountain grades; their trains were comparatively short and light, and their interchange of freight cars with other roads was comparatively small. But for two or three years there had been a great and fast-growing agitation amongst the people for means to reduce the dreadful list of casualties to freight-train hands. The popular leader in this agitation was Mr. L. S. Coffin, State Railroad Commissioner of Iowa. He had the fiery energy of a Hebrew prophet and the engaging gifts of a Yankee politician. He was saved from being a fanatic by a moderate but sufficient sense of humor, and he really loved the "railroad boys." A good cause, with such a leader, was bound to prevail. There were two perfectly obvious means of keeping the "boys" off the roofs of freight cars while running and from between them while coupling, namely, continuous brakes and automatic couplers. Both of these would have come into universal use in time for technical reasons, but Coffin's movement forced the situation, and concerted and definite action by the railroad companies began.

There are in the United States several organizations of operating officers of railroads which have been working for years to improve practice and especially to develop standards. The free interchange of freight cars is a necessary feature of our operating methods. A car of the Boston and Maine Railroad is on the Southern Pacific and needs repairs; or a car of the Canadian Pacific is on the Texas Pacific. It is obvious that, for good service and cheap service, the parts of all these cars must be reduced to a few standards. It is equally obvious that for progress, contrivance must not be put into a straitjacket. It is the ancient principle of compromise. With this ancient principle, these groups of railroads officers have been laboring for more than a generation. The Master Car Builders' Association and the Master Mechanics' Association have to do especially with rolling stock, and when the use of continuous brakes on freight cars began to seem possible, it was taken up for systematic study.

The first report of the Committee on Automatic Freight-Car Brakes was made to the Master Car Builders' Association in 1885. In it, the statement was made that a complete report on Automatic Freight-Car Brakes should be accompanied by an elaborate and thorough series of comparative trials and tests which were quite beyond the field of the committee. Four types of brakes were suggested for investigation buffer brakes, friction brakes, air brakes, and electric brakes with a brief description of each brake of these various types that was at the time in actual service and had been observed by members of the committee. These included the American, the Rote, and the

Prescott brakes of the buffer type, the Widdifield and Button friction brake, and the Westinghouse automatic air brake.

At the convention of 1886, the committee made no formal report but announced that arrangements had been concluded for two series of tests on the Chicago, Burlington, and Quincy Railroad at Burlington, Iowa, in 1886 and 1887. The competitors in the first series of tests, which were run from May 29, 1886, were the American Brake Company's direct buffer brake, Eames automatic vacuum brake, Rote direct buffer brake, Westinghouse automatic air brake, and the Widdifield and Button friction buffer brake. The succession of violent shocks experienced with all forms of buffer brakes, which increased inversely as the length of the stop, soon eliminated this type from competition and left the field to Westinghouse and Eames, the automatic air brake and vacuum brake.

Nor did the more successful competitors escape criticism and temporary rejection for the same reason. The expected delays in charging and releasing continuous brakes were shown to be of no moment, and the performance of the Westinghouse brake was satisfactory in service work, but emergency applications of the brake produced such violent shocks, due to slow serial action, that the committee reported adversely as to the adoption of any existing brake as standard for freight-train operation. At the same time an invitation was extended to all brake manufacturers to take part in a second series of trials in the spring of 1887. This was done in the hope that meanwhile such improvements might be made in the speed of emergency applications as to overcome the admitted deficiency in the air brake, or that some other form of brake might be submitted that would satisfactorily meet all the conditions imposed.

The situation was serious, not to say alarming, for the great unoccupied field was in freight braking, and that field was immensely greater than the passenger field already pretty well cultivated. The cars in freight service, including "company" cars, are from forty-five to fifty times as many as those in passenger service. Many of the air brake men in the Brake Company and on the railroads were gloomy. But it was the kind of situation which Westinghouse enjoyed. He at once started lines of inquiry and experiment that culminated in the production of the so-called quick-action triple valve. Let the reader carefully note this, for it was an epoch, not only in the history of the brake, but in the history of land transportation.

THE QUICK-ACTION TRIPLE VALVE

The first form of this valve was covered by U. S. Patent 360,070, issued March 29, 1887. The improved form which later became the standard quick-action triple was covered by U.S. Patent 376,837, issued January 24, 1888. Both forms were involved in the litigation that followed efforts made to share in the commercial success attained as a result of the great invention they embodied.

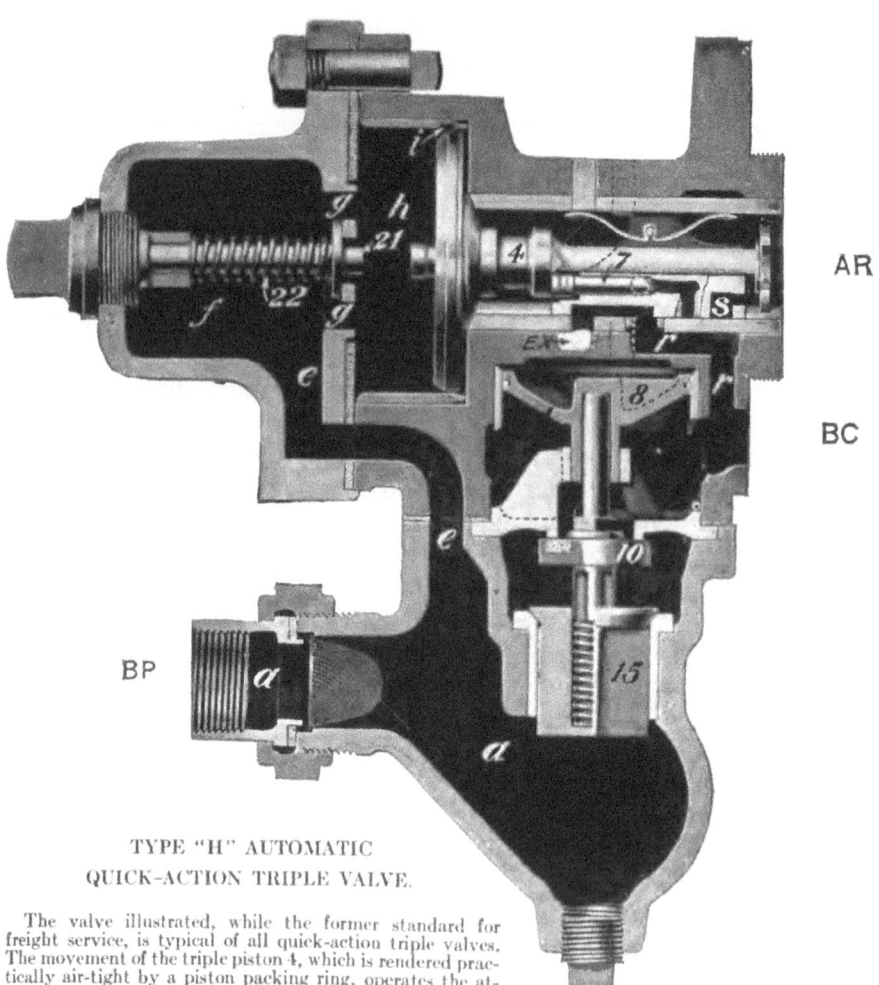

TYPE "H" AUTOMATIC QUICK-ACTION TRIPLE VALVE.

The valve illustrated, while the former standard for freight service, is typical of all quick-action triple valves. The movement of the triple piston 4, which is rendered practically air-tight by a piston packing ring, operates the attached slide-valve mechanism and thereby controls the flow of compressed air from the auxiliary reservoir at AR into the brake-cylinder at BC, also from the brake-cylinder to the atmosphere through the exhaust-port EX. In "full release" position, as shown, standard brake-pipe pressure, entering at BP, fills the passages a, e, f, g, and h and charges the auxiliary reservoir to the same pressure through the feed-groove i. A partial reduction of brake-pipe pressure through the engineer's brake-valve reduces the pressure on the face of triple piston 4, and the higher pressure on the auxiliary reservoir side of this piston causes it to move to the left about one-half of its full traverse, closing the feed-groove and shifting the position of the slide valve attached so as to open a port into the passage r leading to the brake-cylinder. Sufficient air pressure to apply the brake to the desired degree thus passes into the brake-cylinder, reducing the air pressure in the auxiliary reservoir until the pressure on opposite sides of triple piston 4 is again in substantial equilibrium. The triple piston then moves toward its former full-release position sufficiently to close the port opening into the brake-cylinder by means of the graduating valve 7, though not enough to move the main slide valve. By additional reductions of brake-pipe pressure the graduating valve 7 can be opened and closed and brake-cylinder pressure gradually increased at will to the maximum amount. By restoring normal brake-pipe pressure the triple piston is at once forced to full-release position, carrying the slide valve with it, closing the connection between the auxiliary reservoir and brake-cylinder and opening the free passage from the brake-cylinder to the atmosphere, thereby releasing the brakes.

An emergency application of the brakes is obtained by a sudden and heavy reduction of brake-pipe pressure, which forces the triple piston 4 rapidly to traverse its full stroke to the left until stopped by the stem 21 and spring 22. The large port S through the slide valve is thus uncovered and full air pressure previously stored in the auxiliary reservoir rushes into the brake-cylinder and at the same time forces piston 8 downward, unseating the valve 10, and brake-pipe air pressure, being still somewhat in excess of the depleted auxiliary reservoir pressure, raises valve 15, and passing directly into the brake-cylinder still further increases the pressure by which the brakes are applied.

In all probability, the only thing that prevented the elimination of all competition in this field during the life of these patents was the fact that one of the methods of obtaining quick serial action, while clearly Westinghouse's invention and, in fact, the most obvious and the first method considered by him, was not patented because of the more effective method which at once claimed and absorbed his attention. Fundamentally, serial quick action of the brakes was obtained by locally venting brake-pipe pressure at each triple valve. The obvious method was to vent to the atmosphere, and at first this was done; but Westinghouse immediately saw the saving of air and other benefits to be gained by venting this pressure directly into the brake cylinder, and this feature was effectually covered by patent 360,070. A dozen words would have covered venting to the atmosphere also. These words were not written into the claim, and a competing company has built up a handsome business on a quick-action valve venting to the atmosphere. Ben Franklin has called our attention to the fact that for want of a horseshoe nail the rider was lost. Perhaps society has profited by the competition, and perhaps it was as well for the world that Ben's rider should have been lost.

The great significance of the invention of the quick-action brake may be illustrated by the fact that comparing it with the plain automatic brake used in the 1886 trials, the rate of serial action was so increased as to cause a reduction in the time of full or emergency application of the fiftieth brake in a fifty-car train of approximately fourteen seconds, that is to say, from twenty seconds to six seconds. There was also marked increase in resultant cylinder pressure, as well as in the rapidity with which air was admitted to the brake cylinder in such applications, due to the larger opening from the brake pipe to the brake cylinder.

These improvements in the speed and effectiveness of the Westinghouse brake led to the belief that the problem had been solved, and as there was no opportunity to test the new brake on a fifty-car train before the opening of the second series of trials, the Westinghouse people appeared at Burlington in May 1887, confident of complete success. They were again disappointed. The individual efficiency of each brake had been so greatly increased as to completely overbalance the increased rapidity of serial action, with the result that while the stops made were much shorter, the shocks sustained in the rear cars were even greater than in the trials of 1886. Observers and recorders in the rear car were shot promiscuously the length of the car, and there was at least one leg broken. Some of the members of the committee were quite cross at being so hustled, and the chances of a favorable report faded away. Fortunately, an alternative had been provided in electrically operated vent valves in the hose-couplings at four points in the train. These valves were connected by wires running through the pipes and energized by batteries on the locomotive. The engineer's valve was provided with contact points, so that in emergency applications only, the electrically operated vent valves could be opened instantaneously throughout the train and the brake applied with almost absolute uniformity. At that time Westinghouse had no faith in the practicability of electrically operating brakes on freight trains. It was not a question only of immediate reliability, but of maintenance. He used to say: "A freight car has no father or mother." It must wander over a continent and stand for weeks at a time on remote sidings. The electrical apparatus had not then been made that would remain operative in such conditions. But the electric vent valve showed that his brake could be worked that way, and so he kept his position on equal terms with his competitors who exhibited electrically operated brakes.

In the 1887 trials, besides the Westinghouse automatic air brake and the Eames vacuum brake, there appeared the Carpenter electro air brake and the Card electric brake. The Carpenter brake used compressed air as the braking force, and the Card brake was purely an electric device. Both depended entirely upon electricity for the operation of the braking mechanism. In the cases of Westinghouse and Eames, electricity was employed as as auxiliary to a braking device complete in itself. The performance of the Carpenter brake was ideal when it worked, but in the last stop of the test, a broken wire caused a complete failure. This incident confirmed Westinghouse in his opinion that electricity, as then applied, was not a sufficiently reliable agency upon which to depend for stopping trains. Its use as an adjunct, however, seemed established, and while the committee declined to make any definite recommendation as to what freight-train brake should be generally adopted, and suggested that the subject of automatic freight-train braking should be continued for further investigation, with special reference to the reliability of the electrical element, it reported as follows:

First, that the best type of brake for long freight trains is one operated by air, and in which the valves are actuated by electricity.

Second, that this type of brake possesses four distinct advantages:

a. It stops the train in the shortest possible distance.
b. It abolishes shocks and their attending damages to equipment.
c. It releases instantaneously.
d. It can be graduated perfectly.

This report, while eminently fair, was a verdict against brakes operated by air alone, and again Westinghouse was faced by a situation critical to his fortunes and dangerous to the best interests of the railroads. Most of his associates in the brake company and his best friends on the railroads thought that he was beaten at last. An editorial writer of the time, very friendly to Westinghouse, but professionally bound to form and express correct opinions, so far as light was given to him, said: "The most remarkable feature of the trials has been the general adoption of electricity, which has been proved capable of operating the valves of air brakes so as to secure greater quickness of action, less shock, and better graduation...When we consider the great variety of purposes for which it is now used, the constant increase of its application, and the very rapid growth in the electrical art it does not seem very sanguine to prophesy that it may be successfully used in train braking." Writing four months later, after the astonishing thing that Westinghouse had done in the meantime, the same writer said: "At the conclusion of those trials it is probable that there was only one engineer living who believed that the triple valve could be so altered as to stop a fifty-car train, at forty miles an hour on a fifty-three-foot grade in less than half the length of the train without a shock...When he announced that he would certainly eliminate the shock in the emergency stops by the use of the air alone, he was listened to with incredulity by the best informed students of this great mechanical problem...We have long regarded the eminent services of Mr. Westinghouse to the railroads as sufficient to place him on a level with the foremost of those who have benefited the world by mechanical inventions, and we now tender to him our hearty congratulations on this new and most important achievement whereby the necessity, or even the desirability, of an electric complication of the air brake is completely avoided." What had happened was that Westinghouse went back to Pittsburgh, in three months changed the air brake to the form which endured for twenty years without important modification, and in four months proved to the world that the longest freight trains could be handled with air and without electrical complications. And it was so simple!

The form of quick-action triple valve was produced which afterward became standard as the "376,837," and in which friction, due to the use of the emergency slide valve, was eliminated. One-and-a-quarter-inch brake pipe and hose were substituted for the one-inch pipe and hose previously employed, with enlarged angle cocks, hose couplings, and other fittings. These changes reduced the time of serial action on the last car to about two and one-half seconds as compared with six seconds, and an empty train of fifty cars was stopped from twenty miles an hour without shock in 200 feet or less. The enlarged brake pipe and fittings also materially improved the service functions of the brake, especially in grade work.

After experiments that demonstrated these facts to the satisfaction of Westinghouse and his associates, the same train which was used in the 1887 trials, refitted with modified and improved apparatus, was sent on a tour during October, November, and December 1887 (the Burlington trials had been late in May), and a series of unofficial trials was made at a dozen cities. Mr. Godfrey W. Rhodes, who was Superintendent of Motive Power of the Burlington at the time of the trials, and who was chairman of the Master Car Builders 7 Committee, writes: "Mr. Westinghouse's wonderful optimism and confidence in the principle of air power, after the early failures were very marked. After the first collapse, in rapid succession, three different triples were invented. Finally came the gem, and then, greatest of all acts, it was exhibited all over the country in operation on a fifty-car train, making stops with no shock in the fiftieth car, not enough jar to upset a glass of water, a marvellous condition when one considers the wreck and disaster that used to take place in the fiftieth car." These trials were attended by many hundreds of railroad managers, motive-power officials, press representatives, prominent citizens, and technical students. The results were so successful that the committee of the Master Car Builders' Association on freight-train brakes reported to the meeting of the Association in June 1888, as follows:

In our report to the convention last year the main conclusion we arrived at was that the best type of brake for freight service was one operated by air, and in which the valves were actuated by electricity. Since that time your committee has not made any further trial of brakes, but the aspect of the question has been much changed by the remarkable results achieved in non-official trials which have taken place in various parts of the country, and have been witnessed by many of the members of this Association. These trials show that there is now a brake in the market which can be relied on as efficient in any condition of freight service.

The present position of the freight-train brake is briefly as follows:

First. - Brakes can be, practically speaking, simultaneously applied, without electricity, throughout a train of fifty freight cars.

Second. - Other inventors are working at the problem of making an air brake which will be rapid in action and suitable for service on freight trains. We also understand that inventors are working at buffer and electric friction brakes, but we have no reason to hope that brakes on these principles can successfully compete with air brakes.

In view of these conditions, your committee does not recommend the adoption of any particular brake, but considers that a freight-train brake should fulfil the following conditions:

First. - It shall work with air of seventy pounds' pressure. A reduction of eight pounds shall set the brakes lightly, and a restoration of pressure shall release the brakes.

Second. - It shall work without shock on a train of fifty cars.

Third. - It shall stop a train of fifty empty freight cars when running at twenty miles per hour within 200 feet on the level.

Fourth. - When tried on a train of fifty cars it shall maintain an even speed of fifteen miles an hour down a grade of fifty-three feet per mile without variation of more than five miles per hour above or below that speed at any time during the descent.

Fifth. - The brake shall be capable of being applied, released, and graduated on the whole train by the engineer, or without any assistance from brakemen or conductor.

Sixth. - The hose coupling shall couple with the present Westinghouse coupling.

All of the conditions of this report fell well within the demonstrated performance of the Westinghouse automatic freight brake, and the battle was won. It was one of Westinghouse's swiftest and most brilliant victories, and it is a classic in railroad history. Thus the standard freight brake for the ensuing twenty years established its title to supremacy. When the next broad advance in the art of freight braking came, through the invention of the quick service or "K" triple valve, Westinghouse, while still President of the Westinghouse Air Brake Company and the director of its general policies, was not personally active in the development of this improved device.

Any fairly complete investigation of the subject leads to the conclusion that the greatest original contribution to the art of power braking was made by Westinghouse in the invention, development, and perfection of the triple valve. From its beginning, that device was, and it still remains, the heart of the air brake system. It seems a far cry from the plain triple of 1872 to the universal valve of today, but the trail is clearly marked and the development of the one into the other is no more or less remarkable than the development of Stevenson's *Rocket* into the Mallet compound locomotive of today, or of Fulton's *Clermont* into the modern Atlantic liner. Beyond mechanical modifications of more or less importance, the invention of an improved engineer's brake valve in 1896 and of a quick-service triple in 1907, Westinghouse's direct personal contributions to the air brake art ended with the perfection of the quick action triple valve in 1887. When, in order to cope with the changing conditions of transportation, the next step forward became necessary, he was so deeply engaged in other work, largely, but by no means exclusively, of an administrative character, that the Air Brake Company was forced to rely upon the engineering talent that in the meantime had been developed in its own ranks or acquired by additions thereto. While it is not within the province of this biography to describe these later developments, it is proper here to record that the inventor chiefly responsible for the later devices by which the art was still further advanced, referring particularly to the K type of freight triple valve, and LN passenger brake equipment, and finally the universal valve, was W. V. Turner, in many respects a worthy successor of the pioneer whose genius was his constant inspiration. Touching his own inventions in relation to the prior art, Mr. Turner has well said: "It is truly remarkable that through all subsequent improvements not one of the original functions of the triple valve has been discarded, but that they have been extended and expanded, and many new functions added."

ENGLISH EXPERIENCES

The beginning of the air brake and its development were in the United States, and we have followed the story so far with but little mention of what was done abroad. But Westinghouse's doings in England and on the Continent were an interesting part of the history, and some of the things done were not only interesting but of distinct importance in the engineering development of the brake. They destroyed a law of mechanics which had almost the standing of a law of nature, and they exploded an ancient mechanical fallacy which to many minds was a law. They established principles which are. useful not only in braking but in other fields of applied mechanics.

We have seen that the first air braked train was run out of Pittsburgh in September 1868, and that less than three years later Westinghouse was in England with his brake. We have also seen that in that first visit an impetus was given to the idea of making the brake automatic. The next year, 1872, the Westinghouse Continuous Brake Company was organized for handling export business. This company, a Pennsylvania corporation, maintained a technical and sales force in England, with some shop facilities, but until the latter part of 1881, when its corporate successor, the Westinghouse Brake Company, Limited, was chartered under the English Companies' Act, practically all brake equipments supplied for the European trade were made in America. At the time of his second visit, March 1874, 148 locomotives and 724 car equipments of the straight-air system had been so furnished, and the Westinghouse name and product had become well known in railway circles. The introduction of the Westinghouse automatic brake, the principal object of the 1874 trip was, therefore, a much less difficult task than that of 1871. Consequently, when he returned to England for the third time in May 1875, the automatic brake was in service on several important railways. In the meantime, other ambitious inventors had been busy and continuous brakes of various types were in service or were claimants for recognition.

In England, the most dangerous competitor of the compressed-air brake was the vacuum brake, originally brought out in the United States under a patent issued to John Y. Smith of Pittsburgh hi 1872. The principle of vacuum brake operation was used by Nehemiah Hodge of North Adams, Massachusetts (patented 1860, extended 1874, reissued to George Westinghouse, Jr., assignee, 1879), but Smith, by substituting an ejector, or what he calls an injector-exhaust, for the vacuum pump specified by Hodge, greatly improved the chances of the vacuum brake in competition with the straight-air brake. Westinghouse had promptly entered the vacuum-brake field, and besides securing the assignment of the original Hodge patent, he took out patents on improvements and refinements both in the United States and abroad, so that in England, in 1875, he was prepared to furnish either vacuum or compressed-air brakes as might be required.

The conflicting claims of the various inventors and manufacturers were vocal in England at that time, and led up to the first and most important series of competitive brake tests of early days. These tests, known as the Newark trials," took place on the Nottingham and Newark Division of the Midland Railway in England, June 9, 1875. On complete trains of thirteen carriages and two vans continuous brake equipments were installed, representing mechanical, hydraulic, vacuum, and compressed-air brake systems, as follows: Fay's hand brake and Clark & Webb's chain brake, Barker's and Clark's hydraulic brakes, Smith's and Westinghouse's vacuum brakes and Steel &; McInnes's and Westinghouse's automatic compressed-air brakes. These tests were conducted by the Railway Companies' Association under the direction of the Royal Commission on Railway Accidents.

Comparing the best stops made, the results demonstrated the superiority of the Westinghouse automatic brake, with a stop of 777 feet from fifty miles an hour, as compared with 901 feet by Clark's hydraulic brake, 1158 feet by Steel & McInnes's compressed-air brake and 1477 feet by the Smith vacuum brake. In commenting on these results, *Engineering* of June 25, 1875, says:

Lastly, we come to the Westinghouse automatic arrangement, and this, we think we may safely say, is shown by the recent trials to possess all the requisites of a thoroughly efficient continuous brake. This brake proved more prompt and powerful in its action than any of its competitors. ... Its performances as they stand were far beyond those of any other brake. As regards durability and general reliability in every-day practice also it should be remembered that no brake sent to the trials has been so thoroughly tested as the Westinghouse, and this is a fact which it is well to bear in mind.

Surely this is a remarkable tribute for that day to an American invention in the face of strong English competition. It should be noted, however,, that notwithstanding this early demonstration of the superiority of compressed air brakes over vacuum brakes, which was repeated in later tests, the vacuum brake is still used on a much larger mileage of English railways than the compressed-air type. On the other hand, in America, vacuum brakes long ago completely disappeared from service.

The three or four years following the Newark trials passed without any outstanding incident in the development of the art of power braking beyond the gradual evolution of the plain triple valve into its final form, the modification of various subsidiary devices, and the relatively slow introduction of the automatic brake, including the change over from straight air. The latter, so far as new business was concerned, practically concluded its American career in 1878. Meanwhile, in England, the proponents of straight-air, automatic-air, and vacuum brakes, continued to wage vigorous warfare on behalf of then-favorite systems. Westinghouse, after returning to America in 1875, was again in Europe for his longest stay, extending from July 1876, to August 1879, and naturally took an active interest in the controversy.

THE GALTON-WESTINGHOUSE EXPERIMENTS

During the discussion of a paper relating to brakes which was presented at a meeting of the Institution of Mechanical Engineers late in 1877 or early in 1878, Westinghouse called attention to the fact that in testing the action of several kinds of brake shoes, he had observed a very marked difference in the friction of the shoes upon the wheels at high speeds and low speeds. Let the reader note this and keep it in mind. Westinghouse believed that a determination of the facts was of great importance and volunteered to design and make the necessary automatic recording apparatus, and to carry out a system of experiments under the direction of any person who should be appointed by the President of the Institution to supervise the tests and report them. The Institution immediately delegated Captain Douglas Galton, who directed the experiments; which took place on the London, Brighton, and South Coast Railway during the year 1878. Thus originated the famous Galton-Westinghouse tests or experiments, which were the first investigation of this character to be carried out on a practical scale and the results of which may still be considered the most reliable experimental data in existence on the relations of friction, speed, and weight. Galton achieved distinction and became Sir Douglas Galton, C.B., D.C.L., F.R.S.

Three papers entitled "The Effect of Brakes upon Railway Trains," submitted by Captain Galton at meetings of the Institution of Mechanical Engineers held in Paris June 13, 1878, in Manchester October 24 of the same year, and in London April 24, 1879, fully describe these remarkable experiments, and the discussions that followed in each case are scarcely less interesting. These papers and discussions were reprinted by the Westinghouse Air Brake Company in a publication issued in 1894, bearing the same title, copies of which may be found in most technical libraries.

The part taken by Westinghouse in these investigations is suggested by the following sentences from Captain Galton's papers, and from the minutes of the meetings at which they were presented:

Experiments connected with the action of brakes on railway trains require very delicate apparatus, and the author wishes to explain that the credit of the design of the apparatus used in these experiments, and of the successful manner in which the apparatus was applied, belongs entirely to Mr. Westinghouse. (Galton's first paper.)

He has to repeat his thanks to Mr. Westinghouse for the beautiful apparatus contrived by him, and for the very valuable assistance he has rendered in carrying out these experiments. (Galton's second paper.)

The President said that in moving a vote of thanks to Captain Galton for the very great labor he had undergone in bringing before the Institution the results contained in his paper, he thought he ought not to omit the name of Mr. Westinghouse. They had just heard from Captain Galton, that in devising the means of arriving at the conclusions, Mr. Westinghouse had done the greatest possible service.

The way in which Mr. Westinghouse had gone to work, directly he found that something was wanted, to design precisely the thing that was wanted, was as good an illustration of the spirit in which engineers ought to work as could be found anywhere. (Discussion of Galton's third paper.)

The most surprising fact established by these trials was that the friction between two bodies, one or both being in motion, varies inversely as their relative speed. Westinghouse had already observed this phenomenon, and that observation brought about the trials, as we have seen. The following report of his remarks in discussing Galton's third

The first conclusion is that exploding of an ancient fallacy of which we spoke above. It will astonish some to know that such a fallacy persisted as late as 1878. But that it did then persist is certain. In the discussion of one of Galton's papers a speaker said that the result mentioned in the paper as to skidding was certainly somewhat surprising after the deductions drawn by the Royal Commission on Railway Accidents to the effect that when wheels were skidded they retarded the force of the train more than when revolving.

During the further discussion the Royal Commission found supporters, but one speaker said that it had been well known by every practical engine driver for the last twenty-five years that the skidding of wheels was a great mistake. That depends somewhat perhaps on the definition of the word "practical." Many old-time railway-operating men will testify that the Royal Commission theory was not only ancient but was existent years after the Galton-Westinghouse trials, and we find a United States Patent granted to T. E. Sickles as long ago as 1857, which in part reads as follows: "If he (the engineer) wishes to stop as suddenly as possible, he opens to its full width the communication to the atmosphere, whereby the weights acting with their full force, cause the brakes to be applied and the wheels of the car to slide."

It was useful, even if hardly necessary, to prove and emphasize the facts about skidding. It was well worth while to show to men deeply interested that the stopping effect of sliding wheels is less than one-third of the stopping effect of the brakes while the wheels revolve. That was a good thing to know, but the fifth conclusion, that the coefficient of friction increases as the speed falls, is very important. It radically limits and modifies one of Morin's laws of friction, which had been accepted since 1834 by writers, teachers, and practitioners. It shows that to get ideal brake performance the greatest permissible pressure must be used at high speeds, to be gradually reduced as the speed fell. This sets a mark toward which to advance in building up the ideal brake system. It sounds simple, but the physical conditions of braking are extremely complicated.

We shall consider now for a moment the practical deductions from the vital fifth conclusion from the Galton-Westinghouse trials; the friction between brake shoe and wheel is less as the speed of the train is greater; to produce the maximum retardation so far as speed is concerned, the pressure should be greatest on first application and should be diminished as the speed decreases; this to keep the shoes from seizing the wheels and sliding them on the rails. The reader has noted, no doubt, that the stopping effect of a skidded wheel is about one-third of the stopping effect of a wheel braked but still turning. He may have seen this in running his automobile. The obvious thing was to use a relief valve, the action of which should depend on time or the speed of the train. But wheels slide easier on a wet rail than on a dry one. The best rail is clean and dry. The worst rail is one wet with drizzling rain or fog, and still having on it dirt and oil from passing traffic. Between is the rail washed clean but still wet. The conditions may be modified by sanding the rail with clean sand, well screened. Nobody has yet been able to make a relief valve intelligent enough to discriminate between all these varying conditions, although the triple valve can almost talk. Westinghouse took out two patents in 1879 for a pressure-reducing valve, designed to reduce the brake-shoe pressure as the speed falls, and in 1893 Messrs. Parke, Clark, and Hogan of the Brake Company took a patent for an apparatus "in which a higher degree of braking power than heretofore may be made available for emergency application of the brakes in the operation of trains at exceptionally high speeds." At the time the movement for very fast passenger trains was under strong headway. This was especially true in the United States, but some trains famous for speed were running in England and France. The writer, being a somewhat "reactionary" person, and having been considerably influenced by the conservative teachings of Westinghouse, ventures to express here the hope and the belief that it will be a long time before the railroads return to the wasteful and dangerous passenger-train speeds of the last decade of the last century and the first decade of this.

The inventors of the Parke apparatus say: "Our invention is particularly designed for trains which are run at extremely high speeds. We provide means whereby the ordinary graduated application may be made when running at ordinary speeds...and a very powerful application may be made when the train is moving at high speed and the wheels are revolving at their greatest velocity. We also provide for the gradual reduction of the force of such powerful applications as the speed of the train slackens in order to prevent the sliding of the wheels."

The expectations built upon the various reducing contrivances were only partly realized. This was due not only to the impossibility of endowing a mechanism with intelligence, but also to actual physical and financial reasons. The brake rigging in universal use would not stand greatly increased strains, and the railroads could not reasonably and properly rebuild all their passenger brake gear to fit the requirements of a few very fast trains. So an ingenious and fair compromise was reached which served excellently for many years until the standards of practice were slowly built up to the high-efficiency brake now in general use in this country.

We say "in this country," and it has been said elsewhere, that the vacuum brake is still considerably more used in the British Isles than the compressed-air brake. That is by no means due to the invincible prejudice of the Britisher. He naturally prefers the slower and more comfortable stop that goes with a relatively light braking force, and his conditions permit him to enjoy it in safety. He has no level crossings; his right of way is protected from trespassers - man or beast; his lines are all well signaled, and there is higher discipline amongst the men, and more general respect for orders. The need for quick stops is not nearly so frequent, or so great, as with us, although the passenger train speeds are quite as great and the freight-train speeds are greater. On the other hand, the conditions that make the need of emergency stops greater in this country are not due to American recklessness, any more than the use of a less powerful brake hi Great Britain is due to British prejudice. The railroads here were built to create cities in a wilderness; there they were built to serve cities already existing, in a settled and populous land. Here labor and money were scarce, and wages and interest were high; there they were relatively cheap. All the essential differences in the railroads of the two countries may be explained by these fundamental economic facts.

By the compromise spoken of above, provision was made for high-speed braking without disturbing the brake apparatus as it existed. For high-speed braking air was supplied to the train line at 110 pounds per square inch; for ordinary service braking at 70 pounds. Two pump governors were put on the locomotive, one or the other being cut in as high or low pressure was required. A relief device was attached to each brake cylinder, and this was very ingenious. It kept the cylinder pressure from rising to the point of skidding wheels in service stops, and permitted the high pressure to be used in emergency stops; then the emergency pressure was gradually and automatically reduced to service pressure. This seems to be a good deal for an unintelligent machine to do. An expert, after describing the device, says "this seems a very crude adaptation of the refined methods and results indicated in the Galton-Westinghouse tests, but in practice it worked admirably and served a useful purpose for many years, and ultimately became standard on passenger equipment." One's notions of crudeness and refinement depend upon the stage of civilization that he has reached. Most of us who have looked at half a dozen drawings of this relief device, and read several pages of Patent Office specifications describing it think of it as sufficiently refined.

But the reader who has had the patience to read what is here written of the air brake has discovered that the art of train braking is an elaborate structure, the building of which has taken fifty years of high effort. The inventions of Westinghouse and of other men in the organization were the foundations of the art, but only that. On these foundations a structure of applied science was built through fifty years of effort. Research, design, experiment, and test went on, and brilliant things were done in the gradual development of a delicate and complicated apparatus. Not the least important matter was the education of the users. In 1888 the Brake Company put in service an instruction car which wandered over the continent for thirty years, giving free education to the men who handled the brakes in service. It is believed that no university in the country has a larger body of graduates than this travelling school. Closely allied to it was the systematic investigation of accidents. If a collision occurred, Westinghouse men were sent to the spot to help the railroad men to find the causes. The quick explanation of a collision used to be "the air brakes failed to work." In nine cases out of ten, perhaps in ninety-nine cases out of one hundred, this was not true; but it was the easy refuge of a negligent engineer or flagman, and being so simple, was accepted in the newspaper offices. The process of education was tedious. The instruction car was one of Westinghouse's personal helps to the process. After thirty years it was dismantled, for the Air Brake Association, born in this car in 1893, had grown to be a serious and influential body, including makers and users of air brake equipment, and the railroads had established their own brake schools.

This car carried the brake apparatus for a thirty-car train, complete from the engineer's brake-valve to the connections with the brake gear under the cars. The pupils could be taught to handle the brakes and could see many of the results better than on a train. The car carried a steam boiler and air compressor, a water pump and a dynamo to generate its own lighting current. It had an office and bedroom for the instructors, so it was quite at home on a prairie siding. On the walls were valves, cylinders, air pump, and other apparatus, the actual parts cut through in section. Four classes a day of engineers and firemen, and two classes of conductors and trainmen, were run through the car. They were taught, then quizzed and rated, and finally got such certificates as they deserved. Keen students sometimes followed the car 400 or 500 miles to get more information and higher rating. Several presidents of big railways and men eminent in other places started in the engine cab, and it is impossible even to guess how many general managers, division superintendents, and so on, were graduates of the instruction car. The sum of it all is that we have now in America far and away the best braking apparatus and systems in the world; but the ideal brake has not even yet been realized.

In closing the air brake chapter, attention is asked to a fundamental thing which will be suggested in various ways before we have done with this book. Westinghouse was an idealist. Probably he would have resented such a charge. He would have said he was a practical man. Emerson said that he "found that genius left to novices the gay and fantastic and ostentatious and itself pierced directly to the simple and true; that it was simple and sincere... All great actions have been simple." So of Westinghouse's idealism. It was not vague or fantastic or expressed in sounding phrases. It was never expressed in words at all; it was expressed in facts. The instruction car and the elaborate system of investigating accidents of which we have just written were expressions of his idea of what folks nowadays call "service." We see many such expressions as we go through his life, for the idea was in his nature. He never ceased to think how the product of his mind and the product of his shops could be of more service to his customers, to his employees, and to the world. To that end he lavished money and effort. It was enlightened selfishness, if you please, but that seems to be a good basis for working ethics. At any rate it was enlightened and we call it applied idealism.

[1] Mr. Moore contributed substantially to the brake and friction draft-gear arts, both as an independent inventor and as co-inventor with Westinghouse.

Chapter Three - Friction Draft Gear

A GREAT railroad president, an engineer by profession and a man of imagination, Mr. Cassatt, said that the friction draft gear was a more important invention than the air brake, and Westinghouse himself sometimes said the same thing. How many readers of this book ever heard of the friction draft gear, or have a definite notion of its construction and its functions? Even railroad men were slow to appreciate it. Other inventors and manufacturers, usually quick to see, and diligent to seize opportunities, long failed to understand that a new field for profitable enterprise was opened by this invention, although Westinghouse advertised it widely in print and by public demonstrations.

This situation came about partly because the immediate need of the friction gear at the time of its invention was not urgent, and only a man with the foresight of Westinghouse could expect the future need. That involved foreseeing something of the mechanical effects of the air brake in handling long and heavy trains. Such foresight required engineering knowledge and insight, and it required also considerable applied imagination, a combination not very common. The need of the air brake at the time of its invention was tolerably obvious to all men, and inventors were busy with schemes for brakes, continuous through the train, and controlled by the engineer. The time was ripe for a revolution in brakes; only a few gifted men suspected that a revolution in draft gear was impending when Westinghouse brought out the friction gear. Perhaps another reason for the reluctance to use the new device was failure to grasp the consequences to flow from dissipating energy by friction instead of storing it in springs.

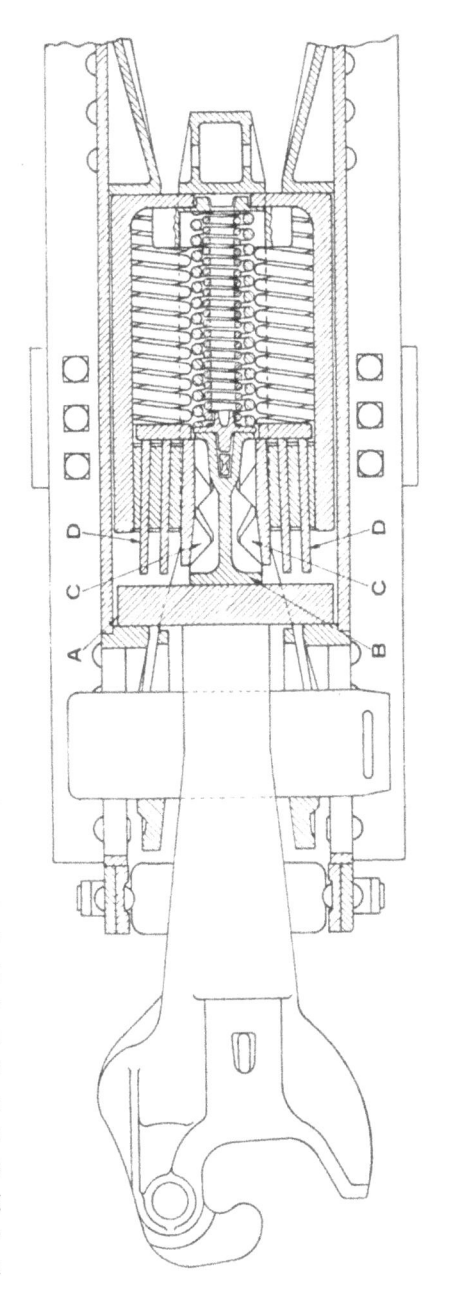

WESTINGHOUSE FRICTION DRAFT-GEAR.

The coupler abuts against the follower-plate A. This follower-plate when driven back forces back the wedge B and the wedge plates CC which are opposed by the springs, causing the wedge plates CC to be thrust sidewise. In the meantime the follower-plate A has engaged the friction-plates DD, carrying them back. The greater the backward movement of the coupler, the greater the side thrust on the friction-plates and the greater the frictional resistance. Similar action takes place in pulling.

It is much too soon to attempt any estimate of the relative effect on human progress of those two inventions. Few men would now venture to say that

51

the friction draft gear is nearly as important as the air brake, but it was a more novel conception. It introduced into railroad practice a new principle; the air brake applied new means to an old principle. The spring gear mitigates by spring action alone the shocks and stresses due to coupling, starting, running, and stopping trains. The energy developed is stored ready to react when the springs are released. In the friction gear the energy is dissipated as heat and there can be no reaction. This was the great conception of the invention. The consequences of spring reaction depend upon the quantity of energy stored and the period of release. If that quantity is large and release sudden the consequences are serious. If the recoil of a great gun on shipboard were taken up by springs the reaction would throw the gun out of the ship if it were not stopped by the turret walls. At best it would wreck things. In the stirring old frigate actions which we read about when we were boys, the recoil of the guns was managed by block and tackle. The gun crews manning the leads checked the recoil and ran the gun forward to firing position again. In the course of time hydraulic recoil gear came in, and Westinghouse designed and patented hydraulic gear for railroad use, but it was costly, and the mechanical difficulties of fitting it to cars were great, if not insuperable.

As cars increased in weight and as the length of trains grew, heavier springs were used, and the effects of their reaction became more and more severe, particularly on air braked trains. They increased not only in number and in degree but in kind. Things happened that had never happened before. The freight engineer discovered that with the best intentions he was liable to break his train in two or in three parts without actually stopping and starting but by variations of speed while running, and the old hand knows that a broken freight train is not merely inconvenient, it is extremely dangerous. Attempts to make matters better by still further increasing the capacity of the springs made them worse. An excellent demonstration of this particular way of breaking a train in two was made in a series of skilfully conducted tests made on the Southern Pacific Railway in 1908. Incidentally the reader may note that this was twenty years after the issue of the friction-gear patent and twenty-one years after the most important single improvement in the air brake. The report of these tests says: "Probably more damage to equipment and lading has been caused by engineers...attempting to release brakes on freight trains...after slowing down than from any other one cause over which operating officials have control." To ascertain the effects of different gears in such cases trains were run at twenty miles an hour and slowed down to about eight miles; then brakes were released and the engine throttle opened wide. The result was that with the friction gear "the train remained intact and was again accelerated as intended, but in the attempts to accomplish this much-desired result with the spring gear the train was parted sometimes in several places and in no case was the train again put under way." The conclusion was that "it is absolutely impossible to permit engineers to make a practice of attempting to release brakes and apply steam with long freight trains under way which are equipped with spring gear and quick-action brakes."

Now we will look for the genesis of the friction gear. In 1878 certain air brake trials were made under the personal supervision of Westinghouse in England. In foreign practice there is much greater movement between the cars in a train than in the United States because of a quite different arrangement of couplers and buffers. The train used in these trials consisted of a locomotive and twenty vehicles, the buffer springs having a total motion of from eight inches to ten inches, to each car. When completely compressed, they, therefore, reduced the length of the train by about sixteen feet. The trials had proceeded successfully, and a final stop was made at a station in London in which the brakes were applied with full force with the train moving at comparatively low speed, and the buffer springs on each vehicle were fully compressed when the train came to a standstill. As the passengers were alighting, the engineer released the air from the brake cylinders. The exhaust ports were unusually large, so that the air escaped quickly, permitting the springs to react suddenly, causing the separation of the cars to the extent of the spring motion, and the movement was so violent that many of the occupants of the train were thrown down and some slight injuries resulted. Westinghouse said that the buffers required a brake, and the need in this instance was supplied by exhausting the air from the brake cylinder slowly enough to permit the springs to react gradually. In this incident, Westinghouse said, was the germ of the conception of the friction draft-gear mechanism, for it clearly demonstrated to him the destructive tendencies of unrestrained reactive effect of springs used in connection with draft and buffing devices. The idea lay dormant until the necessity for something of the kind in the United States was brought forcibly to the attention of Westinghouse in connection with the brake experiments at Burlington in 1887. The experimental train used at Burlington had ordinary draft and buffing springs with a capacity of about 20,000 pounds, and in addition these cars were also fitted with auxiliary buffer springs of about the same strength, placed directly above the draft mechanism, and contacting with a horn on the coupler head, this spring acting only in compression.

As long as the serial brake operation was so slow that the front part of the train was stopped before the brakes in the rear became effective, the cars were pushed together by the crowding in of the unbraked rear portion of the train, and there was no dangerous reactive effect of the draft springs. When, however, the rapidity of serial brake action had been increased so that the last brake was fully applied while the train was still in motion, the reaction of the springs became effective, and at speeds above thirty miles an hour it was impossible to make an emergency stop without parting the train by the braking of the coupler mechanisms. The parting usually occurred about one-third of the length of the train from the locomotive. An excellent opportunity for observation repeated many times showed quite clearly this effect of spring reaction. As stated before, the reactive effect in the particular train in question was about double that ordinarily present, due to the use of the auxiliary buffer spring, which it was expected would in some measure reduce buffing shocks caused by serial brake operation. It was without value for its intended purpose and proved a positive disadvantage because of its reactive effect, and when it was removed coupler breakages ceased. The experiment, however, served an excellent purpose in demonstrating the objectionable effect of the reactive effort of high spring resistance.

The subject becomes somewhat complex, as it deals with long and heavy trains and not with short ones or individual cars, and because it is also connected with the serial operation of brakes. If all cars were of the same weight, equally loaded and fitted with brakes that applied simultaneously with uniform force, there would be no coupler strains tending to cause train partings, as there would be uniform speed deceleration of every portion of the train. The objectionable reactive effect only occurs when it becomes sufficiently cumulative, as in a long train, and then mainly in connection with brake applications; for it is the serial application of brakes that causes the springs to be compressed one by one, thereby putting them in a state to react together and with destructive effect.

The term "long trains" is necessarily inexact, for the variation in weight of individual cars and of their loading enters into the problem; but the invention of the friction draft gear was based upon the observed performance of a fifty-car train in 1887, and at the same time it was demonstrated that with a train of half the length the reactive spring effect was practically negligible. The draft devices then in use were strong enough to absorb without breaking the strains and stresses produced by the movement and stopping of twenty-five-car trains.

Some of the serious elements in the cost of railroad operation are repairs to draw gear and underframes, and damage to lading due to energy which ought to be dissipated harmlessly instead of being stored to do mischief. Understanding all this involves a pretty complicated group of ideas not so familiar then as they are now. It must be borne in mind that in 1887 trains of fifty cars were comparatively rare, and the average number of cars per train did not then exceed thirty. Furthermore, they were of relatively low capacity and of wooden construction, as the steel car had not yet appeared. The tendency toward longer trains was, however, manifested at the date of the Burlington trials, and its effect began to appear in heavy draft-gear repairs and frequent train partings. Perhaps in no other instance was the capacity of Westinghouse for a long-range vision better exemplified than in the one in which he foresaw the great increase in train lengths and weights, and their loading, and what was demanded in improved draft appliances to make this controlling factor of car construction adequate for the purpose it serves. He clearly foresaw increased stresses in the draft appliances, and as clearly identified the fact that stronger springs intended to meet the requirements would augment reactive effect which had already been demonstrated to be so great as to cause frequent train partings under normal conditions of operation. He, therefore, invented and devised a mechanism which included a high frictional resistance to movement, combined with a moderate spring resistance. The frictional resistance was effective in both forward and backward motion, and entirely counteracted the reactive effect of the spring. The chief function of the spring was to create frictional contact of the moving parts of the device and restore them to normal position when the stresses of operation were removed. So certain was Westinghouse of his inferences and assumptions that he began without delay to develop various forms of the basic idea and submit them to practical tests.

His first friction draft-gear patent was issued in 1888, and it disclosed the broad principles upon which all subsequent friction gears have been designed. The structure shown and described in the patent was built, and it was tested on a train of thirty cars in February 1890. This train was in charge of the late R. H. Soule, a distinguished railroad officer who had entered the service of Westinghouse to develop the first friction gear, and who was an excellent mechanical engineer. The apparatus was shown in several important railway centers and a few of the devices were put in general service, but the construction was such that it was unfavorably affected by an accumulation of rust, so that it did not prove entirely successful. A further study of the problem resulted in a change of form that remedied the defects in the first type, and after three years of development and experimental work a train of forty-five cars in the coke traffic was placed at the disposal of Westinghouse by the H. C. Frick Coke Company, and these cars were fitted with the new device and kept together in one train. The train was put in service between the Connellsville coke region and the Carnegie Works at Homestead and was under daily observation, and some slight changes were developed by use and made. It was operated many months under extreme conditions as to load and speed, and therefore furnished the best possible opportunity to demonstrate the value of the invention in its application to freight equipment, proving, as it did, that the principles involved in its construction were sound, and that the purpose for which it was designed had been attained. Before its use it needed great skill and care on the part of the engineer to avoid train partings and rear-end shocks that were of destructive intensity. When the friction gear was attached it was impossible to so operate the locomotive as to cause serious shocks or strains.

So far we have considered the functions of the draft gear in taking care of the stresses set up in stopping, as observed, for example, at the Burlington brake trials, and in taking care of the stresses set up in a running train by changes in speed, as in the Southern Pacific tests. But it performs an important duty in starting trains also. To start a long and heavy train free slack is necessary. , If such a train were tight-coupled, with no play between the cars, the locomotive would simply spin its drivers and the train would stand still. Actually it is started serially, one car at a time, and the momentum of each moving car helps to start the car next behind. This necessary slack is provided in the draft gear. In the spring gear it is spring slack, and the effects of spring reaction are developed in starting trains as well as in stopping them. The friction gear provides the necessary starting slack without reaction. It has been found in practice that a train fitted with the friction gear can get up to twenty miles an hour by the time that a similar train fitted with the ordinary spring draft gear can be entirely put in motion. This is due to the greater care required to start a train fitted with the ordinary gear, to avoid the destructive reactions from stresses in excess of the cushioning capacity of the spring gear. It is probable that the greatest commercial value of the friction gear is found in the reduction of strains of extension to a point within the strength of the car couplings, strange as that may seem to one accustomed to think of it only as a buffer.

The first commercial application of the draft gear was to 1000 steel cars on the Bessemer & Lake Erie Railroad, exactly nine years from the date of the original invention. This was almost immediately followed by its adoption as standard by the Baltimore & Ohio Railroad. A dozen years after the invention of the air brake Westinghouse was rich and famous. It took nine years or more to put this other brilliant invention in such a place commercially that the manufacturers began to get a reasonable return on the costs of development and promotion. The struggle for the recognition of the principle is now over. In the four years ending in the spring of 1920 some 90 per cent of all freight cars built were fitted with the friction gear, and the Westinghouse Air Brake Company had shipped over a million friction gears.

Regarded as an example of mechanical design the friction draft gear in the form in which Westinghouse left it is one of the most ingenious of his structures, and those who have looked over his many hundreds of patents will agree that this is saying a great deal. When we consider this; when we consider that the parting of trains has long been a fruitful cause of bad accidents; when we consider the great and constant cost, directly and indirectly, of maintaining draw gear and underframes, and finally when we consider the new and fundamental conception, we cannot wonder that Westinghouse sometimes said and that Mr. Cassatt said that the friction draft gear was a more important invention than the air brake. A forgotten" philosopher said that the main obstacles to human progress are friction, gravity, and natural depravity. Obviously he was not an engineer; perhaps that is why he is forgotten.

Chapter Four - General Sketch of Electric Activities

THE air brake and its allies and dependencies have been considered. We shall now take up Westinghouse's electrical activities in a general way. Later chapters will show in more detail how they developed in the gradual building up of a new art.

The general development of the electric art came on in great waves; first arc lighting, next incandescent lighting, then the trolley and the single-phase alternating current at about the same period, and finally polyphase alternating current and transmission of power. Of all these stages Westinghouse was conscious; in all of them he had a part; in one of them, the most important, he took a commanding place. The most important stage was the use of alternating current. This story will be told in detail later. Let us consider here in a general way the relations of Westinghouse to the new art of harnessing electricity for the use and convenience of man.

But first it may not be out of the way to glance at a few very elementary things. Much will be said about direct current and alternating current, and it will be found that Westinghouse's greatest electrical achievement was to hasten the use of the alternating current, a long step in human progress.

"Current" is a conventional and arbitrary term, accepted years ago, to express the passing of electric energy from one place to another. It is said to "flow" through, or on, a conductor. Just how fast it flows nobody seems to know, but the speed varies with the kind of conductor. So far as anybody knows now, light is the fastest thing in our part of the universe, at say 186,000 miles a second, and electricity comes next. For working purposes we may take the speed of the electric transmission on a good copper conductor at 100,000 miles a second, although very much greater velocities have been observed in experiments. In longitude work the time of transmission of electric signals must be considered, but in transmission of power by electricity time does not enter. This matter of the speed of the electric impulse will be interesting when we take up the balancing of current in certain heavy railroad work in a later chapter.

Direct current flows always in one direction. The flow of alternating current is periodically reversed in direction. In much of the early practice these reversals, "alternations," took place 16,000 times a minute. Lower frequencies are now standard.

There is no essential difference in the effects produced by these two different kinds of current in work done. There are some uses to which one or the other is specially applicable; but generally speaking, when the current reaches the place where the work is to be done, by a motor or by a lamp, one kind of current when suitably applied is about as effective as the other. The essential differences are in generation and transmission, hi manufacturing the current and taking it to the work, and in the means of utilization. These differences have brought about the fact that ninety-five per cent of the electric energy generated and transmitted is by alternating current. It is to the everlasting glory of George Westinghouse that he saw the meaning of these differences before it was seen in a big way by any other man who combined in himself the qualities and the capacities to make use of them. This was so true that in the middle eighties alternating current was spoken of in the United States amongst students and experimenters as the "Westinghouse current." Few others than students and experimenters spoke of it at all.

We shall now try to state very simply what those essential differences are. An elementary fact about transmission is that the quantity of current passed economically over a conductor at a fixed pressure, or voltage, depends on the size of the conductor, and conversely if the size of the conductor is fixed the power passed economically can be increased by raising the voltage. If the power conveyed is great and the voltage is low, the conductor must be large. If the distance to be covered is considerable the cost of the conductors becomes prohibitive. This is exactly the situation that had come about when Westinghouse took up alternating current. Direct current had to be conveyed at low voltage, because it had to be used at comparatively low voltage, and it does not lend itself to ready reduction from high transmission voltage to low working voltage. Therefore, the cost of copper conductors set a narrow limit to the quantity of power conveyed and the distances. Alternating current can be readily transformed from high transmission voltage to low working voltage with but little loss of energy in the process. Therefore, a larger amount of power can be carried at high voltage on a small conductor and stepped down to low voltage at the place of use. Furthermore, alternating current can be converted into direct current at the place of use with little loss.

The other important difference mentioned above is in generation. The direct-current generator does not lend itself to very large capacities, relatively, nor is it well adapted to the high speed of the steam turbine. Alternating-current turbo-generators, driven by steam or water, are now built up to 60,000 horsepower or more. This leads to economy in the manufacture of power.

An old Westinghouse engineer writes: "The greatest possibilities of alternating current seemed to lie in its flexibility of voltage transformation. This one feature alone always impressed Mr. Westinghouse as important enough eventually to make the alternating system the dominating one. However, it is doubtful whether even his great imagination foresaw the complete extent to which the alternating-current system actually would supersede all others."

So much for the elementary things; now we may proceed with the story of George Westinghouse.

In the field of electricity he was not an inventor of fundamentals. He invented many useful details, but his great work was in stimulating, combining, and directing the work of other men. When he entered the field he was already a world figure; a loadstone attracting from all directions. No other man combined the resourcefulness, the contact with scientists, the ardor for engineering development, the manufacturing plants, the organization of men in many groups, the vision, the optimism, the courage, and the will to bring things to pass. Known the world over, he was the receptacle of the thoughts and ideas of scientists and inventors everywhere. He was the captain of them all, the man who received and coordinated and executed.

A mind so active and inquiring as that of George Westinghouse could not fail to be interested in electricity. As a boy in his father's shop he amused himself taking sparks from a belt and charging a Leyden jar; but for many years the incentives and the opportunities before him were much more mechanical than electrical. There were useful things to be done with mechanisms in endless variety, while the only important use of electricity was in telegraphy. As the years went on, Westinghouse gave some thought to the possible use of electricity in railroad braking. Later he took out patents for an automatic telephone exchange, disclosing principles suggestive of some features of modern practice. When he took up railroad signaling and interlocking he soon began to use electric circuits for control. Meanwhile electric lighting was developing slowly; the distribution of power by electricity was but a dream of a few speculative philosophers. AU effectual uses of electricity in the arts were by direct current; the alternating current as a useful form of electricity was not known. In the early eighties the few important uses of electricity other than in telegraphy were for street-lighting by arc-lamps and for indoor lighting by incandescent lamps. There were a few private lighting plants in hotels and other large buildings, and in 1882 central stations for commercial lighting current began operation, but it was soon seen that the cost of copper wire for transmission would be prohibitive for distances more than a few hundred yards.

Late in 1883 Westinghouse began to think somewhat seriously about direct-current lighting. He began to gather about him a staff, and soon had several men busy in study of methods and in development of details; but not until he had his vision of the possibilities of the alternating current was his interest thoroughly aroused. He had but just started on his way to Damascus. The road was somewhat long and the vision did not come so abruptly as it came to Saul.

Although the arc lamp came into commercial use earlier than the incandescent lamp, Westinghouse took up incandescent lighting first. A difficulty found early in that art was automatic regulation of dynamo voltage to conform to varying loads on the lighting circuit. In 1881 Westinghouse had taken out a patent for automatically regulating either the engine or the dynamo in response to changes in load. The pursuit of this object soon brought about relations with William Stanley, who later became a famous figure in electric development. Mr. H. H. Westinghouse, a younger brother, had invented a high-speed engine and formed the Westinghouse Machine Company to make it. This engine had inherent self-regulating capabilities, and negotiations were begun with the Brush Electric Company looking to its use with the Brush dynamos. Brush was an able and enterprising pioneer in electric lighting. While negotiations were going on, H. H. Westinghouse happened to meet Stanley, then a young and unknown electrical engineer, and learned that he had invented a self-regulating dynamo. Stanley with E. P. Thomson had also invented an incandescent lamp with a filament of carbonized silk. The immediate result of this accidental meeting was that Stanley went to Pittsburgh, in the employ of Westinghouse, to manufacture his dynamo and lamp and to develop a complete electric-lighting system, and Westinghouse entered upon a careful study of the art. This happened in the first months of 1884, just when he was starting his natural-gas company and thus creating another new art, in which he brought out thirty-six patents in two years. At the same time he was active also in the affairs of his new company which was introducing railway signaling and interlocking.

To appreciate the task before Westinghouse when he considered taking up the electrical-manufacturing business, it will be helpful to outline briefly the condition of the business as it then existed.

The exploitation of direct-current arc and incandescent lighting had gained considerable headway in the early eighties. The more prominent producers of such apparatus were the Brush Electric Light Company, the Swan Incandescent Light Company, the Consolidated Electric Company, the Edison Electric Lighting Company, the United States Electric Lighting Company, and the Thomson-Houston Electric Company. Each of these companies owned numerous patents relating to the electrical art. It thus became necessary for Westinghouse to learn whether the Stanley silk-filament lamp and the Stanley self-regulating direct-current dynamo would involve the use of adversely held patents.

Until the metal-filament lamp was developed, the essential of the universal incandescent lamp was the arch-shaped illuminant of carbonized organic material. For many years vain attempts had been made to produce an incandescent lamp having as an illuminant a metal of high melting point, such as platinum. In 1878 Sawyer and Man succeeded in carbonizing paper and other fibrous materials in the form of an arch. They applied for a patent thereon in 1880. After extended Patent Office interference proceedings with an application of Edison, the patent was granted in 1885 by assignment from Sawyer and Man to the Electro-Dynamic Company. That company, incorporated in 1878, was the earliest company organized in this country for carrying on a general system of incandescent electric lighting. In 1881 its patents and assets were sold to the Eastern Electric Company, which, in turn, in 1882 sold them to the Consolidated Company. By the purchase of this company the Westinghouse Electric Company became the legitimate successor of the first incandescent-lighting company.

Meanwhile, Edison, although he was ultimately defeated in his contest in the Patent Office with Sawyer and Man upon the filament, secured a patent in 1880 upon a carbon filament in an exhausted container made entirely of glass. Sawyer and Man had shown in their application a container in the form of a tube closed by a stopper, sealed into the end. This "stopper lamp" became famous in its relation to the lighting of the Columbian Exposition in 1893. Of that something will be said when we come to treat particularly of the Exposition. Two other inventions of moment should be here mentioned, one patented by Sawyer and Man in 1879 for treating carbon conductors in an atmosphere of hydrocarbon, and the other an invention of Hiram S. Maxim for making a filament out of carbonized cellulose. These and other adversely held inventions cast doubt on the expediency of Westinghouse entering the incandescent-lamp field. We shall hear more of this when we come to the story of the Chicago World's Fair.

The status of the generator was less complicated, although a patent issued to Weston in 1883, and assigned to the United States Company, upon a self-regulating dynamo, appears to have caused Westinghouse to doubt the propriety of manufacturing the Stanley dynamo. Numerous other patents on the direct-current generator and systems of distribution were also held by the United States and other companies.

Through Franklin L. Pope, an eminent electrical patent expert, and Thomas B. Kerr, one of his patent lawyers, Westinghouse was advised as to the probable bearing which these various patents might have upon his operations, and particularly upon the Stanley incandescent lamp and dynamo. The results of these investigations apparently caused Westinghouse to hesitate at the time, but in March, 1885, he, with some apparent reluctance, consented to the organization of a company to take over the business previously carried on by Westinghouse as a personal undertaking at a cost of about $150,000. Westinghouse proposed that the company if formed should be known as the Stanley Electric Company. This plan, however, was not then carried into effect, and Westinghouse showed no great enthusiasm for electric ventures until the alternating system had made its strong appeal to him.

But direct-current development was by no means abandoned. Research work, design, and experiment went on, and early in 1886 a Westinghouse direct-current incandescent-lighting plant was installed in the Windsor Hotel in New York. About the same time a similar plant was placed in the Monongahela Hotel in Pittsburgh. The first central-station Westinghouse equipment was at Trenton, N. J., the installation of which was begun in the latter part of May 1886, by the construction firm of Westinghouse, Church, Kerr & Company, and practically completed late in August of that year. The generating plant consisted of six 100-volt, 300-light, direct-current, shunt-wound dynamos of the Siemens type. Similar direct-current plants were soon after placed in Plainfield, N. J., and in Schenectady, N. Y., the present home of the General Electric Company, and installation in many other cities followed. In August 1889, more than 350,000 incandescent lamps were in service in connection with the central-station plants installed with apparatus produced by the Westinghouse Electric Company requiring about 40,000 horsepower. Of these lamps a large number, perhaps the greater number, were alternating current.

The beginning of those activities of Westinghouse in alternating-current development, which were to revolutionize the electric art, was late in 1886; but we will go on now with some further details and return shortly to the alternating current.

In course of time Westinghouse decided to take up arc lighting, and in November 1888 he bought the entire capital stock of the Waterhouse Electric and Manufacturing Company. This was more than ten years after the installation of arc lights in the Place de l'Opera in Paris, and the people of many cities, in many lands, had become familiar with the dazzling glare of enormous lamps. The Waterhouse system, direct current, was supposed to be well developed and the company had established a considerable business. It gradually appeared that a system that would do pretty well on a small scale was not necessarily fit for large-scale operation. The Waterhouse apparatus when in service demanded too much personal attention from experts. After considerable redesign the system was dropped.

Meanwhile, Stanley, a versatile and clever man, thought that he had discovered a principle in alternator design that might be the basis of a system of arc lighting by alternating current. Westinghouse was much taken by some features of this new system, which were indeed plausible, and the company spent a great deal of money developing it and pushing it commercially. Many difficulties developed. One of these, and a serious one, was the fact that the alternating-current arc lamp of those days was inferior to the direct-current lamp. The light of the alternating-current arc lamp was from the incandescent tips of the carbons. In the direct-current arc lamp of those days much of the light was from a glowing crater formed in the upper carbon. From this crater a big part of the total light developed by the arc was projected downward. In the alternating-current lamp of the time craters formed in both carbons, and the light from the lower carbon was projected upward and much of the total light was wasted. This fundamental difficulty was corrected in later years by radically different lamps. Furthermore, the noise of the early alternating-current arc lamp was objectionable.

For these reasons this Stanley system of alternating arc lighting was given up, and effort reverted to direct current. But there were strong engineering reasons pointing to the alternating-current system, particularly the possibility of using larger generating units in central stations. Slowly came radical changes in lamps. The flaming arc lamp came in; the arc flame itself was used as the source of light instead of the craters. The energy expended in the arc became the important thing; not the kind of current. Detail improvements went on in the lamp itself and in regulation until generation for direct-current arc systems almost disappeared from the market so far as new apparatus was concerned. This must have been a pleasing outcome for Westinghouse, who never let the alternating-current idea sleep.

On the whole, the Westinghouse Company did a good deal for arc lighting in original research, in developing lamps and other apparatus, and in commercial effort; but arc lighting never became either a specialty with the company or a very important part of the business. In the nature of things, this was logical, for it was obvious almost from the start that immensely the greater part of the artificial lighting of the world must be by something capable of indefinite subdivision into small units, and to this the incandescent lamp lent itself admirably. We shall see later that Westinghouse gave much attention to the development of various forms of glow lamps.

With the coming of the gas-filled or nitrogen lamp the arc lamp is gradually disappearing from the active field. Unless something new and surprising develops, the arc lamp evidently is doomed. For the same energy expended, the nitrogen lamp probably gives but little more light, if any, than the arc lamp, but, like all incandescent lamps, it requires practically no attendance except for replacement in case of breakage. It can operate directly from the alternating-current system, with regulators for constant current. Therefore, it may be said that lighting by arc lamps, practically the earliest branch of the electric-lighting business, has now been superseded by incandescent lamps.

The Westinghouse Electric Company went steadily forward in developing and producing machinery and apparatus for lighting, and in a few years railway work began to look important. As time went on the Company carried out an enormous development, and it has brought about some of the greatest advances in the direct-current field. Particulars of some of these will be told when we come to speak of the Company's activities in transportation.

In 1890 the Company built a 250-horsepower direct-current generator for railway service. Possible customers came hundreds of miles to see one of the largest machines in the world. There was some discussion as to whether a larger generator would ever be built. Certain things happened in the tests which the visitors did not see. For instance, parts of the armature winding shifted on the smooth, cylindrical core as much as an inch. The armature was tinkered up, the machine was shipped, and gave satisfactory service. This incident led to one of the very important improvements in direct-current dynamo construction, the use of slotted armatures in large dynamos; they had been used before in small ones. After the building of a machine of this type was well under way the opinion of high authorities was taken, in Europe and America. They agreed that it was absolutely impossible to make satisfactory large-capacity, slotted-armature railway dynamos, and that it was a waste of money to attempt it. The Westinghouse people went on, and when this first machine was tested the results surprised even the designers, and it was evident that a big step forward had been made. The slotted armature soon superseded all other types in large direct-current work, and several manufacturers were temporarily driven out of the field. For a time the Westinghouse Company was the pace maker with its slotted-armature, multipolar generator.

About this time, in the early nineties, came the direct-connected generator, followed quickly by the engine-type machine. Theretofore the generator had been driven from the prime mover by a belt. The direct-coupled set was a generator complete, with its own bearings, connected to a standard high-speed engine. In the true engine-type machine the armature is on the engine shaft. This construction called for many changes in details, but the development was rapid, and generator units quickly increased in size. By 1894 machines of 1500 kilowatts were built, and by 1898 generators of 3000 kilowatts were in hand. In this development the Westinghouse Company had a great part, but about 1899 it gave the large direct-current generator its death blow. The rotary converter had been developed by Westinghouse's engineers, and they had brought forward the alternating-current machinery and apparatus. The combination made it unnecessary to build large direct-current generators for the special places where large volumes of direct current were required. Electric energy could be developed and transmitted as alternating current and converted as needed. An account of the origin, nature, and functions of the rotary generator will be given later. The economic consequences of what had happened will become clear as we go on.

Let us now go back a few years and try to find the origin and trace the development of the alternating-current conception in the mind of Westinghouse. While in Italy in the early part of 1882 he had formed a close friendship with Doctor Diomede Pantaleoni, an eminent Italian physician, whose son, Guido Pantaleoni, recently had been graduated from the University of Turin. Through this acquaintance Westinghouse became interested in a process, invented by an Italian, for making artificial marble from gypsum, and he arranged with Guido Pantaleoni and Albert Schmid, a young Swiss engineer, to come to America for the purpose of manufacturing this product. The process was never of commercial utility, and Westinghouse placed Pantaleoni in general charge of certain activities of the Union Switch & Signal Company which brought him into contact with the electrical work upon which Stanley was engaged.

Pantaleoni was called back to Italy in May 1885, by the death of his father, and having occasion to visit his old professor, Galileo Ferraris, at Turin, he there met Lucian Caulard, who had installed between Lanzo and Circe an alternating-current system of distribution, patented by himself and John Dixon Gibbs. This meeting had great consequences. Leonard E. Curtis, an eminent patent lawyer, who later became associated with Thomas B. Kerr, counsel for the Westinghouse Company, and was for twenty years in the thick of the movement, writes: "It was in 1885 that Mr. Westinghouse became interested in the inventions of Gaulard and Gibbs relating to the use of single-phase alternating currents for distribution by means of what they called secondary generators (now called transformers), and that was the starting point of the great development of the alternating-current system. All of us who knew anything at all about the practical application of electricity, knew that the induction coil was necessarily the most inefficient transformer of energy possible, and we also thought we knew that there were other objections to the use of alternating currents, which would make their commercial use wholly impracticable. It required the combination of an erratic Frenchman, Gaulard, as an inventor, and a sporty Englishman, Gibbs, as a financial backer, to make the necessary experiments to show that that was not necessarily so, and it required a man of wide vision and adequate resources for making his dreams come true, like Mr. Westinghouse, to introduce the alternating-current system into the wide field it was destined to occupy." No one knows just when Westinghouse began to think of the immense results to flow from the transformation of voltage and current; but it is certain that very early he appreciated that the limitations of the low-voltage direct-current system might be overcome by such transformation. He foresaw quite clearly a broad field for electric power, and this was the vision of which we often speak.

As regards Gaulard and Gibbs, the impression conveyed by Mr. Curtis is neither just nor adequate. Gibbs speaks of Gaulard as a "talented young Frenchman," as he undoubtedly was. It is true, however, that he died insane. Gibbs may have been sporty; he was a "good sport," and he lost his fortune like a man. Neither of them was an electrical engineer. Gibbs says he "conceived the idea that it would be a great step, if it should be possible, to convey an electric current capable of lighting a small incandescent glow lamp at a considerable distance, perhaps some miles from the dynamos, as was already possible with arc lamps, while the more generally useful incandescent lamp could not be lighted beyond 500 yards from the power station." He hired Gaulard, and they soon "discovered and demonstrated that the actual transformation of alternating current practically costs no expenditure of energy." Their first transformer is now in the South Kensington Museum. They took out patents, organized companies, took lighting contracts, and made exhibitions. Their patents were attacked, and the suits finally went to the House of Lords on appeal. Here after seven years of litigation Gibbs was defeated. He says: "I left the House of Lords a ruined man." But he died hard. With the help of Schneider of Creusot he organized a French company to distribute electric power on the left bank of the Seine, but he does not seem to have recouped his fortune.

The "secondary generator" (or transformer) of Gaulard and Gibbs was first shown in public in 1883 at the Royal Aquarium in London. It was exhibited in Turin in 1884, and a plant was installed at Tivoli to send lighting current to Rome. For this installation the Italian Government gave Gaulard and Gibbs a gold medal and a prize of 400.

Pantaleoni was so much impressed by what he saw and learned at Turin that he cabled an account to Westinghouse, who promptly requested Pantaleoni to secure an option upon the American rights of Gaulard and Gibbs. Accordingly Pantaleoni proceeded to London and there met Gibbs, and secured from him an option which he brought back with him upon his return to the United States in 1885. Westinghouse at once accepted the option in principle, although asking for certain changes in detail.

Westinghouse instructed Pope to make a careful investigation of the Gaulard and Gibbs patent situation and to study the possibilities of their system. Pope, in testimony given in 1887, in connection with the Gaulard and Gibbs patent litigation, said:

My own impression at first sight was, like that of everyone else, an unfavorable one. The knowledge which I had gathered in the ordinary course of my professional experience led me to expect that the loss of energy in conversion would be so great as to render the scheme commercially unprofitable, and that this lost energy, appearing in the form of heat, would quickly destroy the apparatus, or at least render it useless; and it was not until I had gone carefully through the published researches of Hopkinson and Ferraris that I found reason to change my opinion. I followed up the matter by personal investigations of the apparatus in operation, and was convinced of its novelty and industrial value.

The extracts which I have quoted are but fair samples of the communications and articles which appeared in many of the technical periodicals, and in fact I may say that, so far as I now recollect, all these journals, without exception, whenever they took any notice at all of the work of Gaulard and Gibbs, did so in a spirit of hostile criticism, which continued not only long after the successful installation of the plant in many places, but continues in many quarters up to the present hour.

Westinghouse instructed Stanley and his assistants, Schmid and O. B. Shallenberger, to make tests to determine the commercial value of the Gaulard and Gibbs system. He also arranged to have a number of the transformers and a Siemens alternating-current generator forwarded from England to Pittsburgh. This apparatus was brought over by Reginald Belfield, an assistant of Gaulard and Gibbs, who arrived in this country late in November 1885.

In the meantime considerable progress had been made abroad. A plant had been installed at Aschersleben, Germany, which appears to have been moderately satisfactory. A bit of the Metropolitan Railway (London) had been lighted, from Netting Hill Gate to Aldgate. The Grosvenor Gallery Company had been formed to light the Bond Street and Regent Street districts. This is now one of the largest lighting companies of London. In the spring of 1885 the Inventions Exhibition (London) had been opened with Mr. Belfield in charge there of the Gaulard and Gibbs apparatus. The installations of the Gaulard and Gibbs "secondary generators" at Turin, on the Metropolitan Railway, and at the Inventions Exhibition received much attention in the technical press of Europe. As one result of the knowledge thus spread abroad Zipernowski, Deri, and Bldthey, engineers in the employ of Ganz of Budapesth, brought out transformers which were shown at the Inventions Exhibition. These were designed and wound to run with their primaries in parallel, an arrangement which Westinghouse adopted from the start although the Gaulard and Gibbs apparatus was designed for operation in series.

Immediately on the arrival of the Gaulard and Gibbs apparatus at Pittsburgh, Westinghouse began his study of it. Those who knew him will understand the energy he threw into this work, and how practical were his suggestions on the mechanical side, and how readily he grasped the theoretical lines necessary, applying his mechanical knowledge and skill to the information he obtained, with the result that in an astonishingly short time the uncommercial secondary generator was correctly started on the direct line of development into the modern transformer. A great step had been taken. It led directly to the enormous electrical advance that we have seen during the past three decades, and the essential conceptions were formed and pretty well developed within about three weeks - from December 1 to December 20, 1885.

Those who watched Westinghouse and worked with him through the years ceased to be surprised at his capacity to do extraordinary things and to do them quickly. They learned too, that this capacity was not only a matter of intellectual gifts, but also a matter of dogged industry and of power to work fast and to make other men work fast. Through the long evenings he worked in his private car and in his house, designing, sketching, and dictating. In his car any corner of a table would do, in his house he worked on a billiard table. Seated and leaning uncomfortably over the rail, he drew rapidly and with accuracy and completeness of detail, while those around him watched and answered questions and made suggestions if they could. Probably he had no pencil but borrowed one from the nearest man. As these pencils were never returned one wondered what became of them. His trail through the world was blazed with other men's pencils. An instance of his speeding-up other men is told by Mr. E. M. Herr, now President of the Electric Company, and some time General Manager of the Brake Company. Mr. Herr says:

George Westinghouse at work.
(From a snapshot photograph.)

In all my experience with and work for Mr. Westinghouse, I never but once succeeded, in doing a piece of work for him quicker than he thought it could be done. On this occasion he sent me a pattern to Wilmerding (the Air Brake Works), which arrived there Sunday morning. He had notified Mrs. Herr in my absence on Saturday that this would be at Wilmerding on Sunday, and that she should be particular to see that I got this information immediately on my return, Sunday morning. On getting the information, I called up the superintendent of the foundry at Wilmerding, told him of this pattern and asked him to get it at the station, and see if he could get one of our moulders to mould it Sunday afternoon so that it could be poured the first thing Monday morning. Owing to the continuous process of moulding in use at the Air Brake Company's foundry, unlike other foundries, the pouring of metal began at seven o'clock in the morning. I was at Wilmerding before seven o'clock that Monday morning, and saw that this pattern was poured of the first iron out of the cupola, as I expected Mr. Westinghouse would be out on an early train to see what progress we had made on this casting which he had told me he wished to have sent to the Electric Works at East Pittsburgh as soon as it was cold enough to be hauled down there. As soon as the metal had hardened in the mould, we took it out, put some sand in one of our delivery wagons, and put the red-hot casting in it and sent it to the Electric Works. The wagon had hardly got out of the yard when Mr. Westinghouse appeared. In his usual pleasant manner he greeted us, wished us good morning, and asked me if I had got word about the pattern he had sent out on Sunday. I told him I had and he then asked when it would be moulded. I told him it was moulded. "Indeed. When will you have a casting?" "The casting is made," I replied. "That so? That's good. How soon can you send it to the Electric Company?" I said: "It has gone." Mr. Westinghouse looked at me, hesitated a moment, turned around and started off at a brisk pace. "Then I will go down there and hustle those fellows," and off he went.

An old employee tells this: "The drum rolled off and broke in two pieces, so we had to hustle and make a new one before Mr. Westinghouse got around. We worked all night, but did not succeed in finishing the work before Mr. Westinghouse got to the works the following morning, so our foreman had to tell him what had happened. All he said was: 'It is a good thing such accidents happen, just to see how fast you fellows can work.'

There are many tales of this sort floating about in the various companies.

It is not to be understood that Westinghouse, in a miraculous three weeks, by a flash of genius, made the transformer. The way was long and hard and many fine minds were enlisted. What happened was that the swift and penetrating insight of Westinghouse, and his keen and experienced mechanical faculty, discerned what must be done to change a scientific toy into a commercial tool, and the way to do it.

A general word about the transformer may help us to appreciate what follows. The transformer is not interesting to look at. It is a mere mass of metal, dull and motionless. It is not even graceful in outline or proportion. But it is the heart of the alternating-current system. The reason for being of the alternating-current system lies in its capabilities for simple transformation of voltage over almost any required range, from hundreds of thousands of volts down to almost nothing. Without this ability to transform voltage, the alternating-current system probably would not exist today, or at least it would doubtless hold a position secondary to direct current. This capability of voltage transformation lies in the transformer itself. It will be said many times in this narrative, and in many ways, that the development of the art of distributing electric energy by means of the alternating current has already changed the face of society, and still greater changes are yet to come. Therein is the meaning of that three weeks at East Pittsburgh and of the later work of Stanley, Shallenberger, and Schmid in developing the transformer. Stanley's part in this development will be told in some detail as we proceed. A word in passing is due to Shallenberger and Schmid, both dead now. They were highly gifted men of particularly fine character. They were young in years in 1886 and young in the electric art, but they made an impression on the product of the company which lasts to this day. The present Chief Engineer says that "it was due to Shallenberger that the early Westinghouse transformers were brought to a practical commercial condition. He was a good analytical man and was able to take very scanty data and get practical results." The memory of Shallenberger and Schmid is held in affection and esteem by those who worked with them in the pioneer years.

The "secondary generator" as brought to the United States was designed by Gaulard, who had discussed it with some of the most prominent scientists in Europe, and it should have been, from the advantages M. Gaulard enjoyed, further developed than it actually was. The original apparatus was the old and well-known induction coil. It was not a practicable commercial apparatus from the standpoint of the manufacturer or of the user. Westinghouse, as soon as he grasped the fundamental electrical facts underlying the working of the instrument, applied himself to the production of a piece of apparatus which could be wound on a lathe, discarding the unpractical soldered joints and stamped copper disks for the more commercial form of ordinary insulated copper wire, and it was then a question of only a few days before he had evolved the H-shaped plate built up, and then the primary and secondary were wound in place on a lathe, and the ends were closed by means of intervening I-shaped plates. These are the essentials of a modern transformer. It is interesting to look back and realize that with the time that this invention had been before the public and the many minds working on it, no simple and practical solution should have been found, whereas it took Westinghouse only three weeks to work out those leading features of mechanical design which have been standard ever since.

Stanley, working under the direction of Westinghouse, devised a further improvement, which consisted in securing the enclosure of the coils by making the core of E shaped plates, the central projections of each successive plate being alternately inserted through prewound coils from opposite sides, thus permitting separate winding and consequently the better insulation of the coils. This form was further improved by Albert Schmid, who extended the ends of the arms of the E to meet the central projection. When inserting these plates the extensions were temporarily bent upward, and upon being released each plate formed a closed magnetic circuit about the sides of the coils.

In the early transformers the core-plates were made of very thin sheet iron commonly called tintype metal, having one side covered with thin paper to prevent the flow of eddy or Foucault currents. Pasting paper on the plates was highly objectionable as a manufacturing process, and this led Albert Schmid to build a transformer without the paper. To the surprise but greatly to the gratification of the electrical engineers of the company it was found that the oxide formed upon the surface of the iron sheets served as a sufficient insulation and, with the decreased separation of the sheets, resulted in increased efficiency. The use of paper was then discontinued.

Mention should also be made of two other important early contributions to the development of the transformers made by Westinghouse in 1886, one of which is the ventilated core for preventing overheating by permitting the circulation of air; the other is the well-known oil-cooled transformer of the present time. The patent secured by Westinghouse on the latter device was the subject of extensive litigation, which resulted in the patent being broadly sustained.

These various inventions and discoveries led up within a year to commercial production of transformers of high efficiency and excellent regulating qualities. The development was a fine engineering performance in speed and in quality. The most important single contribution was by Stanley. He brought out the parallel connection in which the transformers are connected in parallel, across the constant-potential alternating-current system, instead of being arranged in series, as in the Gaulard and Gibbs connection. He obtained patents on the method, involving the construction of transformers in which the counter electromotive force generated in the primary of the transformer was practically equal to the electromotive force of the supply circuit. This is obvious now, but in 1886, when the principles and characteristics of the alternating current were practically unknown, it was a wonderful invention, and revolutionary in character. On this invention Stanley's fame largely rests. Of course Stanley did not discover or invent a theory of counter electromotive force before any one else had thought of it. Such fundamental things seldom happen in invention. His claim to great and original merit rests on the discovery of a theory which was new to him and the use of it in making a structure of immense importance in the affairs of men. Westinghouse's situation as an original inventor of the air brake is exactly similar. Briefly, all transformers now made are built upon practically the same principles as those that were developed in these early products of the Westinghouse Company.

According to the Gaulard and Gibbs system as at first announced the transformers were arranged in series. As to the broad principle of parallel connection of transformers instead of the Gaulard and Gibbs series arrangement, it is of interest to note that under date of June 2, 1883, an article by Rankin Kennedy appeared in *the London Telegraphic Journal and Electrical Review* in which he demonstrated that with transformers having their primaries arranged in parallel rather than in series, "the secondary generator is a beautiful self-governing system of distribution"; apparently, however, Kennedy had not then in mind the possibility of using high-potential primary and low-potential secondary coils, and was thus led into the error of closing his article with the expression, "but what about the size of conductors for such a system? Prodigious." Fortunately, the engineers at Pittsburgh were not led into like errors, and Kennedy himself soon corrected his views.

To sum up in a few words: Gaulard and Gibbs considered, developed, and demonstrated crudely the general principle of transformation of electrical energy. Déri, Bláthy, and Zipernowski of Budapest early began research in the same direction. Westinghouse took the crude ideas and, with his engineers, worked out a commercial system and revolutionized the electric art.

The swift development in December 1885, and in the first months of 1886 satisfied Westinghouse as to the great merit of the system and of its tremendous possibilities. He quickly realized that the alternating-current system was the solution of the problem of economically transmitting through long distances, inasmuch as it could carry large quantities of electrical energy in the form of high voltage and low amperage, and that the transformers supplied the means for locally readjusting the voltage to consumption requirements.

Having decided that the capabilities of the system warranted using every endeavor to secure proper patent protection in the United States, Westinghouse in January 1886, sent Pantaleoni and Pope to England to complete the negotiations with Gaulard and Gibbs and prepare the necessary patent applications. This was accomplished in February. The article of Rankin Kennedy above referred to also presented possibilities in the patent direction, and later Westinghouse bought the Kennedy American rights. Zipernowski, Déri, and Bláthy had obtained a British patent in 1884 for "Improvements in transforming and distributing alternating current and apparatus therefore." Some negotiations were had by Westinghouse looking to the purchase of these rights, but it was later found their opportunity of obtaining in the United States any patents of value had been forfeited, and negotiations with them were dropped.

Early in the work upon the alternating system there was brought to the attention of Westinghouse the fact that Philip Diehl, of Elizabeth, N. J., then Superintendent of the Singer Sewing Machine Company, had done some early work with alternating currents, particularly in the line of producing an incandescent lamp without leading-in wires. DiehTs plan was to enclose within the lamp globe the secondary of an induction coil and induce currents therein by an externally located primary coil. Diehl had obtained patents upon these devices, and because of the possible bearing which Diehl's work might have upon the whole alternating-current system, Westinghouse in 1887 bought these patents as a precautionary measure, but not with the thought that this form of incandescent lamp in itself would prove to be of practical worth.

When Westinghouse became convinced that the alternating-current system would be of the very greatest importance to mankind in enlarging the field for the use of electrical energy, he became possessed of a strong desire to take up and carry on the work of its development. On December 23, 1885, he, in company with H. H. Westinghouse, John Caldwell, Frank L. Pope, John Dalzell, John R. McGinley, C. H. Jackson, and Robert Pitcairn, executed articles of association and an application for a charter for a corporation to be known as the Westinghouse Electric Company, the capital stock of which was to be $1,000,000. Among the assets of the corporation were twenty-seven patents and applications relating to the electrical art including those of Gaulard and

Gibbs, Stanley, Shallenberger, and others. The charter was granted January 8, 1886, and the practical organization of the company was effected March 8, 1886, Westinghouse being made President, H. H. Westinghouse, Vice-President, A. T. Rowan, Secretary, and Guido Pantaleoni remained General Manager until September 15, 1886, when he resigned and H. H. Byllesby, who had been the electrical executive of Westinghouse, Church, Kerr & Company, was elected to that office.

Late in 1885 Stanley's health having been impaired he had moved to Great Barrington, Mass., and Westinghouse assumed the expense of conducting there a laboratory for the purpose of further developing and practically demonstrating the utility of the alternating system. Belfield, who had brought over the Gaulard and Gibbs apparatus and who had spent a few weeks with Westinghouse at Pittsburgh, helping in the design of the new transformer, went with Stanley. Their chief work was to develop the transformer commercially. They designed, built, and installed an experimental plant at Great Barrington, comprising a dynamo sent over from England and wires extending to various stores in the center of the town, where were placed transformers feeding lamps for lighting the stores. The operation of this experimental plant began March 16, 1886. This was the first operating alternating-current transformer installation in the United States. The first commercial plant employing the alternating-current system was installed by the Westinghouse Company in Buffalo, N. Y., where it was put in operation November 30, 1886. This was rapidly followed by other installations scattered throughout the country.

Coincidentally with the development of the transformer, the company brought out a new alternating-current generator designed by Stanley. This was a much more practical and efficient form than the old Siemens type. Many other devices required in connection with the system were produced with surprising rapidity by the corps of brilliant young engineers who entered the employ of the company during the first two or three years. The contributions of Shallenberger and Schmid proved to be of inestimable value to the company, and the high regard which Westinghouse held for both of these brilliant inventors and their aides he manifested at every opportunity. Among the devices which immediately found extensive use was a voltage regulator invented by Lewis B. Stillwell, a young engineer just graduated from college, who at the suggestion of Byllesby was employed by Westinghouse late in 1886. Stillwell explained the regulator to Westinghouse as a device adapted to raise the alternating-current voltage at any desired point. Westinghouse was greatly pleased and at once christened it the "Stillwell booster," a title which became the popular name of this type of apparatus, technically called the Stillwell regulator. Various other important adjuncts to the system were devised by Byllesby, Shallenberger, Belfield, and others of the company's force.

As soon as it became evident that Westinghouse proposed to exploit extensively the alternating-current system great opposition was developed. Looking back at history, one is surprised at the stupidity and the puerility of some of this opposition. Men of great repute gave their names and their help to methods of which they must now be thoroughly ashamed. They know now that if they had succeeded, the progress of civilization would have been delayed - how much and how long we cannot even guess. Lord Kelvin said: "The electric development we know today would long have halted without his daring and resourcefulness." Assertions were made that the alternating current was dangerous and deadly, that its use should not be permitted commercially, and numerous articles appeared in the newspapers and elsewhere designed to prejudice public opinion against the system. The most popular electrician in the world wrote in the *North American Review,* November 1889: "There is no plea which will justify the use of high alternating currents, either in a scientific or commercial sense...and my personal desire would be to prohibit entirely the use of the alternating current."

If anything was needed to urge Westinghouse to greater effort, this antagonism served the purpose, he being well convinced from his own observations and the counsel of his electrical associates that of the two the direct current brought greater risk to life and property. This was not because one form of current was, in its nature, more dangerous than the other, but because of the conditions of use. This contest, long and acrimonious on the part of the opponents, Westinghouse met with smiling calmness and justified confidence. It is needless to enlarge upon this aspect of the development. Every well-informed human being knows Westinghouse was right, the alternating electric current being now used to generate and convey about 95 per cent of the electric energy used in power and lighting in the United States. The latest information available at the time of writing is from the United States Census of Electrical Industries for 1917. The census of equipment of central stations (commercial and municipal) and of electric railways shows that the kilowatt capacity of direct-current generators "forms a negligible part of the total." In fact it was about 5 per cent in 1917. An exact statement is not possible, for the returns from electric railways are not complete, and the census report gives no figures for the "isolated plants" operated solely for the benefit of the owner and none for plants owned and operated by the Federal and State governments. It does not seem important, however, to elaborate the point. Some notion of the present size of the business of distributing electric power may be got from the fact that in 1919 the central power stations of the United States generated 40,000,000,000 kilowatt-hours of energy. This was carried to the users over 87,000 miles of high-tension transmission lines. And yet there is scarcely a central power station which can meet the demand upon it for power for industrial uses.

This is briefly the history of the beginning of the industrial and commercial use of the alternating-current system. For transmitting power electricity has no economical competitor. Its limitation is the cost of conductors; this is less if the volume of current is small and the voltage is high. This is seen in the early struggles of the direct-current central station to increase its area of distribution. The increase from 110 to 220 volts by the so-called three-wire system and the unsuccessful endeavor to devise other systems by which higher voltages could be used indicated the need of higher voltage and set the limit of the direct current. The transformer in permitting a small current, transmitted at high voltage, to be transformed into a large current at low voltage by means of stationary apparatus supplies the essential factor in electric transmission. This Westinghouse early appreciated. The whole story of electrical progress is the story of advancing voltages. Each increase has been followed by transmission to longer distances and the economic use of power on a larger scale.

Westinghouse's conception of what had been done may be summed up in a few words to be found in a paper presented by him at a joint meeting of engineering societies in London in 1910:

As an illustration of the wonders of the laws of nature, few inventions or discoveries with which we are familiar can excel the static transformer of the electrical energy of alternating currents of high voltage into the equivalent energy at a lower voltage. To have discovered how to make an inert mass of metal capable of transforming alternating currents of 100,000 volts into currents of any required lower voltage with a loss of only a trifle of the energy so transformed would have been to achieve enduring fame. The facts divide this honor among a few, the beneficiaries will be tens of millions.

We have now traced in a general way the growth in the mind of George Westinghouse of his interest in the uses of electricity, and we have traced also some of the steps taken in putting that interest into practice. It remains to consider some specific developments; but first let us note the big fundamental thought that gradually took possession of his mind and eventually came to dominate it. Around this thought was built the great structure of his electrical industries, and it influenced later the nature and direction of his mechanical industries. For convenience we may call this the central power-station idea, the idea of manufacturing power in quantities, at advantageous places, and distributing it for use. It is one phase of the era of manufactured power into which mankind entered when James Watt made the steam engine a tool for the conversion of energy for convenient daily use, which began a new era in the history of the race. The reader will of course observe that we do not say creating power, which is manifestly absurd, but manufacturing power, which is merely changing matter and energy, in form and place. It is the world-old (universe-old) process of transforming energy. Until steam was harnessed, man had transformed energy, for his own use and convenience, by hand and by help of his tamed animals and, in favored localities, by wind and water. When he learned to use steam, he acquired a new capacity, the capacity to transform energy by machinery, and this is called for convenience manufacturing power. Harnessing the alternating current was the next great step in enlarging this new capacity, as will be shown in some detail as we go on.

Westinghouse's conception of the place hi the affairs of man of central power systems became great when he realized the possibilities of the use of alternating current. That realization was an inspiration of genius. It did not come overnight; it was not a bolt out of the blue; it had a background of thought and experience, and we are told that genius is a manifestation of the capacity to "toil terribly."

It is not possible to say when the thought of central power systems first took a great place in the mind of Westinghouse. He did, however, develop early the idea of converting energy into useful power, on a large scale, at suitable places, carrying it to greater or less distances, and distributing it for the "use and convenience of man." This is the conception at the bottom of one of the most important advances in production, transportation, and comfort. Watt and the steam engine made the manufacture of power possible and changed society. The next great step was to concentrate the manufacture of power at points where for one reason or another it could be manufactured cheaply, and that could only be done when cheap transmission was provided. Westinghouse more than any other one man opened up the way for cheap transmission of power; this by the use of the alternating current.

In his case there was nothing apocalyptic in the central power-system conception. It was a slow growth and took several shapes. For years he thought of piping compressed air along the lines of railroads to handle, not switches and signals alone, but cranes, capstans, riveters, hammers, and other tools. It was an alluring notion which was in his mind long before he began to think of the uses of alternating current, and lingered there long after the epoch-making developments in electric transmission at Niagara Falls. He thought, too, for a long time of piping gas to gas-engine stations, and there developing power for manufacturing and transportation. Of course, he had no monopoly of such notions. Compressed air had long been distributed in Paris for operating small machinery, and in 1889 an American writer said: "It is now known to be practicable to distribute from one central station to another all the light and mechanical power used in any city" - practical but not yet practicable, for the revolution in electrical transmission had hardly begun. This was four years after Westinghouse began to develop alternating-current machinery and three years before the successful transmission at Telluride and six years before the first operation of the Niagara plant. It has been said that our ancestors stole all our best inventions. The difference between Westinghouse and his ancestors and contemporaries was that he saw his vision in a big way and followed it in a big way. It was a matter of difference of mental stature.

Having now the key to the major activities of Westinghouse for the last half of his life, we are prepared to consider those activities in some detail.

Chapter Five - The Induction Motor and Meter

THE transformer showed the way to transmitting alternating current at high voltages and using it at low voltages. A necessary step was to convert it into direct current for local use. This led to the development of the rotary converter, of which something is said in the next chapter.

Conversion would make it possible to use direct-current motors, but if the alternating system was to become general, alternating motors must be used and a meter must be provided to measure the current consumption. These two classes of service devices, the motor and the meter, did not exist.

THE MOTOR

May 1, 1888, patents were issued to Nikola Tesla for those brilliant inventions which have made his name famous and which disclosed to the world the alternating-current motor. A writer of authority has said: "The invention of alternating-current motors, and the system for operating them, was one of the greatest advances ever made in the industrial application of electricity." No one will dispute that; in fact, he might have gone further and specifically included the field of transportation. Westinghouse immediately saw the meaning of these patents, and on July 7 he secured an assignment of the exclusive rights under them, and in course of time the Tesla motor became one of the most valuable assets of the Westinghouse Company; but not at once. The way was long and costly. In 1893 the induction motor (Tesla) was still experimental, although the development cost to that stage was one element in the financial embarrassment which nearly swamped the Westinghouse Electric Company that year. A year or two more passed before it had become a commercial machine.

There were two underlying reasons why seven years should pass from Tesla's invention until it was brought to usefulness, and why a great deal of money should be spent in developing it.

The Tesla motor was polyphase. That is, it required two or more currents whose periods of alternation were not simultaneous; in the language of the art they must be out of phase with each other. The alternating-current system as then developed was single phase. One current was generated and transmitted over one pair of main conductors.

The second reason was a matter of frequency; that is, the rate at which the direction of the current is reversed. In the alternating system, as then developed, the standard frequency was 16,000 alternations per minute or 133 cycles per second. But it was discovered as experiment and research went on that a frequency so high as 133 cycles was not suitable for any kind of alternating current motor.

Westinghouse and his engineers stood face to face with three fundamental facts of which the magnitude and the meaning were not at once obvious. The motor itself must be designed from the ground up; a system of polyphase generation and transmission must be created; some frequency lower than 133 cycles per second must be agreed upon by engineers, manufacturers, and users. Phase and frequency will be considered when we take up the Chicago World's Fair and Niagara Falls episodes; now we shall speak of the development of the induction motor.

The story of the induction motor is one of the great and splendid chapters in electrical history, but it cannot be written here. It would take us into deep waters of physical science and mechanical art and it would require space beyond the plan and scope of this book. The subject has attracted analytical and mathematical writers who have produced a copious literature which can be enjoyed only by those who have considerable gifts to start with, and who have had a special training. The writer has a friend who at the age of seventy-one still carries a heavy administrative load and works incessantly. When asked how he amused himself he said: "Often of an evening I read some pure mathematics." It is not to be assumed that many readers of this book have the background for that kind of amusement.

The induction motor and the rotary converter made possible the prodigious development of the alternating-current system, which has profoundly influenced the direction and advance of industry and transportation the world over. These two machines had their earliest practical development in the Westinghouse Works, and engineers still active there, who saw the beginning, have seen the induction motor grow from little experiments to machines of 23,000 horsepower. We may doubt if even the imagination of Westinghouse foresaw such things in 1888 when he bought the Tesla rights.

The reader should not get the impression that Westinghouse contributed much as an engineer or as an inventor to the induction motor. He did not. He did contribute imagination, courage, and force of character. It is hardly necessary to suggest which was the greater contribution. Sir James Fitz James Stephen, in one of his delightful essays, now forgotten by most men, says: "The real greatness of Newton's achievement was not that he did a very hard sum and did it right, but that he had an imagination so powerful that he could conceive the possibility of devising a classification which should fit the motions of all heavy bodies whatever, from a sun to an apple." The hard sum was done by the man who discovered a new planet by mathematical analysis of the phenomena of the known planetary system. Astronomers know the name of Adams and admire his deed; Newton is one of the immortals.

The first three years of work on the induction motor were mostly valuable in showing what could not be done. The engineers played a losing game against high frequency and single phase, and they simply developed something that could not be used until standards of phase and frequency were changed. Moreover, certain necessary knowledge of motor construction was not in existence, and the engineers started with some wrong fundamental conceptions.

In 1890 and 1891 a direct-current motor was developed in the Westinghouse Works which had a great effect on the advance of railway work. This was the single reduction-gear motor, of which some account will be given when we come to speak of electric traction. A new feature of this railway motor, the slotted armature, was found to be suited to alternating-current work. The results which followed led to the analytical calculation of a new kind of induction-motor, Stephen's "hard sum," and an experimental motor was built and turned out to be the first motor of the modern type constructed by anybody. By the middle of 1893 a group of low-frequency, polyphase apparatus was built for the Chicago World's Fair and the way was now reasonably clear, but the induction motor was not yet commercial. This World's Fair installation was a great event in the story of the electric art and it will be described later at some length.

By this time it was well recognized that the immediate need was for polyphase supply circuits. In a conference between Westinghouse and his engineers on the polyphase situation in general, and induction motors in particular, the question was considered as to how to approach the induction motor development from the commercial standpoint. The suggestion was put forward that if a fad were made of polyphase generation and the country filled with polyphase circuits, the motor situation would take care of itself. Orders were issued at once to bring out a line of sixty-cycle polyphase alternators, which the company was to push in place of the single phase. This was done and the public accepted the polyphase quite quickly; in fact, so quickly that the resulting demand for induction motors to use on these polyphase circuits came before the motors were ready. In consequence, a line of motors, which was being planned, was rushed on the market with all possible speed. This motor was known as the Westinghouse type B, a collector-ring type of machine with starting resistance. In spite of the speed with which it was got out, it was quite successful, and some of these motors are operating even today, after twenty-five years' service. The induction motor had changed from an experimental machine in 1893 to a commercial machine in about two years' time. Industrial plants were buying polyphase generating equipment and induction motors for changing over to electric drive.

During this time the General Electric Company had also been developing induction motors. On account of the Tesla patents, however, that company got out a new system called the "monocyclic," which they claimed was really a single phase system and which, their engineers insisted, avoided the Tesla polyphase patents. This monocyclic system consisted, primarily, of a main circuit and a "teaser" circuit, the latter principally for the purpose of furnishing the polyphase excitation. This system was fundamentally an unbalanced polyphase system, and the Westinghouse Company always claimed that it was an infringement. Probably if it had gone through the courts it would have been declared to be an infringement, but the two companies made their well-known patent agreement, and the induction-motor patents were covered by the cross-licenses between the two companies, and the General Electric Company was able to take up the straight polyphase system. This company developed the induction motor in parallel with the Westinghouse Company, although their constructions were quite different in many ways. Both types of motors, however, were considered thoroughly successful.

The motor of 1895 was hardly settled as standard when a revolution came with the introduction of the type C motor. The characteristics of this motor were materially different from those of the motors in use and it was much criticised, even inside the Westinghouse organization. The engineers and salesmen of competing companies adopted a general formula of disfavor. "It is as bad as the Westinghouse type C motor." This new contrivance was said to rest on a fundamental absurdity; namely, its starting torque was "necessarily small," but the designer had introduced an autotransformer to reduce the torque during starting. The absurdity was as obvious to the sceptics as the multiplication table. But, like Whistler's pictures, "the stuff sold," and presently competing companies began to put more or less accurate copies on the market. The Westinghouse type C motor soon became the preferred type, and eventually took a prominent place in Europe. It advanced the induction-motor business enormously and created a reputation for reliability and durability of the induction motor, compared with the direct current, which placed the alternating motor far ahead of the direct current for general industrial purposes.

Engineers will be interested in Mr. Lamme's short statement of the beginnings of this one element in the growth of the art. "In developing the various Westinghouse motors which were under my charge, I had gone quite deeply into the analysis (that is, deeply for those days). In working out the various conditions upon which the starting torque depended, I uncovered what seemed to me to be some hitherto unrecognized conditions in the construction, which, if carried far enough, would allow a very great simplification of the motor itself. In working out the characteristic curves of the motor I found that if I could reduce the motor reactance to a certain point, I could make it develop relatively high starting torques, with a pure 'cage-type' winding on the secondary, the simplest type of winding possible. Heretofore, it had been believed, very generally, that the cage type of induction motor necessarily had poor starting torque. My analysis of the reactance and other conditions indicated that I could get any starting torque I pleased by properly reducing the reactance. Others may have recognized this same thing, but did not know that the reactance actually could be reduced sufficiently, in a motor of commercial proportions. My calculations of my former designs had shown me how to reduce such reactance to almost any desired value. In consequence, I figured out certain motors with a view to making them two or three times full load starting torque with less expensive constructions than the then existing types. However, the figures also showed that such motors would take very large starting currents. This immediately led to the idea of introducing a small autotransformer at start for reducing the voltage, and, consequently, the starting current. Mr. Schmid was quite in sympathy with this scheme for simplifying the motor, and he authorized the construction of several sizes. In fact, several of these motors were sold for operating cranes before the first ones were completed, the speed control on these first motors being obtained by varying the voltage supplied to them. However, when the motors came through, the tests bore out all the calculations, and this construction was very quickly put on the market."

It may not be impertinent to suggest that this is a pretty instance of the application of two of the qualities of the complete engineer the gift of seeing things and the power to do a hard sum.

THE ALTERNATING-CURRENT METER

The alternating-current motor was provided as is told above, but no instrument existed to measure the quantity of current supplied to the user. Westinghouse took this matter up personally, and in June 1887 he applied for a patent on an alternating-current meter. In October he filed another application jointly with one of his engineers, Philip Lange. Patents were issued in May 1888. This meter would have served very well if a better one had not been devised. That soon came in a most interesting and important invention by O. B. Shallenberger, chief electrician of the company. No doubt his mind was pretty well saturated with the problem when an accident gave the slight agitation which crystallized the invention.

Late in April 1888 Shallenberger was examining an alternating-current arc lamp which had just been completed under the direction of Lange. By chance a small coil spring got loose from the mechanism and lodged on a plate at the top of a coil surrounding a protruding soft-iron core. Lange was about to replace the part, when Shallenberger noticed a slight movement of the spring, which was unaccounted for. By analyzing the influences he discovered that the spring was being subjected to a shifting magnetic field. Directly he said to his assistant Stillwell, who also was present, and to Lange: "There's a meter in that and perhaps a motor." Within two weeks he designed and built a most successful alternating-current meter of the induction type, and within a few months these were being produced in quantity.

Although this meter operates on the same fundamental principle as the Tesla motor, neither Shallenberger nor the public had knowledge of Tesla's work till some days later. Shallenberger had thus independently invented a form of induction motor. It should be added that Tesla on learning the facts not only added his congratulations to Shallenberger on his skill in devising the meter but expressed sympathy in the natural disappointment which came to Shallenberger on finding that he was anticipated by Tesla in the invention of the motor itself. Another incident is worthy of note as illustrating how different minds in widely different localities independently think along like lines. Within a day or two after Shallenberger's conception in Pittsburgh, Galileo Ferraris in Turin published a lecture which he had delivered to his class in the University of Turin as early as 1885, describing a like form of alternating-current motor. These occurrences were in the latter part of April 1888, and Tesla's patents then pending in the Patent Office at Washington were issued May 1, 1888.

Chapter Six - The Rotary Converter

THE story of the development of the transformer has been told in earlier pages and told at some length because of its immense importance in the electric art. It is now well understood that the transformer is an instrument for changing the voltages of alternating current, and so making the current transmitted at one potential available for use at another potential. It is a fundamental tool and has made possible the prodigious development of the use of electricity in the last quarter of a century. But the transformer was not enough. To transmit electric energy over considerable distances, high-potential alternating current must be used; but there are many important uses for direct current which alternating current does not meet. Moreover, in the dawn of the alternating-current art there were great investments in direct-current motors which would be sacrificed reluctantly, if at all. For example, all electric railway work was then direct current. The economic distance to which direct current could be carried had not yet been fixed; but it was already clear to the seeing eye that a great extension of electric railroads would demand numerous power stations to keep the generation of power within practicable distance from its work if direct current were used. The same set of facts was met in electric lighting and in various minor uses of electric energy. So arose the problem of transmitting energy by high-potential alternating current and converting it for use into low-potential direct current. This situation faced Westinghouse and his engineers, to complicate the negotiations and designs for the hydroelectric project at Niagara Falls.

The consideration of the Niagara project by Westinghouse began in 1890. The serious and active consideration at East Pittsburgh of alternating-current-direct-current converters, to change alternating current into direct current, began a little earlier. This was pioneer work. It was the beginning of a course of research, invention, design, and manufacture which has had, and still has, great effect on the use of electric power in transportation, manufacture, and the arts. The motor-generator was already known and used to convert alternating current to direct current; but the rotary converter promised greater economy and efficiency, and that promise gave direction to the development at the Westinghouse Works. The successful demonstration of a rotary converter made at the works, before the engineers of the Niagara commission, was an important influence in the decision to adopt alternating current at Niagara. That decision fixed the direction of electrical development for all time. It was a landmark in the history of the manufacture of power.

The conception of the rotary converter, so timely in its coming and of such continuing value, seems to have entered the minds of several people at about the same time, as generally happens in inventions. A rotary converter was shown by Siemens & Halske at the Frankfort Exposition in 1891. We do not know when the studies for that machine began. In May 1887 Mr. Charles S. Bradley filed an application for a United States patent on a rotary converter and in October 1888, a patent was issued to him. In the late eighties, Mr. B. G. Lamme, of the Westinghouse Electric Company (now Chief Engineer), began studies in the same field and in course of time he worked out design specifications for an operative apparatus. Until he encountered Bradley in the Patent Office he believed that he had made a new invention. He has been more persistent and resourceful than any other man in the development of the rotary converter, and in the Westinghouse shops it first became a real working element in the structure of the art. A 375kilowatt rotary was shown in the Westinghouse exhibit at the Chicago World's Fair in 1893, and when we come to read of the first hydroelectric plant at Niagara Falls we shall see the place that it had in that tremendous historical enterprise. We may apply here Carnot's rule: "The honor of a discovery belongs to the nation in which it has acquired its growth and all its development." The same may be applied in distributing honors amongst men as well as nations.

In a few years after the rotary was first put on the market as a commercial machine it had practically driven the large direct-current generators out of business. The first rotary converters were put in service about 1894. By 1899 electrification of the Manhattan Elevated Railway in New York was decided upon, with one huge alternating-current-generator station and with twenty-six 1500-kilowatt rotary converters, in a large number of substations, for supplying direct current for operation of the cars. This one contract for converting machinery was larger than any single contract for direct-current generator machinery that had yet been undertaken, showing that, even at this early date, the alternating-current generating system combined with the rotary converters had already forged ahead of the direct-current generating system for railway work. The same held true for many of the large three-wire Edison systems, where the handicap of transmission at 220 volts for supply was felt very early, and the advent of the rotary converter permitted generation and transmission by high-voltage alternating current, and thus allowed great extensions of the three-wire system by means of suitable distributing substations with rotary converters. All this means that within a period of, say, five years the source of direct current, for large plants in particular, had shifted from direct-current generation at low voltage to alternating-current generation at comparatively high voltage, with transmission at high voltage and with conversion, by means of the rotary converter, to any desired direct-current voltage at any desired place. Surely this was revolutionary.

It does not appear that Westinghouse had much personal part in the early studies of the converter. Mr. Lamme says: "Strangely enough, it appeared to me that Mr. Westinghouse never took any strong interest in the rotary converter as affording a means for extending the field of direct-current traction, and yet this has been possibly the greatest single step in overcoming the early limitations of the 600volt system. He did not ask me many questions regarding rotary-converter development and operation, as he did with other developments. He seemed quite pleased with the success of the rotary and its rapid growth after it had passed through its earlier experimental stages." Perhaps he took it as a matter of course, as an inevitable step. Perhaps he was satisfied that it was in competent hands. Perhaps there was a small and passing dark spot in his imagination just here. Or perhaps it was something of all three. For present purposes the essential things are that the coming of the rotary converter was an opportune event in the course of the growth of the universal power system, the conception of which was steadily forming in Westinghouse's mind; and this event took place within the organization which he had built up.

Chapter Seven - The Chicago World's Fair

THE Columbian Exposition at Chicago in 1893 was an interesting incident in the life of George Westinghouse and in the history of the Westinghouse Electric Company, and there were picturesque, not to say dramatic, situations, which brought out daring and resource. A certain shrewd university president said that we must think of arctic exploration as a high form of sport. There was some high sport in this World's Fair adventure.

On May 23, 1892, the Westinghouse Company took the lighting contract at a price much below the bid made on behalf of the Edison General Electric Company, its only serious competitor. The story is that the saving to the Exposition Company was something like $1,000,000, which may well have been, as the unit prices were about as one to three. The Edison General Electric Company counted on its strong patent situation, and Westinghouse set high value on the advertising element. His company lost money directly, but its technical success had a great effect on the Niagara Falls contract then pending, and on the whole struggle between direct current and alternating current, and it is hard to exaggerate the world importance of that struggle.

This exposition was one of the famous world's fairs, in the supreme beauty of buildings and grounds, in the number and variety of exhibits drawn from all the world, and in the number of visitors. Never before had so much artificial light been produced in one place, and it was beautifully used to emphasize architectural effects. It was a strategic opportunity which Westinghouse and his engineers seized and used. The lighting was only a part of their exhibit. The new machinery, apparatus, and methods were more impressive to the scientific visitor than the picturesque effects. The appeal to the scientific imagination was powerful; the demonstration was complete to those who knew enough to understand it.

It had not been easy to get this contract, notwithstanding the great difference in the bids. The patent situation was dangerous, and when bids were first invited Westinghouse refused to submit one. Finally, he became interested in a bid which the Exposition Committee on Grounds and Buildings had refused to consider, as the bidder was obviously not in a position to carry it out. With a rejected bid as a basis and with an obviously strong patent in the way, he began negotiations rather heavily handicapped. His frank and genial manner, no less than his ingenious arguments, gradually won the committee; but before that he had won over the Chicago newspapers, which became insistent that Westinghouse should have consideration. The upshot was that new bids were asked for and the Westinghouse Company got the contract.

The patent situation in which the Edison General Electric Company had well-grounded confidence may be explained in a few words. Suit was brought on an Edison patent. The first claim was very broad, for the combination of a carbon filament with an exhausted glass globe. This claim was not sustained by the court.

The second claim was narrower, for a globe "made entirely of glass." The context of the specification showed this to mean a globe made in one piece with the glass fused on to the leading-in wires. This is the type of lamp now in universal use. It is as familiar to us as was the tallow candle to our grandfathers. It was one of Mr. Edison's most fortunate inventions. The court sustained this claim and refused to require the Edison Company to license the Westinghouse Company or to sell lamps to them. Proceedings were begun to get an injunction which would restrain the Westinghouse Company from making a lamp which was in course of development. The story goes that one evening in New York, Westinghouse and Mr. Terry, of the legal department of the Electric Company, took an uptown train on the Elevated Railway and found themselves seated by Mr. Lowrey, chief counsel of the Edison Company. In course of casual talk Lowrey said that Mr. Fish, also of counsel for Edison, had gone to Pittsburgh. Westinghouse and Terry soon left the train, and when they were out of hearing Westinghouse said: "What's Fish gone to Pittsburgh for?" The immediate result was that Terry hunted up Curtis (another of the Westinghouse patent attorneys) at his home in the suburbs; Curtis wired Christy in Pittsburgh, and the next morning when Fish entered the court room he found Christy seated there. The further result was that the Edison Company's application for a restraining order was denied.

Nevertheless, matters were critical, not to say dangerous. The Westinghouse Company was committed to the contract for lighting the Chicago World's Fair. It had already equipped many plants which must .have lamps for renewals. Unless a non-infringing lamp could be furnished, the company could sell no more incandescent-lighting material. The need for such a lamp was immediate and urgent.

The events here related took place in 1892. In 1888 the Westinghouse Company had come into possession of a Sawyer-Man lamp patent, for which application had been filed in 1880 - a good patent so far as it went. As early as 1891, perhaps earlier, the Westinghouse engineers were working on a two-piece Sawyer-Man lamp - that is, a lamp in which the part holding the wires was put in the globe and the opening was sealed as the air in the globe was exhausted. This was the lamp which by the ruling of the court did not infringe the Edison patent. Just when the seal was changed to a glass stopper ground in, it is impossible to say, but some time before the World's Fair contract was a matter of negotiation Westinghouse was pushing work on a two-piece lamp as a precaution. Thus originated the famous Westinghouse "stopper-lamp," a kind of lamp which other men had tried to make and failed. It was not at all clear that it could be made to hold a high vacuum for long, and as things turned out, it could not, and the World's Fair lamps had to be often renewed. But the emergency lamp was good enough to light the World's Fair and to supply other needs until the Edison patent expired.

It was not enough to have designed an emergency lamp. It is usually a long way from design to large-scale manufacture. Details must be designed and experimented with. Small tools must be made. In this case facilities must be created to produce within a very few months 250,000 lamps for the Fair and to supply a reliable stream of replacements for that and for other lighting plants. Westinghouse organized a glass factory to make the bulbs. He designed and made apparatus to grind in the stoppers and an air pump to exhaust the bulbs. It was a quick job, but the opening of the Fair on May 1 following was not delayed an hour. In this emergency Westinghouse was well served by his patent lawyers and his engineers. Particularly should be mentioned the late Mr. Thomas B. Kerr, for many years an able and faithful adviser in patent matters, and Mr. Leonard E. Curtis, who practised for years in electrical patents and so helped to advance the art. Amongst the several excellent engineers who took part in this lamp development, one name stands out conspicuously, that of Frank Stuart Smith, then in charge of the incandescent lamp department. His zeal, industry, and ingenuity were highly appreciated by Westinghouse. But it was essentially one man's job, and it was perhaps the most audacious of the many daring enterprises of Westinghouse. He won by those qualities which we often think would have made him a brilliant general if fate had turned his lot that way.

But this spectacular lamp episode, interesting and useful to the student of George Westinghouse, was, after all, only an episode. In itself it had no lasting consequences. The historical element in the Westinghouse participation in this Chicago World's Fair was hidden away in the machinery; hidden away from all but a few seeing eyes. They could see there the faint dawn of a new era; that is, they could see it if they had enough knowledge and imagination. Here was taken one of the first long steps in the use of the alternating current, to be followed shortly by Niagara, of which we shall speak presently.

The generating plant for the World's Fair lighting was the largest alternating-current central station then in existence. There were 12 generators, each of 1000 horsepower, each unit was two 500-horsepower alternators. These were single phase, with toothed, rotating armatures, and were placed side by side, with separate fields. The field-poles were in line with each other, but the two armatures were displaced half one-tooth pitch from each other. Therefore each unit consisted of two single-phase rotating-armature generators, but with the two circuits 90 degrees out of phase. Westinghouse proposed this scheme in order to be able to supply two-phase current. These machines were 200 revolution, 36 pole, 7200 alternations (60 cycles). The nominal voltage was 2200. The rotating armature, toothed-armature construction and 60 cycles were both old features, but the displacement of the armature to give two phase was a new feature, and in fact these were the first large polyphase generators built and installed in this country. Furthermore, these were the largest alternators either single phase or polyphase that had been built up to that time in America. Ganz & Company, at Budapest, had built 1000horsepower alternators, single phase. The General Electric Company showed at the Fair a 1500-kilowatt direct-current generator, and the Westinghouse Company was building 1500-horsepower direct-current machines.

Quite apart from the lighting plant, the Westinghouse Company showed at the World's Fair a complete polyphase system. A large two-phase induction motor, driven by current from the main generators, acted as the prime mover in driving the exhibit. The exhibit, then, contained a polyphase generator with transformers for raising the voltage for transmission; a short transmission line; transformers for lowering the voltage; the operation of induction motors; a synchronous motor; and a rotary converter which supplied direct current, which in turn operated a railway motor. In connection with the exhibit were meters and other auxiliary devices of various kinds. The apparatus was in units of fair commercial size and gave to the public a view of a universal power system in which, by polyphase current, power could be transmitted great distances, and then be utilized for various purposes, including the supply of direct current. It showed on a working scale a system upon which Westinghouse and his company had been concentrating their efforts; namely, the alternating-current and polyphase system.

It has been maintained with some plausibility that the most important outcome of the Centennial Exposition of 1876 was that the people of the United States there discovered bread. So it may be maintained, with even more plausibility, that the best result of the Columbian Exposition of 1893 was that it removed the last serious doubt of the usefulness to mankind of the polyphase alternating current. The conclusive demonstration at Niagara was yet to be made, but the World's Fair clinched the fact that it would be made, and so it marked an epoch in industrial history. Very few of those who looked at this machinery, who gazed with admiration at the great switchboard, so ingenious and complete, and who saw the beautiful lighting effects could have realized that they were living in an historical moment, that they were looking at the beginnings of a revolution.

Chapter Eight - Niagara Falls

LATE in the eighties a local project for the development of power at Niagara Falls began to take definite shape, but the necessary money could not be raised locally and the enterprise soon went to New York and was taken up by a group, amongst whom were Mr. D. O. Mills, Mr. John Jacob Astor, Mr. Edward D. Adams, Mr. Francis Lynde Stetson, and Mr. Edward A. Wickes. The Cataract Construction Company was created and Mr. Adams became its President. Doctor Coleman Sellers, of Philadelphia, was appointed Chief Engineer. In 1889 Mr. Adams and Doctor Sellers went to Europe to observe hydraulic developments and methods of transmitting power. There as well as at home they made a broad study of methods of power development and utilization that might be adapted to the Niagara situation, calling to their aid some of the most eminent physicists and engineers.

Westinghouse had sent one of his young engineers, Mr. Lewis B. Stillwell, to England that autumn to help in the start of the British Westinghouse Electric Company and to inform himself on the state of the electric art, particularly the progress in generating and distributing alternating current there and on the Continent. In November, Mr. Stillwell and Mr. Reginald Belfield, electrician of the British Westinghouse Company, were asked to meet Mr. Adams and Doctor Sellers and to give their views on the Niagara power problem, as representing the Westinghouse interests. This was the beginning of the relations of Westinghouse with the Niagara development.

In 1890 the Cataract Construction Company appointed an International Niagara Commission to consider projects and designs for the utilization of power from the falls. The members of the commission were Sir William Thomson (afterward Lord Kelvin), President, Doctor Coleman Sellers, M. E. Mascart, Colonel Theodore Turretini, and Professor W. C. Unwin, Secretary. It seems almost superfluous to say more about those gentlemen. Lord Kelvin was not only one of the most famous physicists in the world but an engineer of varied and eminent practical achievement. Doctor Sellers, long associated as engineer and inventor with the well-known firm of William Sellers & Company, of Philadelphia, was also professor of engineering practice at Stevens Institute and professor of mechanics at the Franklin Institute. M. Mascart was member of the Institute of Paris and professor at the College of France. Colonel Turretini was President of the city of Geneva, Director of Works for the Utilization of the Rhone, etc. Professor William Cawthorne Unwin, of London, was a distinguished physicist, scholar, and author. The reader of this volume will not fail to recognize the high authority of these names. The officers of the Cataract Construction Company were wise in handling an enterprise so great in cost and so vast in its consequences in a way to bring to their service the ability and experience of so distinguished a group of scientists and engineers.

Projects were invited for a central hydraulic power station to be located above the Falls and to develop as much power as the section of the discharge tunnel (490 square feet), the head of water, and the hydraulic slope would permit, and for the transmission and distribution of this power overhead or underground by electricity, compressed air, water, cable, or other means, to a manufacturing district to be built up within a radius of four miles, and to the city of Buffalo, distant about twenty miles.

At this time Mr. Stillwell was again in London, and the British Westinghouse Company was amongst those asked to submit plans. The broad possibilities of alternating-current transmission had been realized by Westinghouse and his staff from the time of the purchase of the Gaulard and Gibbs patents in 1885, and much work had been done at Pittsburgh toward producing practicable methods and apparatus. The enthusiastic young men in London were eager to have the company enter into the competition and submit plans, and wrote and cabled to Westinghouse. He refused permission. He evidently felt that the project was still much in the air and that his company would not be justified at that time in disclosing comprehensively the results of its studies and the knowledge gained at great cost. Mr. Stillwell says: "My disappointment was great, but I came to realize the reasonableness of Mr. Westinghouse's view."

More than three years passed before the first order for machinery for Niagara was placed with the Westinghouse Company and meantime important things happened. Those were epoch-making years in the electric art, which means that they were epoch-making years in industrial history. During those years the Cataract Construction Company, upon the advice of the International Niagara Commission, arrived at two decisions of far-reaching importance; namely, that the power should be developed in a single large power plant and that electricity should be used for its transmission and distribution. When these decisions were made, the question whether alternating current or direct current should be used was left open, but after further study and investigation by the Commission, it was decided to adopt the alternating-current system. Unquestionably the decision of the Cataract Company to use alternating current influenced greatly the rapidity and direction of electrical development throughout the world. Professor George Forbes, of Glasgow, was amongst those who had appeared before the Commission as advocates of alternating current, and subsequently he was appointed Consulting Electrical Engineer to the Cataract Construction Company.

At Pittsburgh for about two years, beginning in 1890, the development of the polyphase alternating-current system was considerably retarded by financial difficulties in which the Westinghouse Company became involved through lack of adequate capital, but nevertheless research, design, experiment, and construction of alternating-current apparatus went on. The electrical engineers of those days were all young, surprisingly young, but they were creating a new science and a new art, the laws were unknown and the language was new, and older engineers shrank from the task of learning the laws and language. Westinghouse, however, had the gift of youth. None of his young engineers surpassed him in eager enthusiasm. None approached him in imagination. They brought to the work greater knowledge of physics and mathematics than he had, but he supplied the steady flame. He supplied, too, courage, persistence, coordination, and driving power, and he brought into the new art fertile invention and unparalleled mechanical experience and skill.

At a fortunate moment in 1890 a group of these young engineers, and especially Stillwell, Shallenberger, and Scott, persuaded him to authorize a contract for a hydroelectric plant at Telluride, Colorado. It was a small plant, only 100 horsepower, but it served a large purpose. The plant comprised a single-phase generator driven by water power and a single-phase alternating-current motor started by a small "split-phase" induction motor. The generator and motor were wound for 3000 volts, and this was the line potential adopted. The transmission distance was only about three miles, but the amount of copper required for the circuit was extremely little as compared with the direct-current plant proposed by Mr. Edison, whose company also had been invited to bid on the project. The installation was a decided success in commercial and engineering results, and these results had a distinct influence upon alternating-current development and in deciding the system of generation and transmission adopted for Niagara.

The Telluride results had also a certain specific and interesting effect on the thought of Westinghouse. In his early conferences with the Cataract Construction Company he was much inclined to think that power could be best transmitted to Buffalo by pneumatic means. This is quite understandable. For twenty years he had been carrying power by compressed air. Neither he nor any one else knew much about electrical transmission. But his education was quick and complete. The success of the Telluride plant and the progress at Pittsburgh in the autumn of 1892, particularly in the development of the rotary converter and of two-phase motors, definitely changed his mind.

But Westinghouse had not been alone in considering compressed-air transmission. It was amongst the means mentioned in the call for projects, and, besides the tentative suggestion of Westinghouse, five definite plans were submitted. In the list of projects received by the Commission is one from Professor Reidler, of Berlin, and M. Victor Popp, of Paris, employing air compressors "studied chiefly with respect to transmission of power to Buffalo." Others were from Mr. H. D. Pearsall, of Orpington, England, using air compressed to 150 pounds per square inch; Professor Lupton, of Leeds, and Mr. Sturgeon, of Chester, England, "hydraulic motors and compressed-air plant to utilize 125,000 horsepower"; Messrs. Escher, Wyss & Company, of Zurich, "a compressed-air plant for part of the power"; and from the Norwalk Iron Works Company, South Norwalk, Conn. When the Commission, in the spring of 1891, awarded its premium for projects worthy of further consideration (Westinghouse did not compete), four of those in Class A were for compressed-air transmission. The Commission reported generally in favor of electrical distribution with perhaps a partial use of compressed air as an auxiliary method.

It should be particularly noted that the Commission then expressed a preference for distribution by direct current. This opinion governed some time longer. Lord Kelvin, President of the Commission, and without question the greatest mind amongst them, was the last to accept alternating current, which he finally did without reservation, and in May 1893 the Board of Directors of the Cataract Construction Company approved the adoption of alternating-current generators. This is an important date in history and an important date in the life of George Westinghouse. It was the triumphant end of a brilliant struggle.

But to go back a few months. On December 6, 1892, rotary converters of 150 horsepower were tested at Pittsburgh with extremely satisfactory results, and Westinghouse notified the Cataract Construction Company that the Electric Company was ready to submit definite plans and proposals. The converters were tested January 10, 1893, by Doctor Sellers and Professor Rowland, of Johns Hopkins. From that time negotiations went on actively. The officers of the Cataract Construction Company continued an intensive study of their problems, with the assistance of additional expert engineers. The Westinghouse and General Electric Companies were also active in their preparation, and in March 1893, both companies submitted proposals for three 5000-horsepower alternating-current generators of the vertical-shaft type to be placed in a power house above the wheel pit and direct connected to the shafts of turbines placed at the bottom of the wheel pit. They submitted also plans of the systems which they proposed for transmitting and distributing power.

The Westinghouse Company proposed to wind the generators for 2200 volts and to use this potential for distribution of power in the immediate vicinity of the falls. For transmission to Buffalo a potential of 11,000 volts was to be used until such time as line insulators adapted to 22,000 volts might become commercially available. The step-up transformers proposed, therefore, were so wound as to deliver either 11,000 volts or 22,000 volts.

The power was to be transmitted to Buffalo by circuits consisting of bare copper wires carried on insulators of the pin type. At the Buffalo end of the line, step-down transformers to reduce the line potential to voltages suitable for various local purposes were to be installed. In that same year came Mr. Charles F. Scott's invention of his ingenious method of converting from two-phase to three-phase current by a special winding and grouping of transformers, and three-phase transmission to Buffalo was thus accomplished, although the generators were wound for the two-phase current.

To convert alternating into direct or continuous current for operation of trolley lines and for electrolytic and other purposes requiring that type of current, rotary converters were proposed, and for the development of mechanical power for general industrial purposes two-phase alternating-current motors of the induction type were recommended. It was pointed out, also, that synchronous motors could be driven by power from the alternating-current circuits, and that direct-current motors could be operated through the intervention of rotary converters.

While the Westinghouse Company proposed two-phase generators, the General Electric Company recommended a straight three-phase system. After examination by the engineers of the Cataract Construction Company, the tenders of both manufacturing companies were declined, and the Cataract Construction Company instructed its engineers to prepare an alternative generator design.

Before referring further to either of these designs, it is necessary to refer to the question of frequency or periodicity of current.

Westinghouse was probably the first man of strong influence in electric development to realize the importance of adopting and adhering to a standard frequency of alternations. Very early he pointed out to the staff at Pittsburgh that a standard frequency was important in the same sense that a standard railroad gage is important. Upon his return from Europe in 1890, Mr. Stillwell had reported that the Ganz Company was using a frequency as low as forty-two cycles per second. It was obvious that the direct connection of alternating generators to the reciprocating engines then in general use was very difficult, if not absolutely impracticable, unless a frequency much lower than 133 cycles was adopted, and Westinghouse gave instructions for an investigation of the subject. Messrs. Stillwell, Shallenberger, Schmid, and Scott were specially charged with this study. Before the end of 1892 they selected two frequencies as standards for the Westinghouse Company, 30 cycles per second and 60 cycles; 60 cycles to be used where the principal load was for lighting, and 30 cycles where a large part of the power was to be converted and utilized in the form of a direct current. In preparing the plans upon which the first proposal to the Cataract Company was based, the engineers of the Westinghouse Company found it impracticable to wind a two-phase generator to produce 30 cycles because of the fact that the Cataract Company already had placed its order for hydraulic turbines to run at 250 revolutions per minute. This fact forced them to choose between a 16-pole machine which would produce 33 1/3 cycles and a 12-pole machine which would produce 25 cycles. They selected the former, and the first tender of the Westinghouse Company was based on this frequency. Professor Forbes, consulting electrical engineer for the Cataract Construction Company, proposed 16 2/3 cycles (an 8-pole generator). Finally, as a compromise, 25 cycles were adopted, and such has been the influence of the Niagara development that this is today the standard low frequency throughout the United States. After an experience of more than a quarter of a century, electrical engineers are practically unanimous in their opinion that it is unfortunate that 30 cycles is not now the standard low frequency instead of 25 cycles. The frequency, 60 cycles, which was first adopted by the Westinghouse Company as a result of Westinghouse's foresight, is today the standard high frequency generally in use in the United States.

The generator as finally adopted at Niagara was also a compromise. The alternator proposed by the Westinghouse Company had an internal revolving armature and an external stationary field. It was a two-phase machine wound for 800 volts. Following the rejection of this design, the Cataract Company brought forward a design by Professor George Forbes comprising a stationary internal armature and external revolving field. It was wound for 20,000 volts, 2 phases, and 25 cycles. Mechanically the general idea embodied in the design was excellent. Electrically it was impracticable. One of the Westinghouse engineers writes: "From our present knowledge of machine design it would have been a monumental failure." It was proposed to cool the armature-coils by forcing oil through them. Analysis revealed that this circulation would have required a pressure of 400 pounds per square inch, a figure far beyond the strength of the material with which it was proposed to enclose the coils. The insulation was inadequate for 20,000 volts. It was found impossible also to design a field ring of sufficient strength for an 8-pole machine without exceeding the limit of weight fixed by the hydraulic elements of the proposed plant. Other features were regarded as unwise and the Westinghouse Company finally declined to accept any responsibility for the results if the machine were built.

In again asking for bids the Cataract Company said, referring to the alternative generator design prepared by its engineers, "any alterations that you may propose in this design will be carefully considered and if acceptable will be appreciated in placing the contract." The fixed specifications eventually agreed upon were: alternating current, two-phase, 25 cycles, 2200 volts at a speed of 250 revolutions per minute, 5000 electrical horsepower. Seven manufacturers in America were asked to bid; we are not informed how many bids were received. The resulting tenders were examined by a special committee of two foreign engineers and two from the United States mechanical engineers as well as electrical. The result was that in October 1893, a contract was executed with the Westinghouse Company for three 5000-horsepower dynamos. The contracts for the switchboard and auxiliaries were made in March and October 1894. The first 5000-horsepower hydroelectric unit was tested in April 1895, and in the autumn of that year the commercial distribution and sale of electric power from Niagara Falls began.

It would be difficult for those whose recollection does not go back to those days to realize the great and widespread interest aroused by this step in power development. The first Niagara hydroelectric installation was a brilliant engineering achievement. It was accepted generally in America and in Europe as the demonstrated solution of the problem of developing hydraulic power for transmission and distribution and its utilization for practically every purpose to which power is applicable. Its results have been far-reaching to an extent which even today is not generally realized.

The Cataract Construction Company undertook and carried to successful completion a power enterprise unprecedented in magnitude at that time and unequalled then or since when measured by its consequences. The methods of investigation, development, and final determination of plans employed by the officers and directors of that company were remarkable for their vision, thoroughness, and courage. That the plans which they finally adopted after world-wide search were in every essential those developed by Westinghouse and his engineers is a fact which detracts in no way from the credit due to the officers and engineering staff of the Cataract Construction Company. The alternating-current transformer is the essential key to transmission of power at low cost. The polyphase motor is the essential key to the reproduction in mechanical form of power transmitted by electricity. In the hands of Westinghouse and his engineers, the crude transformer of Gaulard and Gibbs capable of supplying at low efficiency a few incandescent lamps became in a few years a transformer which could deliver thousands of horsepower at an efficiency exceeding ninety-eight per cent, and the primitive motor brought to America by Tesla in 1888, and loaded to its practical limit when driving a ten-inch ventilating-fan became a motor capable of delivering hundreds and even thousands of horsepower.

Up to the time of the first Niagara generators the largest alternators built were of 1000 horsepower. The step to 5000 horsepower was a long one involving considerable difficulties in manufacture. Many engineers who may read this book will remember the impression, amazing and almost astounding, made by these machines with their prodigious fields revolving at a peripheral speed of 9250 feet per minute, a speed then considered terrific. Some of them will remember, too, the surprise of Li Hung Chang when the point of his umbrella caught a bolthead on the rim of one of these fields. The old gentleman's admirable curiosity was quite gratified for once, and by good luck the umbrella went clear of him in its flight across the room.

In a report on this first Niagara hydroelectric plant the Westinghouse Company said: "The switching devices, indicating and measuring instruments, bus-bars and other auxiliary apparatus, have been designed and constructed on lines departing radically from our usual practice. The conditions of the problem presented, especially as regards the amount of power to be dealt with, have been so far beyond all precedent that it has been necessary to devise a considerable amount of new apparatus. The general organization of the cables, switches, and measuring instruments differs materially from anything of the kind hitherto installed elsewhere. Nearly every device used differs from what has hitherto been our standard practice. Among novel features of importance we may mention the use of compressed air to operate the switching devices, the construction of the 5000-horsepower switches, and the construction of the bus-bars."

Amongst the men at Pittsburgh who were active in the design and development of the machines and apparatus for Niagara were five who should be cited, to use a convenient war word. These were Albert Schmid, Benjamin G. Lamme, Lewis B. Stillwell, Charles F. Scott, and Oliver B. Shallenberger.

Schmid, a Swiss engineer, was in the Westinghouse service many years in America and in France. He died in New York, December 31, 1919, in his sixty-third year. He was a mechanical engineer and designer of remarkable gifts. He had a fine sense of form and proportion as well as a keen mechanical faculty. The influence of his designs is still seen in various classes of electrical machinery. At the time of the Niagara development he was General Superintendent of the Westinghouse Electric & Manufacturing Company. As an engineer he was largely responsible for the mechanical designs, and as superintendent he was responsible for the construction of the machines.

Lamme entered the Westinghouse service in 1888 direct from college, and has been there ever since, being now Chief Engineer. He has made a broader mark in the whole line of Westinghouse electrical machinery than any other man. Under Schmid he had an important part in designing the electrical features of the Niagara generators.

Stillwell entered the service in October 1886, also direct from college. He probably had a broader knowledge of alternating-current development in its early years than any other one of Westinghouse's young men. He was active in the Niagara enterprise from its start, had general supervision of that work at Pittsburgh in the period of design and construction, and was field engineer at Niagara Falls in charge of installation and first operation as Electrical Engineer and Assistant Manager of the Westinghouse Company. In January 1897, he was elected Electrical Director of the Niagara Falls Power Company and the Cataract Company in charge of the construction and operation.

Scott and Shallenberger were very active in research, experiment, and design of details. They also were recently out of college, Shallenberger from the Naval Academy. Their names are part of the annals of the Westinghouse Company. Shallenberger died in 1898, and Scott has been for some years Professor of Electrical Engineering at Yale.

Such, briefly and inadequately told, is the story of the first great hydroelectric plant at Niagara Falls. It produced 15,000 horsepower by three generators. The original plant was soon increased by the addition of eight similar units. The three 5000-horsepower units first installed are still in commercial use. They have been operating day and night practically without interruption since 1895. That they were scientifically designed and carefully constructed is evidenced by the fact that the cost of maintaining them during these years has been less than one per cent per annum. The present generator capacity of the three power houses constructed by the original Niagara Falls Power Company, two on the American side and one on the Canadian side, is 228,000 horsepower. Five of the later generators are 12,500 horsepower, and there are five of 10,000 horsepower.

Of course there has been no change from alternating current, and the frequency of 25 cycles is still used throughout. On the American side the original generated potential of 2200 volts is maintained, with two-phase current. On the Canadian side the potential is 12,000 volts, three phase. The tendency has been to change from the external revolving field to the less-expensive internal revolving field, and now more than sixty-one per cent of the installed capacity is of the internal-field type.

When the original power plant of the Niagara Falls Company had demonstrated its technical and commercial success, other power companies began the development of large plants, and today the aggregate output capacity installed at Niagara is approximately 500,000 horsepower. The latest unit installed is of 37,500 horsepower, and turbines and generators of still greater output are now in course of construction. It goes without saying that experience on such a scale for twenty-five years has had its effect on hydraulic engineering, as well as on electric. When the Cataract Construction Company decided to adopt 5000-horsepower turbines under a head of 140 feet, the largest hydraulic turbine used in America was about 500 horsepower, and few, if any, larger were used abroad. The greatest head under which turbines were used in America was about forty feet, and although much greater heads were used in France and Switzerland, the units were comparatively small in size. The engineers of the Power Company, among whom the late Doctor Coleman Sellers, of Philadelphia, a lifelong friend of Westinghouse, was chief, deserved no less credit for their courage and skill in dealing with the great hydraulic problem which they faced than for their vision and judgment in selecting the electric system best adapted to meet its requirements.

This splendid enterprise so beneficent in its effect is not a monument to engineers alone. Those who risked their money and reputation in it had courage, enterprise, and imagination. Their work at Niagara is a wonderful illustration of public benefit resulting from private initiative. They were patient in procedure and wise in method. They share the glory with the scientists who revealed the underlying principles and the engineers who developed the methods and machinery.

It has been said above that the outcome at Niagara settled for all time the question as between alternating current and direct current. It also had a tremendous influence in interesting capital for power development, at home and abroad. It was a conspicuous example of the practicability of developing cheap power in large central stations and distributing it for manufacturing, lighting, and transportation. One of the earliest examples of long distance transmission was the Niagara, Lockport and Ontario Power Company which soon came into being and to which Westinghouse gave financial support. This company carried electric power eastward 195 miles and westward some 95 miles, serving several cities and towns. The Niagara enterprise hastened forward the epoch of manufactured power. Of this more is said in another place. It remains to say a word about certain special effects.

The largest group of electrochemical workers in the world is at Niagara Falls, and the development of Niagara power was the beginning of the electric-furnace art as a factor in industrial processes. The commercial development of aluminum was made possible by Niagara power, and for years Niagara Falls was the only seat of the aluminum industry in America. The artificial abrasive industry on a commercial scale started at Niagara, and in 1914, sixty-two per cent of the total abrasives used in the United States were artificial. When the Great War came, importation of emery from Turkey and

Greece ceased. How crippled the great metal-working industries of the United States would have been without Niagara carborundum and alundum may be imagined. The total production of ferrosilicon in the United States was, two or three years ago, perhaps still is, at Niagara, and that which we imported came mostly from Canadian works at Niagara. More than half of the ferrochromium consumed here is produced in electric furnaces at Niagara Falls. Ferrochromium is an essential element in the manufacture of armor plate and armor-piercing projectiles, and shell-steel specifications require a percentage of silicon. Ferrosilicon is used in making a great part of our steel production. The production of alloys of tungsten, vanadium, molybdenum, and ferrotitanium depends more or less directly and largely on the electric furnaces of Niagara. All the artificial graphite used in this country and a large proportion of all that is used in the world is produced at Niagara Falls, which is the center also of our chlorine industry with its many variations, and of an important production of phosphorus. All these essential industries so fundamental in our material development and so vitally affecting our civilization have grown up there as a result of the development and sale of cheap electric power at Niagara.

Not long ago a group of enthusiastic chemical and metallurgical engineers displayed at an automobile show in New York the legend "Niagara Falls made Detroit possible." It was not a geological matter but industrial. The line of development shown was water power, cheap electric current, electric furnaces, alloy steels, tool steel, cheaper manufacture, cheaper automobiles, Detroit. They did not say that Niagara Falls made possible our effective part in the Great War. They must have been tempted, but they knew the "eloquence of understatement."

Chapter Nine - Electric Traction

WESTINGHOUSE was not the first man to try to haul cars by electricity, or the first to suggest it. Far from it. Davidson, a Scotchman, tried an electromagnetic locomotive in 1837, and Doctor Werner Siemens actually worked a halfmile of railroad, of two-foot gage, by electricity, at the Berlin Exhibition in 1879. In 1881 he built an electric tramway of one and one-half miles at Lichterfelde, which he followed in the next two years with short mining roads taking current from overhead conductors. In 1883 a tramway, six miles long, was built between Portrush and Bushmills in the north of Ireland.

But electric traction has had its greatest development in the United States. Edison made experiments with an electric locomotive at least as far back as 1880, and Stephen D. Field was experimenting about the same time. In the next few years half a dozen men, whose names became well known and even famous, worked in this field. Of the kind of trolley road now common all over the world the first to be built and worked in a commercial way was the Union Passenger Railway in Richmond, Va. This was designed and built by Frank J. Sprague, who organized a little company which took the contract to build the road in May 1887. About the same time Bentley and Knight built a short line in Allegheny City, Pa. Sprague was a graduate of the United States Naval Academy, and resigned from the navy to devote himself to the electrical art, in which he has made a successful and distinguished career. He was one of a remarkable group of young graduates who greatly influenced the philosophical and practical development of electrical science and art in the last quarter of the nineteenth century, and most of whom are still active. The careers that they have made are good proof of the advanced and sound teaching in electricity at the Naval Academy.

Westinghouse was a little later in the field, but under his guidance and stimulus the Westinghouse Electric & Manufacturing Company quickly became a leader, and rapidly developed types and systems which have had a commanding influence on electric traction. In 1888 or 1889 experiments were made with a Tesla motor with a view to using alternating current for railway working. From the very beginning of his efforts in traction Westinghouse had in mind alternating current, and he never gave up that thought until he died. We are writing at the moment particularly of the kind of electric traction which has been developed in street-railway working and cross-country trolley roads, but from some indeterminate but early time he began to look forward to the general use of electricity on railroads. Writing in 1910 he says: "Believing unreservedly that the increased capacity of a railway and its stations, the economies of operation, and other advantages will bring about gradually the systematic electrification of steam railways, my wish is that the progress of the art may not be hampered and such electrification of our main lines delayed or rendered unprofitable by mistakes which experience, judgment, and foresight may enable us to avoid. It is my intention in this paper to direct attention to the necessity for the very early selection of a comprehensive electrical system embracing fundamental standards of construction." Events have justified him; but the first traction experiment with the Tesla motor failed, and was bound to, for the characteristics of the induction motor were not yet suitable for traction.

Westinghouse had to be content a while with direct-current working. In the fall of 1889 he told Albert Schmid that he was going into the street-railway business, and instructed Schmid to get ready for it. Schmid directed Lamme to make a study of existing systems. A general scheme was laid out and a double-reduction-gear motor was designed and built, and soon became known as a powerful motor. The design of auxiliary apparatus was limited by patents, but a complete system was quickly evolved which was satisfactory for the time and let Westinghouse into the field. The three principal competitors were Sprague, Thomson-Houston, and Short, all active and competent. The only real advantage of the Westinghouse system was the enclosed gear, one of Schmid's improvements, which was a distinct step forward and a great selling point.

Manufacturers and engineers soon recognized that the double-reduction gear was unsatisfactory, partly in undue exposure to the weather and partly in complication, and several companies began designs of single-reduction gear motors independently and simultaneously. In 1890 the Westinghouse Company brought out a single-reduction-gear motor which proved revolutionary, and eventually drove all other types out of the market, and (modified and improved) is used to this day. It is the only one produced at that time which has persisted in type. It was the progenitor of the present direct-current railway motor, and the whole world has come to this type.

This new motor precipitated a serious commercial situation. It came so suddenly and its use spread so fast that the several companies, Westinghouse amongst them, had to scrap large stocks of double-reduction-gear motors. This was a situation which Westinghouse rather enjoyed, for progress was always a good deal more interesting to him than profit. He would have said that progress is profit; which is true in the long run, but it is sometimes a little difficult to finance that view of life and business. One of his old associates says that Westinghouse was a thirty-day man. The profits of the new idea or the new enterprise would begin to appear in about thirty days. This temperament had much to do with the various embarrassments in his affairs, and it was a powerful element in his prodigious successes.

In the early days of electric traction, while people were feeling around for methods and apparatus, the matter of feeding current to the motors was the subject of much invention and experiment. At first current was taken from a third rail and returned through the running rails, or the two track rails were used as outgoing and return conductors respectively. Westinghouse made very early experiments of this kind. One who saw some of these trials writes: "I recall that they used to lead one of the old horses across the track to see whether he would jump if he chanced to get a front foot on one rail and a hind foot on the other while the rails were charged." We may doubt if the phrase "they used to" is precise. It implies a fixed habit.

Before the time of which we are now writing high feeling had been created about the relative dangers of alternating and direct current. Controversy raged in the public prints. Westinghouse and Edison saw each other burning and killing their innocent fellow citizens, but it is entirely fair to say that on the part of Westinghouse this fight was defensive. It began with the short-sighted but determined effort to head off the alternating current, which with him was a prime article of faith. Naturally, the controversy affected in some degree all schemes for supplying current to car motors. Perhaps the real feeling in the Westinghouse group was expressed by Walter C. Kerr, a man of much ability and famous for fluent and abundant talk. In one of the conferences Kerr sat silent, to the surprise of his comrades. At last one of them said: "Walter, what's the matter; why don't you say something?" Kerr answered: "There are so many greater dangers in railroading, and dangers so very much more likely to happen, that this matter seems to me a good deal exaggerated." Nevertheless, reasonable attention must be paid to public feeling and reasonable precautions must be taken against possible dangers.

Serious and somewhat costly experiments were carried on with a so-called "button" system which had attractive features. Contact shoes under the car took current from plates placed at intervals along the track and energized automatically only when the car was over them. Contact was by buttons, hence the name.

Various other ways of taking current were devised and tried, but all yielded to the Vanderpoel underrunning trolley now in universal use. The General Electric Company bought the Vanderpoel patent and brought suit against the Westinghouse Company. It was one of the celebrated cases in the story of electricity. It went against the Westinghouse Company. The counsel for the company, with great disappointment, and some apprehension, told Westinghouse the decision. He said: "That's good; now there is a basis for a trade. They want our Tesla patents and we want their trolley patent." In March 1896, a general exchange of licenses was effected covering essentially the entire field of operations of the two companies, other than incandescent electric lamps. The arrangement was set forth in a carefully considered agreement pursuant to which was established the Board of Patent Control, of which more will be said in another place.

The Westinghouse Company has continued strong, active, and progressive in direct-current street-railway work, but Westinghouse never slept on the idea of using alternating current for heavy traction. Development of apparatus was pushed steadily forward, slowly it long seemed, but never ceasing.

Before going into this matter with some account of specific things done, it is well to say a few words about the state of the art when Westinghouse took up the systematic production and development of heavy-traffic methods and machinery. The standard practice then was the use of direct current, generated and distributed at 550 to 600 volts. To supply large quantities of power over considerable distances necessitated power-generating stations at frequent intervals and the subdivision of the supply system into small generating units. The result must be high cost of generation and distribution. The reasons for this are made plain in the introductory passages of the general chapter on electricity.

A further serious difficulty existed and even yet is not entirely cleared away. That is the difficulty of collecting large quantities of current at low voltage from the conductor delivering it to the locomotive or the motor on a car. Confronted by these hard and fast conditions the electrification of railroads of heavy traffic was at a standstill. Those who knew the elements of the situation saw little promise of electrification on a large scale. Great projects were brought forward, discussed, analyzed, and abandoned because of their cost and the technical difficulties in the way. The situation was like that of the railroads just before Bessemer made the steel rail possible.

Then came the rotary converter. The story of the origin, natures and functions of this important machine is told elsewhere in this book. Alternating current in any necessary quantity can be carried long distances (in present practice two hundred and fifty miles and more) at high potential and delivered to the converter at substations. There it is converted to direct current and carried short distances, at low voltage, to the place of use. Thus the cost of generating and distributing is brought down to commercial limits and the first difficulty has disappeared.

The problem of collecting and handling low-voltage current in large quantities remained. The third rail partly met this. The rail laid alongside the running rails carries the current from the substation, and it is collected by a shoe, hanging from the locomotive or car. The arrangement is simple and strong and well adapted to maintain the necessary close adjustment of conductor and collector.

The rotary converter and third rail gave a quick and strong impulse to heavy electrification, but high cost limited it to situations of very heavy traffic, such as elevated and subway service in large cities, city terminals, and dense suburban .traffic. There were also a few places where the nuisance and dangers of smoke from locomotives more than balanced the greater cost of electric installation and operation, such as long tunnels and city terminal approaches, partly in tunnel and cut.

When the method of electric operation built up on the rotary converter and third rail came to be studied for possible use on long lines with comparatively infrequent service, it was quickly found that it was not a general solution of the problem. Technically it was possible if not easy; financially it was impossible. Such was the situation about the beginning of 1900.

In the last months of 1885 Westinghouse had begun his serious and powerful development of the use of alternating current. In the next ten years he and his engineers had established beyond reasonable doubt or question the fact that for the generation and transmission of power, cheaply and on a great scale, alternating current must be used. They had produced those fundamental things, the transformer and the rotary converter; they had brought forward a commercial line of alternating-current motors and meters, and they had made the conclusive world-demonstration at Niagara Falls. The way was shown. Engineers throughout the world looked hopefully and even eagerly for the alternating-current system to solve the heavy railway problem; not because there were any particular merits in alternating-current apparatus for traction itself, but because here was a high-voltage, flexible system, which, if it could only be used on the trains or locomotives themselves, would at once settle the questions of generation, transmission, collection, and handling of large units of power on a moving vehicle.

But there were lions in the path yet. It was beginning to be recognized that high trolley voltage (high voltage on the conductors feeding current to the motors) was a necessary condition in a general solution. With alternating current it was easy enough to meet the high voltage, but there were other limitations. In the three-phase traction system, as brought out by the Ganz Company in Europe, three-phase motors of large power could be used, but there was the handicap of two overhead wires at different potentials, thus involving a double collection of current. Moreover, this system was apparently limited to about 3000 or 4000 volts, and if one was to use alternating current, there should be no such limit to the voltage. Furthermore, for lighter service, involving relatively small motors, the polyphase induction motor did not seem to be entirely satisfactory. Direct current was recognized, even at this time, as the possible means provided much higher voltages than 600 could be used, but almost everybody had doubts as to the practicability of sufficiently high voltage, either on the generators or on the motor equipment. Thus much thought was given to the possibilities of single-phase alternating current, for here one could use the single overhead trolley with the voltage limitations largely removed. However, engineers were faced by the fact that there was as yet no suitable single-phase motor available. Mr. B. J. Arnold made a noteworthy attempt toward single-phase operation, by trying to use a single-phase induction motor to drive a car through a special variable-speed gear. This apparently was the first published attempt at traction by single phase.

The Westinghouse Company had already been working on the same problem, but along radically different lines; namely, through the development of a series-type, single-phase motor with commutator, resembling in characteristics the series-type, direct-current motor. It had been recognized for years that the variable-speed characteristics of the series-type motor were ideal for traction service, and the Westinghouse engineers tried to keep the fundamental characteristics of the direct-current system. To accomplish this meant the commutation of alternating current on a relatively large scale, something which was then thought to be impracticable. However, the company had had sufficient experimental experience with the commutation of alternating-current commutating motors to indicate that it was entirely possible, especially if the frequency used was quite low.

In 1901 and 1902 the engineers of the company took up the question of building single-phase railway motors, and in 1902 a contract was taken to equip a high-speed electric line between Baltimore and Washington with single-phase, series-type railway motors. This was the true practical beginning of the present single-phase railway system, for although the installation was not made, the plan was put fairly before the world. It was recognized then, and always has been recognized, that the single-phase, commutator-type railway motor is not, in itself, quite as economical or efficient as direct current, but against this it was calculated that the simplification and economy of the transmission system, together with the more economical speed control, would offset the decreased economy of the motor itself. From the speed-control standpoint, the single-phase system was far ahead of the direct current, for the flexibility of the alternating-current system allowed voltage variations for controlling the motor speed, without the use of regulating rheostats for absorbing the extra voltage and power. Here was one of the major advantages, especially for locomotive work.

Like all new things, the single-phase system, when first brought out, was sometimes misapplied. In a number of cases where the direct-current system did not seem applicable, the single-phase system was used and was also found inapplicable, the fault, however, not lying directly in the system of electrification. In a number of cases there was an attempt to use the alternating-current system in connection with large direct-current systems already established, thus involving much complexity in equipment. In fact, within a few years, it developed that the single-phase system was not a satisfactory alternative to the direct-current system in general, but that it had its own field, and this field was where the special characteristics and advantages of high trolley potentials would apply. In other words, the single-phase system really began where the direct-current system was handicapped by limitations of voltage on the conductors and difficulty of speed control. One excellent result of the competition was the development of direct-current systems using comparatively high voltages, running up eventually to 3000 volts on the Chicago, Milwaukee & St. Paul, of which more will be told later.

While there were misapplications of the single-phase system at first, due largely to over enthusiasm, yet within a very few years it began to be used in heavy service, and in all such installations it has persisted, and not only persisted but has enlarged its field. One of the first large installations was in the St. Clair tunnel of the Grand Trunk Railway under the St. Clair River. There were heavy grades at either end of the tunnel, and the locomotives, working hard, emitted much smoke and gas. This was not merely disagreeable; it was dangerous to the lives of trainmen and passengers if trains were stalled in the tunnel. The same things led to electric working of other tunnels. The electric motive power in the St. Clair tunnel was large, slow-speed locomotives, and the first locomotives installed are still in use. The electrical engineering and equipment were by the Westinghouse Company. The tunnel itself was a remarkable engineering achievement bold, enterprising, and attended with some peculiar risks. It was one of the earliest examples of a cast-iron-tube tunnel built by the driven-shield method. This, with the successful alternating-current working, made a combination famous the world over.

The second large single-phase project, begun practically at the same time as the St. Clair tunnel, was the well-known New Haven electrification. This attracted great attention and much criticism and incredulity. After the contract was taken for electrification at 11,000 volts, 25 cycles, single phase many engineers, undoubtedly with all sincerity insisted, privately and publicly, that the thing was a physical impossibility, and that large passenger and express trains could not be handled by single-phase equipment. However, Westinghouse did not worry about the opinions of others in this matter, and was always eager to take up the cudgel in favor of alternating-current traction. He took the New Haven contract before the apparatus was designed and he said to some of his engineers: "Now I have dropped you into the middle of the pond and it is up to you to swim out." They had swimming a-plenty. The real troubles were not where they were expected. The first forty locomotives built were of the gearless types, that is, with the armatures around the axles, but driving through flexible connections. Many wise men shook their heads over these motors, as a gearless, single-phase, commutator-type motor for 300 horsepower had never been attempted before, which might be said of everything else in this system. However, it was not the motors which developed trouble. In fact, these motors made about the best record of any of the elements which made up this great system. Troubles developed in connection with the overhead-trolley system and its protective devices. Short circuits, and voltage and current surges, had been encountered in all alternating-current systems, in connection with power distribution in general, but these were only semi-occasional. In the New Haven system, at first, they were not only of daily occurrence, but sometimes many times a day, and apparatus which might stand a few surges during the year and still have reasonably long life, was found to last only a few weeks on the New Haven system. New circuit breakers, new selective arrangements, new protective devices, new methods of insulation, new problems of trolley suspension, new problems of underrunning trolleys had to be handled. For the first two years some lively work had to be done, but it was seen quite early that most of the difficulties to be overcome were not fundamental in character and the remedies were not prohibitive in cost or otherwise. Behind all this, Westinghouse had full confidence in the system and in his engineers, and the engineers on the New Haven Railway also had confidence. With these powers behind it, the system eventually began to loom up as a success, instead of the failure which many had predicted. In few great undertakings of any kind has there been shown more persistence, stamina, and resourceful engineering than in this New Haven electrification.

The most important example in the world today of working by electricity a railroad of heavy traffic is the New Haven Road; that is, the most important in the amount of equipment and volume of traffic. But far the greatest in mileage worked is the mountain section of the Chicago, Milwaukee & St. Paul. Here also are some matters of special interest in topography, hi equipment, and in methods of operation. Two mountain sections have been electrified, 640 miles, crossing four mountain ranges, the grades running up to two per cent, 104 feet per mile. Current is bought from the Montana Power Company, which has several generating stations, all driven by water power. The Power Company has some 2000 miles of transmission line, carrying current at pressures as great as 100,000 volts. Power is sold to other users than the railroad. This is, of course, alternating current, but the locomotives are operated by direct current, converted by motor-generator sets at substations situated at average intervals of about thirty-three miles, so that the direct-current transmission is short. The motors work at 3000 volts, the highest direct-current voltage yet used commercially in traction.

The machinery and apparatus for the first installation was supplied by the General Electric Company, but the Westinghouse Company has since furnished much important substation and power-control apparatus, and recently it, in cooperation with the Baldwin Locomotive Company, has furnished a number of magnificent passenger locomotives. These are the largest passenger engines in the world, weighing 275 tons, direct current, at 3000 volts, and rated at 4200 horsepower. It goes without saying that the whole enterprise rests on Westinghouse's conception of, and long contest for, the distribution of power by alternating current.

There are two features of this installation that appeal to every intelligence however unfamiliar with electrical engineering. One is regeneration, that is, using the motors, going down grade, as generators, and feeding current to other trains on the same section or putting it back through the motor-generator stations to the alternating-current supply system. This had been done before in a small way in street-railway work and in some minor locomotive service, using direct current. It was done on an important scale in the three-phase alternating-current traction systems installed by the Ganz Company and the Italian Westinghouse Company in Italy. With three-phase operation, however, regeneration is a relatively simple matter. When the three-phase induction motor runs above its synchronous speed it automatically begins to generate power. In consequence, with the three-phase motors, regeneration is an almost automatic adjunct to the system. Regeneration is also used on the Norfolk & Western electrification (a Westinghouse installation), which went into operation eight months before the Chicago, Milwaukee & St. Paul began operation. This is a single-phase system, with phase splitters for developing three phase on the locomotive for use with induction motors. Therefore, the Chicago, Milwaukee & St. Paul regeneration was not new, but it was new in the sense that auxiliary apparatus was necessary in order to produce, more or less automatically, the regenerative characteristics. The usual series-type, direct-current motors, as used on the Chicago, Milwaukee & St. Paul locomotives, are not in themselves capable of feeding power back to the line in a stable manner. Stability in practice is obtained by field excitation derived from a separate source, and the regenerative devices used in these equipments, both on the Westinghouse and General Electric locomotives, are very interesting.

It is an attractive thought that gravity, acting through a train dropping down grade, should generate power to haul another train up grade. The actual saving in the total power consumption in the St. Paul operation is from 10 to 15 per cent. Naturally, regeneration can occur only on grades, therefore the power saving can never be a great part of the total power used on an operating division. But even 10 or 15 per cent is worth saving.

Another important result is in the braking effect. Part of the energy developed in the train going down-hill is consumed in running the motors which are acting as generators. That energy need not be taken care of by the brakes. Thus, wear of brake shoes and wheels is reduced; there is an element of safety in the added braking power; more uniform speed on grades adds to the comfort of passengers and reduced wear and tear on equipment, and, finally, handling heavy freight trains on mountain grades is easier.

The other peculiar feature referred to is the automatic control of current used on an operating division of, say, two hundred miles. If you are in the cab of a locomotive you may see the voltmeter drop. If you are observant and curious you ask the engineer what has happened. He tells you that a train is starting up a grade perhaps one hundred miles away. At that instant the speed of all trains on the same operating division is automatically lowered, regardless of anything that the engineer can do. In this installation the total quantity of power used at any one time must be kept down to a fixed maximum. Due to the extremely variable power requirements of the railway system in general, excessive burdens are liable to be imposed upon the power supply at times, and to limit these a system of power charges has been instituted which puts a relatively high penalty on power excess. A power-limiting system has been devised whereby the peaks of power taken will automatically be lessened. This is done by what might be called "a load-balancing system," whereby power peaks are automatically held down by means of reduction in voltage in any section which is carrying an overload. This power equalizing or limiting system is too complex for description here, but its general effect is to keep down the peaks without unduly affecting the service. This is done automatically by the power indicating and limiting system. The maximum reduction of power obtainable is about thirty per cent of that which could be used if the control system were not provided. This is a very pretty example of flexibility of electric operation. For many reasons this great electrification has become famous all over the world, and it is constantly visited by engineers from many countries.

This is a water-power operation. It is fairly plain that railroads cannot be worked by water power when there is no reliable and sufficient water power to develop. Many water-power projects, designed for manufacturing, have come to grief because the difficulties and limitations have not been seen and analyzed. But as knowledge grows, the radius of transmission lengthens. It becomes practicable, technically and economically, to mass several smallish water powers into one large system and send the combined power long distances. The problem changes, and from year to year it is more and more possible to make use of water powers of small and irregular supply, extending and diversifying hydroelectric projects. It must not be forgotten that all this is at bottom a matter of transmission, and that transmission rests finally on the alternating current.

The economic advantages and disadvantages of electric haulage on railroads of heavy traffic, now worked by steam, are not measured by the relative cost of a unit of energy delivered at the place where it does work. There is the obvious advantage of saving coal for other uses. There is the advantage, not quite so obvious, of releasing miners for other work. There is the advantage, perhaps still less obvious, of saving the transportation of railroad coal, releasing cars, engines, tracks, and men to haul coal to other consumers; to haul wheat, steel, beef, and merchandise. The higher uniform speed possible with electricity permits the same amount of freight to be handled with fewer cars, an item of very great importance, as everybody knows now. Labor is possibly the most important item of all. Increase in size and speed of trains saves train labor. Roundhouse and shop labor is reduced to still greater extent, and labor is the largest single item in transportation cost.

Something will be said later on of the effect on the progress of mankind of the evolution of the art of transportation. In land transportation the continued improvement of railroads is immensely the most important thing. As the needs of organized society grow, the growth of the capacity of the railroad machine becomes more and more urgent. It is said by many wise men that the capacity of a railroad can be doubled by the use of electric power, with present operating methods. It is hard to forecast the further increase in capacity through changes in operating methods that may follow upon the possibility of almost unlimited power on each train. We may look for something like a revolution in railroad practice as a result of alternating-current distribution.

All of these things being so, the drift toward electrification is bound to gain in volume and velocity. At this moment Japan, Switzerland, and Sweden, with mountain railroads, abundant water power, and dear fuel, are working up great projects of railroad electrification, and inevitably they turn to eight or ten successful workings in America for experience and to American engineers for information and opinion; and the shade of George Westinghouse says: "All of this I foresaw and part of it I was."

Along with the development of high-voltage, direct-current motors, as on the St. Paul, the Westinghouse Company has continued to develop the single-phase system with commutator motors, so that it has become capable of meeting all the requirements of freight and passenger service under extremely heavy conditions. Moreover, it can handle multiple-unit and small-car service with equal facility, and it is particularly well adapted for electrification of freight yards, as in the Harlem yards of the New Haven Company, probably the finest example of electrified freight yards that can be found anywhere in the world. Thus we see that Westinghouse's hope for a universal system for handling heavy railway work is realized as he expected by a purely alternating-current system. Time is showing the truth of his opinions.

From what has been written here it may be seen that in the heavy railway field, Westinghouse and the Westinghouse Electric & Manufacturing Company have been at the front in development and progress. The only radically new system brought out, namely, the single phase, originated with the Westinghouse Company. The split-phase system, which is really a branch of the single phase, was experimented with as early as 1896 or 1897, in connection with plans for electrifying the Manhattan Elevated in New York, and a phase splitter and induction motor were so operated on experimental test. Later the General Electric Company took up similar lines of experimentation and published a description of a split-phase system somewhat earlier than the Norfolk & Western, although apparently this system was never applied commercially. Credit for the commercial application of the split-phase system, therefore, lies with the Westinghouse Company. It is interesting also to note that the later three-phase electric locomotives on the Italian state railways were built by the Italian Westinghouse Company. The Westinghouse Electric & Manufacturing Company has had practical operating experience with all systems which have been seriously proposed for railway electrification, and has carried them through to successful operation.

It is written in the sky that sooner or later the railroads of the earth will be worked by electricity. The way has been prepared by those doings which have been related. It has not been the purpose of the narrative to suggest for a moment that Westinghouse and his engineers have been alone in the preparation. Far from it. The General Electric Company has done big things. It has worked with skill and energy and power. Ganz & Company and others in Europe have done important things. Westinghouse and his men have always been amongst the leaders, and in certain fundamental things they have led the leaders. In the origin and development of the use of the alternating current, without which these great things would have been impossible, Westinghouse was first and was always preeminent. His engineers earned and justified the confidence and support that he gave them, generously and steadfastly.

Chapter Ten - Steam and Gas Engines

IT is probable that in the two centuries before the Christian era, Syracuse was rich in legends of the boyish inventions of little Archimedes. Everybody has been told that the steam engine as a tool grew out of the observations and reflections of the boy Watt upon the performances of steam in a teakettle. Likewise the boyhood haunts of George Westinghouse have traditions of the contrivances that occurred to the deep-revolving mind of another boy. But the earliest documentary evidence of Westinghouse's inventive faculty is found in a patent dated October 31, 1865, for improvement in rotary steam engines. This was the beginning of a line of invention, development, and manufacture that interested him and received an important part of his attention throughout his entire life. The patent was issued twenty-five days after he was nineteen years old. There is good reason to think that the invention was well begun some years earlier, before he went into the army.

We do not know the direct inspiration that led to the particular invention shown in this patent, but Westinghouse's environment was such as to arouse an interest in steam engineering in any one having mechanical instincts, and there is reason to believe that he turned to the rotary engine as a means of eliminating supposed losses in converting reciprocating into rotary motion, as was done by then existing types of steam prime movers. It has, of course, been demonstrated that when reciprocating engines are properly designed, there are no serious losses of the kind often assumed by those not fully informed as to the underlying principles involved. If Westinghouse was at first in error with respect to this particular point, it still remained true that a successful rotary engine would have important advantages of compactness, high speed, and light weight, so that the subject forever remained one of absorbing interest to him, and found manifestation in many and various forms of prime movers which utilized either steam or gas for propulsion. The rotary engine described in the first patent was built but never operated. A second one, built on somewhat different lines, also proved to be practically inoperative.

While still in the navy (that is, before he was nineteen), Westinghouse designed and partly built a four-cylinder reciprocating engine with the cylinders placed radially around a central valve casing containing a rotary valve to effect steam distribution. This was a very early example of that arrangement. Construction of this small model engine was completed shortly after he was mustered out of the navy. It is still in existence and is an operative machine. As was to be expected, construction difficulties were developed, but in collaboration with his brother, John Westinghouse, a new form was designed, from which a forty-horsepower engine was built which was used for some years to furnish power for driving the machinery of his father's shop at Schenectady. Compared with the then existing reciprocating engines, it was relatively compact and light in weight, as the heavy flywheel was dispensed with by the use of multiple cylinders and high rotative speed. Structural and operative defects gradually appeared and another engine was built on the same general principle of four radial cylinders, in which many earlier defects were cured. This engine furnished the power to drive blowers that supplied the blast for the steel-melting furnaces in his first industrial undertaking, the making of cast-steel frogs and switches. It is believed that this was the first foundry in the United States to make steel castings exclusively.

Again he devised a variation of the four-cylinder reciprocating type of engine, that was built upon experience previously obtained, and was used to furnish power for the new Air Brake Works at Pittsburgh. It ran satisfactorily for some years, but had no marked advantages over the accepted type of reciprocating steam engines.

As a result of observation during his first visit in England, he became familiar with the single-acting form of multiple-cylinder steam engine, and on his return designed one with certain modifications and improvements that he hoped might make it commercially adaptable to many purposes in this country. This particular engine supplanted the one first used to drive the machinery of the Air Brake Company, and continued to operate for a few years, being finally replaced by a reciprocating engine of the standard type.

That these inventive efforts were regarded by Westinghouse as tentative and experimental is pretty well established by the fact that no patents were taken for any but the first rotary engine. The subject was apparently dormant in his mind until 1891, when he patented another form of rotary engine that for many years thereafter was the object of intense application, resulting in the production of numerous examples embodying various changes and improvements. The 1891 patent contained a clear and concise statement of the reasons why previous efforts by other inventors had failed to produce practical and efficient machines, and proposed a remedy.

While no commercial production of rotary steam engines resulted from these efforts, many machines were made and sold in the form of air compressors, and proved to be most efficient for the purpose. Experience, however, developed that there were certain limitations tending to restrict the field in which they could profitably be employed, and their commercial manufacture was discontinued. An examination of the many patents issued to Westinghouse in this line, or bought by him from other inventors, will satisfy any one sufficiently interested to inquire into the matter, that they disclosed most important contributions to the branch of engineering art to which they relate, although the meritorious character of the intelligence and industry expended upon them has naturally been obscured by the fact that these efforts did not result in large commercial production.

The interest of Westinghouse in the rotary type of engine was not confined to his own inventions. Patent 572,946, issued to C. A. Backstrom December 15, 1896, illustrates a form of rotary engine quite distinct from those shown in the patents issued to Westinghouse. The Backstrom patent was bought by Westinghouse, and the Backstrom principle, with many variations made by Westinghouse, was labored with assiduously and carried through an extensive series of experiments, without, however, reaching a satisfactory conclusion. It all makes a most interesting and important chapter in the field of the rotary prime mover.

GAS ENGINES

Westinghouse's experience in the natural-gas field and his efforts to make and distribute producer gas, naturally brought to his attention the adaptability of gas engines where natural gas or producer gas was available, with the result that the manufacture of gas engines of moderate size was established as a part of the regular product of the Westinghouse Machine Company. The form of gas engine then in general use was the horizontal type, with hit-or-miss speed regulation. This arrangement required heavy flywheel effect to compensate for intermittent explosions, and even then the performance was unsatisfactory for electric-lighting purposes, because of variable speed. His first patented contribution to the gas-engine art was a method of regulation that provided substantially uniform rotative speed, making the engines entirely satisfactory for electric lighting purposes, a use to which they were largely and successfully applied.

The high thermal efficiency of gas engines as compared with the best performance of steam engines led Westinghouse in the late nineties to believe that if gas engines of sufficient size could be successfully produced to meet the increasing demands for central-station production of electricity for lighting and power purposes, they would entirely supplant the use of steam, and he therefore directed his efforts toward the production of relatively large sizes of gas engines with the expectation that they would be supplied with gas from gas producers in much the same manner that steam is supplied by boilers to steam engines. For some years this was one of his many enthusiasms. He had great and fascinating visions of power stations with gas engines, and spent much thought and money in efforts to work out methods of making fuel gas. Two factors in the problem changed with such rapidity that he ultimately became convinced that the field for gas engines was much more limited than he at one time had assumed it to be. These factors were, first, a greatly increased efficiency in steam turbines due to improved design and the use of high-pressure superheated steam with high vacuum, and, secondly, the demand for much larger power units than could by any possibility be produced in the form of gas engines, the largest gas unit not exceeding 5000 horsepower, while turbines varying from 20,000 to 60,000 horsepower are now in large use.

TURBINES

The interest of Westinghouse in the steam turbine came about quite logically and at first gradually; but when he was actually committed he proceeded with his normal energy and boldness. The Westinghouse Machine Company, in response to the demand for increased size of generating units, designed and produced some of the largest reciprocating steam engines made in the United States. There was little novelty about their construction, they being built in accordance with well-established engineering precedent and practice. In performance they were entirely successful. It is not surprising, in view of the experience of Westinghouse in connection with rotary-engine experiments, that the huge weight and bulk of these enormous machines should have directed his attention to the steam turbine.

"Every schoolboy knows" that a reaction steam turbine was described by Hero of Alexandria 130 B. C. Sadi Carnot says: "There is almost as great a distance between the first apparatus in which the expansive force of steam was displayed and the existing machine as between the first raft that man ever made and the modern ship. If the honor of a discovery belongs to the nation in which it has acquired its growth and all its developments, this honor cannot be here refused to England. Savery, Newcomen, Smeaton, Watt, and some other English engineers are the veritable creators of the steam engine." This is a generous word from a great Frenchman. And, strange to say, the steam turbine carries on the same story. In 1884 Sir Charles Parsons made a ten-horsepower turbine, and in 1885 took out his first patents and launched another revolution in steam engineering. From Hero to Parsons more than two thousand years passed, and in those years nothing was done of the least historical or mechanical consequence in the development of the steam turbine. Then, in a very few years, Parsons built up a great art and industry which spread to the continent of Europe and to the United States. De Laval, a distinguished French engineer, must not be overlooked. His first patent seems to have been in 1883, but he confined its useful development to small and very high-speed machines, and Carnot's estimate of relative honors in steam engineering still holds; an English engineer was the "veritable creator" of the steam turbine.

Parsons went ahead fast. By 1889 he had built some 300 turbines, running up to 75-kilowatt capacity. In the next five years he made a number of turbines of 350- to 500-kilowatt capacity, and the historical "Turbinia," the first turbine ship, was afloat.

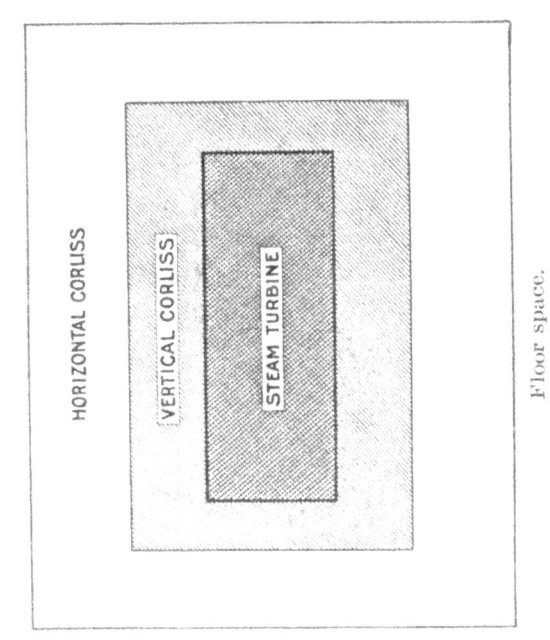

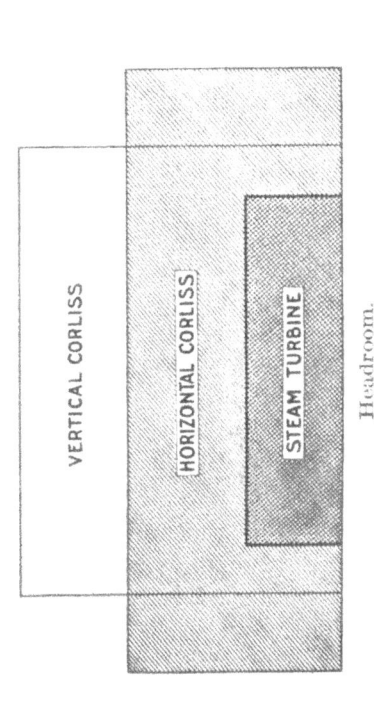

Steam turbine and Corliss engine. A comparison of headroom and floor space; equal powers.

The turbine was then almost unknown in the United States. Some experimental machines had been devised which are known only to students, and a 300-kilowatt De Laval turbine had been imported and installed as an experiment in one of the New York Edison plants. Westinghouse had watched Parsons, and he had become satisfied that the turbine was a suitable prime mover for electric generators which ran at the speeds that are necessary for the economical performance of the turbine. In 1895 he took a license under the Parsons patents for manufacture in the United States for other than marine uses. The Parsons-Westinghouse turbine soon came to pass. Operations were begun in the spring of 1896, and the usual development work was carried on under his direction, resulting in modifications and improvements leading to a greater adaptability of the design to conditions then existing in the United States. In collaboration with the engineers of the Westinghouse Electric Company, who made the electrical end of the unit, the first commercial machines were produced and installed in the plant of the Westinghouse Air Brake Company at Wilmerding, Pa., in 1898, consisting of three 400-kilowatt machines, which are still in operation. Both operatively and in the matter of steam consumption, the performance was satisfactory, comparing favorably with results obtained from the best type of reciprocating engines.

The market for large electric generators had already been established, and Westinghouse believed that great advantage would come from the use of steam turbines if built in adequate sizes to drive them, and in 1899 there was designed and built a turbo-generator of 1500-kilowatt capacity, running at 1200 revolutions per minute, which was installed in the plant of the Hartford Electric Light Company - very much the largest machine of its kind yet produced. The performance of this turbine in reduced steam consumption was surprising, and while certain mechanical difficulties were encountered, that were subsequently overcome, it established beyond question the value of steam-turbine prime movers in the production of electricity. The story of the development of the turbo-generator itself involves a great deal of electrical engineering and is made the subject of another chapter.

The mechanical difficulties which appeared in the Hartford machine were entirely due to its unprecedented size and seemed for the moment to indicate the ultimate limit to the capacity of the steam turbine. In a turbine, whatever its size, the clearances must be small if economy of steam is to be secured, and but little distortion can be tolerated in either the stationary or the moving parts. It is clear that the tendency to changes in the form and relation of the parts, due to weight, motion, and temperature, increases with the size, particularly with the length.

In England these mechanical difficulties were, in a measure, avoided by building the turbine in two sections, one using high-pressure and the other low-pressure steam, a construction equivalent to the ordinary compound reciprocating steam engine. This design, however, was not regarded with favor by Westinghouse, as he felt that it unnecessarily increased size and cost, and his efforts were directed, successfully, to the solution of the problem by a unitary structure. In all this development work he was the leader and inspirer of a staff of highly competent and interested engineers, with whom he actively collaborated.

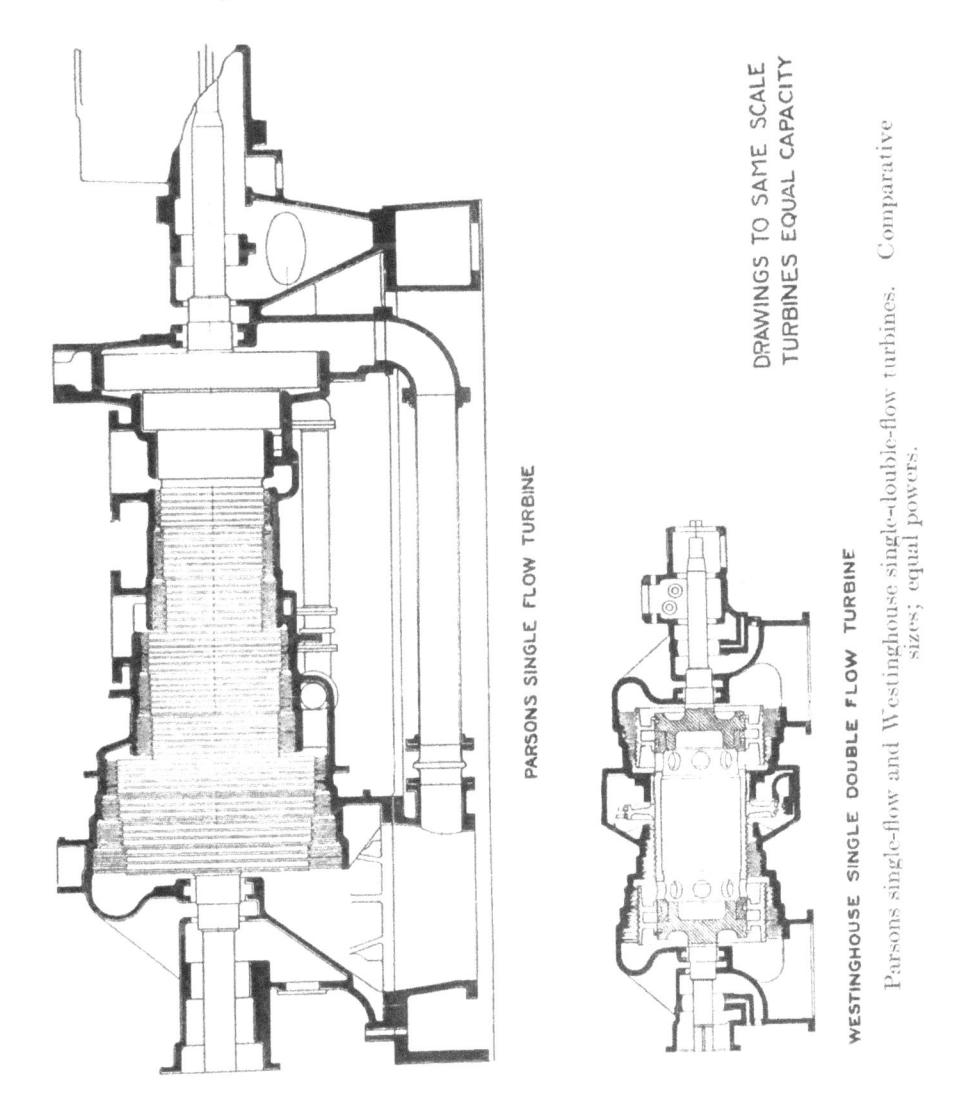

PARSONS SINGLE FLOW TURBINE

WESTINGHOUSE SINGLE DOUBLE FLOW TURBINE

DRAWINGS TO SAME SCALE
TURBINES EQUAL CAPACITY

Parsons single-flow and Westinghouse single–double-flow turbines. Comparative sizes; equal powers.

One of his outstanding contributions, as an inventor, to the turbine art was what is known as the single-double-flow type, which was the natural outcome of experimentation with the double-flow form. This was a distinct advance in the art. The single-double-flow turbine became one of the most successful products of the company, technically and commercially. Somewhat earlier than the development of the single-double-flow machine, Westinghouse produced a type combining in one turbine the reaction and impulse principles. This materially shortened the structure for a given capacity. These two inventions made a standard of practice for high-speed machines of large capacity. Patents were secured on them, and at the time of this writing builders of large turbines on both sides of the Atlantic are seeking licenses to use them.

The terms "single-double-flow" and "impulse-reaction" are not quite clear to us all, and our notions about the turbine itself may be a little vague. The following uncommonly clear and concise explanation is helpful. It is by Mr. Herbert T. Herr, vice-president, Westinghouse Electric & Manufacturing Company, who has long had especial charge of the turbine work:

> The turbine is essentially a machine for developing large powers, and it reaches its maximum economy with large capacity. It is essentially different from the ordinary steam engine in that it converts the energy in steam into mechanical work by utilizing the velocity resulting from the steam expansion, either by action or reaction of a steam jet on the blades, as opposed to the conversion of steam into energy in reciprocating engines by direct pressure of the steam on a piston.
>
> Multiple stages become necessary in the turbine to fractionally extract the energy of steam in its expansion from boiler pressure to the condenser because it is impossible in mechanics of engineering, as now known, to provide materials which would stand the stresses and speed necessary to extract in one stage efficiently the energy of a jet of steam expanding from 200 pounds pressure to 29 inches vacuum, as the steam speed under these conditions would be 4300 feet per second.
>
> In turbines of large capacity, on account of the large volumes of steam to be handled in the low-pressure stages, we again encounter the difficulty of materials in mechanical construction to efficiently handle them through the blading, and it is therefore necessary to divide the steam in such cases, and flow half of it through blading of half the area which would be required if the turbine were single-flow. In other words, by double-flowing you can double the capacity of the machine.
>
> While the double-flow turbine is an old construction, Mr. Westinghouse conceived the idea of using a single-flow construction in the upper ranges of the turbine and then, in the same cylinder casing, dividing the steam and passing it through two independent low-pressure portions; hence the name single-double-flow turbine. Of course, the whole turbine could be made double-flow, but it would mean a spindle of twice the length of a single-flow turbine, and by double-flowing only the low-pressure portion the machine is shortened and cheapened.
>
> With reference to the impulse-reaction combination it is, of course, important to make the number of stages as small as possible, *i.e.*, the number of rows of blades, both from the standpoint of the length of the machine and cost. With equal blade speeds the impulse turbine requires one-quarter the number of blades that the reaction turbine requires, the reason being that the impulse turbine extracts energy from the jet impinging on the blades in the direction of rotation of the blades, and again by reaction of the jet on the blades as it leaves them in the opposite direction. In the reaction turbine there are only the forces from the reaction of the jet as it leaves the blades, since the expansion for each row of

blades takes place in the blades themselves, whereas in the impulse turbine, there is no expansion in the moving row, the steam speed being created by the expansion in the stationary nozzles.

At the time of Mr. Westinghouse's investigation it was quite well known that the impulse turbine was not as efficient as the reaction turbine for a given condition suitable to both types of machines, and that, further, the efficiency of the high-pressure reaction turbine is less than the low-pressure turbine because the blade heights are less and the leakage by the stages is consequently greater in proportion. Mr. Westinghouse therefore devised the scheme of combining in a single machine that turbine which is best suited to the higher pressures, *i.e.*, the impulse type; and that turbine which is best suited to the lower pressures, *i.e.*, the reaction type. This resulted in the so-called impulse-reaction turbine which we have used a good many years.

These are the most important of Westinghouse's engineering contributions to the turbine art. He made hundreds of designs of, and experiments on, details which are of great interest to the student but which it does not seem expedient to describe here, although they further illustrate his tireless industry, and his skill and ingenuity in mechanical design.

Westinghouse's own inventions, although important, were the least part of his work in the turbine field. He stimulated others to invent and he drove development and research. Mr. Herr writes: "Whether he was in Pittsburgh or New York or Lenox, he would invariably call me on the telephone several times a day to inquire how things were going. His usual questions would be: 'How are you now? Did you get that turbine running again?' Then would follow a great many terse and direct questions." He saw that the time had come and his prescience started the turbine industry in the United States. He was the first great manufacturer this side of the Atlantic to take it up. Others quickly followed, and naturally the impulse was felt in England and on the Continent, where the steam turbine has become the most important prime mover in industry and in the navies.

THE REDUCTION GEAR

The use of the turbine in ships brought a new set of problems. The steam turbine to be efficient must run at high peripheral speeds, and this characteristic tends to limit its most favorable application to the direct driving of machinery that also runs satisfactorily at high speeds. The electric generator comes within that class, but a ship's propeller does not. The effective speed of a propeller is slow. When it is run too fast we get slip and cavitation. When directly coupled together, either the turbine speed will be too low or that of the propeller too high for the efficiency of the combination. But even with this drawback so attractive was its use in ships, on account of saving of weight and absence of vibration, that as soon as the success of large turbines was demonstrated in the electrical field, installations were made in some of the greatest fast ships then afloat, notably the *Lusitania* and *Mauritania*. The discordant speed conditions were in some measure corrected by objectionable, but operatively successful, compromise proportions of both turbine and propeller, resulting in a smooth-running and fairly efficient propelling mechanism when the vessel ran at full speed. At reduced speeds the consumption of fuel was prohibitive because of the low efficiency of the turbine, and it was quite clear that propellers directly driven by turbines could not be advantageously used in moderate-speed passenger or cargo ships.

This whole subject was ably and exhaustively dealt with in a special report made to Westinghouse by the late Rear-Admiral George W. Melville and his associate, John H. MacAlpine, a marine engineer of much experience, and with fine engineering attainments. At the time of their investigation almost the only field for research was in English practice, and this was covered very completely.

In the light of the facts, it was obvious that a speed-reducing mechanism, permitting the turbine and propeller to each run at its most efficient speed, would greatly increase the useful range of application of the steam turbine for marine purposes, as by far the larger number of ships are in the moderate- or low-speed class.

Gearing in some form as a speed-changing medium is probably one of the oldest known mechanical expedients, and its successful application in an almost unlimited field when operating at moderate speeds is a matter of common engineering knowledge. De Laval had demonstrated that speed-reducing gearing properly designed; accurately constructed, and with suitable accessories could be operated at very high velocities for transmitting limited powers; but for large powers comparatively slow peripheral gear speeds had been adhered to because of the difficulty of maintaining the exacting mechanical conditions essential to successful high-velocity operation.

A fundamental requirement of satisfactory gear operation is that the tooth pressure of the gears at point of contact must not exceed that at which they can be operated without abrasion. Otherwise destructive wear will quickly render them inoperative. To insure maintenance of adequate contact surface, perfect axial alignment of the driving and driven shafts carrying the gears must be originally produced, and substantially maintained, and this presupposes that there shall be little or no distortion or deflection in the supports carrying the gears and their shafts, and that the results of wear due to operation shall not affect the relative alignment of the two shafts.

That there will be some deflection of the supporting base, however rigidly constructed, is beyond question, for a ship's frame is far from being a stable foundation, neither does it accord with experience that four or more independent bearings supporting fast-running shafts transmitting heavy powers will wear equally.

To overcome the effects of almost inevitable misalignment, with its possible serious consequences, there was submitted by Messrs. Melville and MacAlpine a design of a geared speed-reducing mechanism, in which one of the transmitting shafts carrying the gears was so mounted as to automatically maintain exact alignment between the two shafts under all reasonable working conditions. The design was original and bold. It has been called a perfect mechanical conception, and Westinghouse was sufficiently impressed with the importance and possible success of the proposed plan to authorize the construction of a machine designed to transmit 3000 horsepower, and it was completed at a cost exceeding $75,000. Had he been a man of conservative temperament, there would have first been constructed a small and relatively inexpensive model, but to attack the problem in that manner would have been for him waste of time, with at best an inconclusive result, for he felt that only through the operation of a full-size example, under practical working conditions, could a definite determination be reached. The trial device proved successful beyond all expectation, as it was found to be capable of transmitting 5000 horsepower, and its practical operation and entire adaptability for the purpose for which it was designed were demonstrated by actual service in the United States collier *Neptune.*

The circumstances under which this interesting experiment was carried on are worthy of notice. In the midst of its development and construction the Westinghouse Machine Company was placed under the control of receivers, acting for its creditors, and both engineering and financial pressure was brought to discontinue the experiment, but with characteristic persistence and determination Westinghouse succeeded in having the machine completed. His strong conviction as to the great importance of the object in view, and confidence in the invention of Melville and MacAlpine, were important, if not controlling, factors in making it possible to realize in marine service the important advantages of the steam turbine when substituted for reciprocating engines, and the demonstration made in the *Neptune* came at a most fortunate time, for the steam turbine thereby became available for war ships. By the spring of 1920 this gear was in service in twelve destroyers, three battleships and two auxiliaries of the United States navy, and orders were in process of manufacture for scout cruisers for the United States navy with 90,000 horsepower in each ship, and for battle cruisers of 150,000 or 160,000 horsepower for a foreign navy. There were 211 ships afloat fitted with the flexible gear, and 101 on order. These, naturally, are pretty big ships, although the average is lowered by the destroyers. It was estimated that there was afloat and on order in May 1920, 2,000,000 horsepower in Westinghouse geared-turbine drive.

The advantages of what Westinghouse called the floating-frame gear were summed up by him as: Greatest possible output per pound of metal; automatic elimination of unequal tooth pressures; comparative noiselessness; gears well cut can be put into operation without costly and slow fitting of bearings and scraping of teeth. Use is steadily establishing his claims, with all that they imply, and that is a great deal; but at the moment of this writing a hot conflict of opinion, international in its scope, is going on amongst marine engineers as to the relative merits of flexible gears, rigid gears, and electric drive. The conflict is working itself out in a huge way in naval and commercial ships, some of them of enormous horsepower. Westinghouse would have greatly enjoyed the situation if he could have lived to take part in it.

Westinghouse contributed a number of inventions to the flexible gear. Amongst these is an arrangement that includes a recording dynamometer showing graphically and accurately the amount of power that is transmitted to the propellers. But in this case the credit due to him (and it is great) is not so much for his own inventions as for his quick and tolerant recognition of the inventions of other men, and for the force with which he drove those inventions forward against technical doubt and financial opposition.

SOME BY-PRODUCTS

The by-products of Westinghouse's imagination were always entertaining and often useful. While he was pushing along his plans for revolutionizing marine engineering with the geared turbine, he thought he saw a chance to bring back to us some of the glories and profits of those brave days when our ships carried the commerce of the world, and when sailormen out of Salem took British troops to India and helped save the Empire. It was a pleasant thought to put a little auxiliary turbine in a five-masted schooner. With fair winds the schooner would slip along at eight knots and the screw would idle in the water. In contrary winds and rough seas the turbine would get busy and the schooner would keep up her eight knots. It would be a simple matter (for him) to handle the engine from the pilothouse. He actually designed and built a 750-horsepower turbine and gear calculated for this attractive scheme, and meantime he and some of his friends passed agreeable hours talking about it.

In our brief account of the development of the geared turbine it was said that the efficient speed of a turbine is high; the efficient speed of a propeller is low. These are hard and fast facts that cannot be escaped. But it occurred to Westinghouse that the propeller might perhaps be improved, and he entered upon an extensive series of experiments with propellers. He designed, tested, and rejected a great many propellers in an effort to discover some law.

A concrete tank was built about eighteen feet in diameter and some six feet deep. A propeller shaft was put through the wall of the tank, the propeller being placed close to the inner wall. By the thrust of the propeller the mass of water in the tank was set in motion, revolving in the tank. The speed at which the water moved was measured by suitable apparatus, giving a reading equivalent to the speed of a boat moved through the water by a like propeller thrust. The inside contour of the tank immediately adjacent to the propeller fairly approximated the stern contour of a ship. The propeller was actuated by a 500-horsepower turbine built especially for these tests. The arrangement of this turbine was most ingenious. The stator or casing was free to rotate except for an arm that rested on a weighing machine. As the turning effort on the turbine shaft is exactly balanced by the reaction on the casing, the weighing machine showed the torque, and the revolutions being known, the power developed was easily computed. The turbine shaft and the propeller shaft were so coupled through a thrust block that no thrust from the propeller was transmitted to the turbine rotor, but it was received and measured through the thrust block acting on a weighing machine. Now, having the horsepower delivered, the thrust of the propeller and the speed of the water (or of the vessel through the water), we can find the loss through slip, cavitation, etc. So we have the means of making accurate comparison of different propellers. By making enough tests of enough designs the best may be discovered. The process is costly, but it is cheaper than trying out the propellers in ships at sea.

There were two interesting refinements in these experiments: one an investigation of the effect of lubricating the propeller blades by air, the other an effort to find the differences of pressure on different parts of the surface of the blade.

From the speed with which the propeller cuts through the water, and the considerable blade surface exposed, the friction loss must be quite a factor in the energy wasted. Westinghouse conceived the idea of lubricating the propeller by a film of air. Blades were made with air pockets near the entering edge and small holes drilled into these pockets. Air was forced into these pockets to flow out as a film between the blades and the water. Many tests were made with different air pressures, but the results were disappointing. No gam in efficiency was discovered. Very high authority had warned Westinghouse to expect this result. In one of his letters to Lord Kelvin, written some months before the propeller experiments, he says, quite incidentally: "I am also about to try an idea I have had for many years, viz., the air lubrication of the hull of a ship and of the blades of the propeller. The tests will be made on our electric launch on Laurel Lake. To produce the required quantity of air I have had made a rotary blower in which are incorporated, in a new manner, details which have been in use some years. I find a sheet of air one-half inch thick can be paid out next to the hull, from slots, as fast as the ship moves. The *Lusitania,* for instance, would require less than 600 horsepower (to deliver the air), and this should so reduce the skin friction as to greatly affect the speed. I have discovered, however, that the air in the water will necessitate the use of a special propeller, to avoid cavitation, which I am having made for trial on the launch."

Lord Kelvin replies: "I do not think it possible that good results can be got by air lubrication of the hull of a ship or of the blades of a propeller. Experiments on a small scale on your electrical launch might seem to promise good results, but I feel perfectly sure that it would be impossible to get good results on the large scale of a ship at sea. The air would be washed away, and would make foam, and would, I believe, increase the turbulence of the water close to the bottom and sides of the ship, to which a large part of the resistance at high speeds is due. Air introduced in any way about the blades of a propeller would, I feel sure, largely increase cavitation troubles, which are known to be adverse to the efficiency of the propeller."

To measure the pressure at different places on the surfaces of the blades, passages were cored or drilled in the propeller castings, and the air passages were also used. Experiments were made, too, to determine the effect of different sizes of hubs. Many out of the great mass of notes collected in these propeller studies have been tabulated and plotted for convenient comparison. Perhaps they will some time be generalized by a competent analyst and serve as the starting point for further laboratory investigation of a most complicated art. For Westinghouse this propeller interlude was a fascinating pastime at a time when he greatly needed diversion, in the darkest moments of his life, when some of his companies were going through receivership.

CONDENSER IMPROVEMENTS

It will be recalled that at one time Westinghouse was of the opinion that because of their high thermal efficiency, gas engines might supplant steam engines for the production of electricity, but changed his views when the use of high-pressure superheated steam with high vacuum greatly increased the efficiency of the steam turbine. Before he engaged in the manufacture of turbines, Westinghouse had little experience with condensing machinery for producing the vacuum necessary for the most efficient operation of steam engines. Its importance, however, soon attracted his attention, and as the result of a contract entered into in 1897 with Maurice Leblanc, a French physicist and engineer of high standing, there was developed at the works of the Westinghouse Machine Company, in accordance with the patents of M. Leblanc, an improved type of air pump, to be used in connection with existing types of condensers, either jet or surface. The mechanism employed was relatively light in weight, cheap to manufacture, and exceedingly simple in construction and operation. Added to these meritorious features it possessed the still more important quality of creating a considerably higher vacuum than was obtainable with any other type of air pump in use. The increased vacuum obtainable by the Leblanc system materially reduced the steam consumption of turbines as compared with any other existing device in use at the time the Leblanc air pump was put on the market, and it, therefore, became a most important factor in that overall increase of turbine economy that has for the present, at least, established it as the most efficient type of prime mover for the general production of large powers.

M. Leblanc gives this account of his first meeting with Westinghouse:

About 1897 the owners of my patents started a suit for infringement against the General Electric Company. This suit took on Homeric proportions: the defense was as vigorous as the attack, and it was becoming a celebrated case when, in the year 1901, I was stopped on the Boulevard by an unknown person, who addressed me in the following terms: "Mr. George Westinghouse, who is now in Paris, leaves for London in two hours; he wishes to see you immediately, and has commissioned me to find you and to take you to him, dead or alive." I replied: "Then you mean" to effect an abduction or to kidnap me. Unfortunately this can no longer be regarded as the abduction of a minor. Well then, kidnap me, I have no objection." He conducted me to the Rue de l'Arcade, where, for the first time, I saw the great engineer, who said to me: "So it is you who have sworn to make the fortune of all the lawyers in America. Can we come to terms?" I replied: "I ask for nothing better, and probably my associates will do likewise." That was all for that day. But I had been greatly struck with the great bearing of the man and his easy good humor. Some months later he bought for the Westinghouse and General Electric Companies my patents, and the inventor into the bargain, whom he appointed consulting engineer to the Société Anonyme Westinghouse in France. That was the starting point of a cooperation of which I shall always be proud, my first impression being duly confirmed. He was before all things a perfect gentleman and a great-hearted man, and he was himself a mechanician beyond compare.

He inspired me not only with great admiration but also with a warm affection, which I believe he returned to some extent. He was the best and most steadfast of friends. I could obtain witnesses amongst all his old co-workers whom I knew and whose fortunes he had made. All adored as much as they esteemed him. His vigor and his power of work were extraordinary. He never took any rest. Starting with next to nothing, he became one of the greatest industrial captains in the world. He fell in action, crushed like a Titan, on the eve of the Great War, which he had long foreseen. In fact, in 1903 he said to me that the first United States war would be against the insupportable Germans. His talent as an organizer would have been of the very greatest service, and this for us is a further cause to regret his premature end. George Westinghouse was a great American, and no man had a greater regard for his country. He lived like the type of modern inventors and great realizers. His memory will always be green in the hearts of those who surrounded him and all who loved him.

Chapter Eleven - The Turbo-Generator

THE turbo-generator is the greatest contrivance for the manufacture of power yet produced by man greatest in the capacity of single units, in the extent of its use, and in economy of result. Its usefulness to mankind, already prodigious, has but just begun. In the present state of knowledge one cannot foresee or imagine anything that will even closely approach it in usefulness, much less take its place. In saying this we do not limit the term to its present strict technical meaning, an electric generator driven by a steam turbine, but include also a generator driven by a water turbine, which may or may not be eventually the biggest power unit. A steam turbo-generator of 45,000 kilowatts (60,000 horsepower) is now in service. There is another one in service, a compound turbine of three cylinders, of 70,000 kilowatts (93,000 horsepower). The biggest power station now operating generates 230,000 kilowatts with fourteen units; but there is one building of 360,000 kilowatts, six steam units, and another of 450,000 kilowatts with ten hydroelectric units. There are battle cruisers now building to have 180,000 horsepower on four propeller shafts, which means approximately 218,000 horsepower at the turbines. Working current is now carried 250 miles and more, and men are talking seriously of 800 or 1000 miles transmission. This enormous massing of the manufacture of power and the capacity to transmit it great distances are amongst the most important elements of the new epoch into which mankind has now entered, and of which we shall speak later more circumstantially.

The leadership of George Westinghouse in the origin and development of the turbo-generator was an important part of his life. He took up the steam turbine in 1896, as is told in the chapter on steam and gas engines. He saw at once that the field for the turbine was in heavy power generation by polyphase alternating current, and he began to push the design of complete alternating turbo units parallel with the design of the turbine itself. All this being so, a life of George Westinghouse would be quite incomplete without the story of the turbo-generator. We shall try to tell that story briefly and with as little technicality as is consistent with reasonable completeness. To the reader who is not an engineer that will probably seem too much; to the electrical engineer it will certainly seem too little. Perhaps to the civil and mechanical and mining and chemical engineer the compromise will seem judicious. One of the notorious defects of a compromise is that it is not often entirely satisfactory to any one.

Perhaps it is not superfluous to repeat that a turbo-generator as here spoken of is a machine to generate electric current, driven by a steam turbine. The engine-type generator, which will be often mentioned, is a reciprocating steam engine with the armature of the generator on the engine shaft.

Seven or eight years before the turbine development began, Westinghouse was playing with a rotary engine, direct-coupled to an alternator. It will be remembered that his first patent, taken out when he was nineteen, was for a rotary engine, and he did not drop it until the turbine came along, thirty years later. The experiments of which we now speak were carried on in a little shop occupied by the Electric Company, then about three years old. Power for at least part of the shop was supplied by this experimental unit, which went out of service often and sometimes abruptly, and it was not uncommon to hear the men say "there goes that dashed rotary again." or words to that effect. The apparatus was really a plaything, but Westinghouse took his sports as seriously as he did his work. The difference between work and play was in time used and not in the intensity of interest.

The first turbo-generator units put in service by the Electric Company were three for the Air Brake Company. They were of 300-kilowatt (400-horsepower) capacity at 3600 revolutions per minute, 440 volts, 60 cycles, polyphase. This type had rotating armatures, and at 3600 revolutions per minute the armature end winding would distort into all sorts of shapes under centrifugal force, even when tied down so that it would not burst. Supporting end-bells, if made of bronze, would distort, or even burst; if made of steel, they were magnetically very bad and would overheat. A decision was quickly reached that the future machine would have to be of a rotating-field type, with the field windings so embedded or protected against centrifugal force that stretching or bursting would be physically impossible. The support of the field windings, especially in view of the insulating materials available, was thus one of the earliest problems encountered in turbo-alternators.

By 1899 the rotating-field type was decided on. Westinghouse was personally much interested in this part of the construction, and would telephone almost every day asking whether anything satisfactory or promising had been worked out. He was very prolific in suggestions for the rotor construction, but, not being experienced in the difficulties of insulation, the engineers had to turn down his suggestions daily. However, as good reasons were given, he took it all good-naturedly. Finally it was decided that the rotor must be one with many relatively small slots to subdivide the field winding into a large number of small coils, so that each could be supported without unduly crushing the insulation and becoming displaced. This developed into the "parallel-slot" construction, which was used by the Westinghouse Company for many years, and which really made the Westinghouse type a pacemaker in the race toward higher speeds, which came in the following years.

The 3600-revolutions-per-minute, parallel-slot rotor for the 60-cycle generator, when first designed, was made cylindrical in general form, but with two sides flattened. On test this made such a frightful noise that it was considered impossible. Westinghouse, who was greatly interested, saw this first rotor on test in the East Pittsburgh shops, and was much disturbed by the noise. He asked if this was the best that could be done. The answer was to the effect that this was the best for the present. Westinghouse seemed much disappointed, and when a few days later he was told that the noise could probably be overcome in a very simple manner, he snapped at the suggestion and wanted to know how. It was explained that by making the rotor entirely cylindrical, without the flat sides, and cutting in the parallel grooves and finally turning off the supporting wedges to give a finished cylindrical face after the rotor was wound and wedged, a comparatively quiet construction should be obtained. Westinghouse thought about it a moment and then laughed and said: "Things are easy when you know how." He authorized the improved construction to be taken up at once, and this eventually proved quite satisfactory, and was used for some ten years with great success. With other improvements, such as the bolted-on shaft arrangement and artificial cooling, this type of rotor enabled the 3600-revolutions-perminute turbo-generator to be carried by successive steps from 400 kilowatts up to 6250 kilowatts, an increase of over fifteen times. In the 25-cycle, 2-pole, 1500-revolutions-perminute machine this construction was carried from 750 kilowatts up to 10,000 kilowatts (say 13,400 horsepower), an increase of about fourteen times. This was done within a very few years.

To appreciate the effect of the turbo-generator on other types of apparatus, it is necessary to consider the rapid growth of the turbo-generator when it once got started. By 1902, 6000-kilowatt units were being built. One must remember that, only three years before, in 1899, the huge 6000-kilowatt 75-revolutions-per-minute, engine-type alternators for the Manhattan Elevated were contracted for and were assembled about a year later. Within a year or so the 6000-kilowatt generators for the New York Subway were also assembled. Seventeen of these machines were built for the two stations. The outside diameter of the armature frames was forty-two feet. There was no place in the existing shops at East Pittsburgh high enough to assemble them. A new aisle was built with overhead travelling cranes forty-four feet above the floor. The rings were made in four parts to ship by rail. That involved extreme accuracy in fitting. There were no templates or shop-measuring devices big enough for the purpose, and a transit was used to line up the parts. It is no wonder that the relatively small turbo-generator unit quickly drove these immense machines out of the market. The engine-type generator was right in its prime, but within two or three years it was, from the commercial standpoint, obsolescent. Everybody was waiting for the coming turbo-generator, with the impression that the day of the engine-type alternator was over. In consequence, this business went to almost nothing within practically a year's time, and, in fact, the engine type went down before the turbo-generator was really ready to take its place.

This obsolescence of the engine-type alternator was almost pitiful. Here was a branch of heavy engineering, built up at great cost and backed by years of experience. In the coming of the turbo-generator this experience was mostly thrown away, for the engineering required in the turbo-generator work was so radically different from that of the engine-type generator that the designers had to start practically anew and build up entirely new experiences at enormous expense and through years of effort. However, in the development of the turbo-alternator there was one favorable feature; namely, there was a large field open for the apparatus. It was not a question of building up a new field of use, as was the case of the earlier types of apparatus. Also the call for larger alternators, from 1898 to 1902, indicated that the engine type of construction of the future was going to be hard put to it to meet the demands for still larger units. In fact, the Manhattan and Subway machines of nominal 6000-kilowatt rating (really 7500) were supposed to be almost as large as was practicable, and yet people believed that larger units than these would be necessary at some time in the future. It was, therefore, recognized that the engine type was handicapped for still larger sizes, whereas engineers had a feeling that the opposite might be true for the turbo-alternator, that is, it might eventually make its best showing in the larger units.

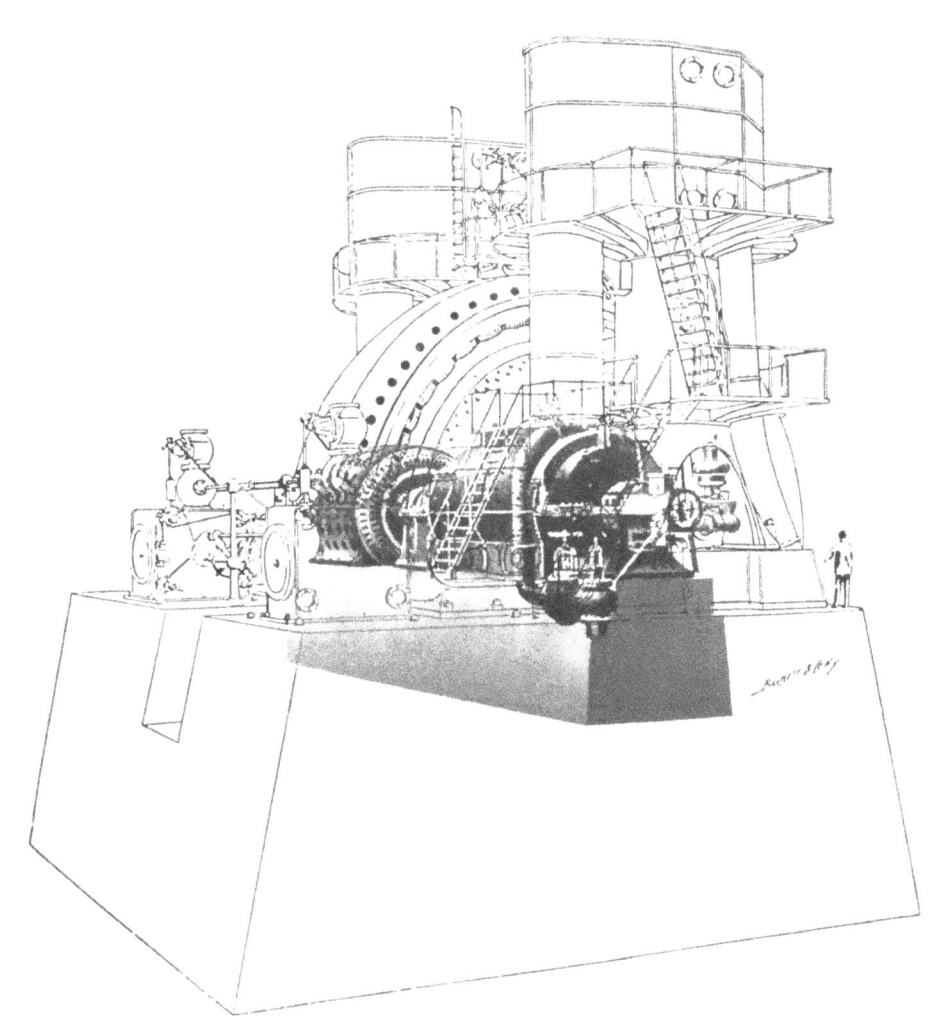

Turbo-generator and engine-type generator. Comparative sizes of machines and foundations; equal powers.

From 1902 to 1906 or 1907 the turbo-alternator had a hard time. It had driven the engine type out of the market, but it was not easy to replace it, not because the turbo-alternator itself was unsatisfactory, but because it was not yet advanced far enough in the manufacturing and commercial end to meet the needs. Each successive large machine pointed the way to something better in the next one. Noise, one of the great objections to the earlier machines, even after the smooth cylindrical rotor was devised, had to be overcome, and this was accomplished principally by enclosing the generator and furnishing artificial ventilation. This was carried out on commercial machines while being got ready for the market. With the enclosure and consequent less noise, and the then necessary addition of artificial ventilation due to the enclosure, a great advance was permissible in ratings, and this accompanied the great growth in capacity mentioned above. To show how fast this work was growing, orders were placed in the shop for an experimental enclosed machine to determine the possibilities of enclosure and artificial ventilation, but before this experimental machine could be completed and tested, the use of such enclosure and artificial cooling had been forced on the standard machines, due to commercial needs, and had become established practice. In this matter of enclosing and artificial cooling, there was much severe criticism. The criticism was made frequently that the Westinghouse machines necessarily were badly designed because they had to be boxed up and big blowers added. No other types of generators, according to such criticism, needed artificial cooling, and, therefore, the Westinghouse machines were very bad, indeed, if they needed such remedies. However, the public accepted such machines and wanted more of them, and before long other manufacturers began to box in their machines and pipe air to them. They went through the same stages as Westinghouse and eventually came to the same general practice.

The two great competitors in this turbo-generator work were the Westinghouse and General Electric, the former with horizontal-shaft units, and the latter with vertical. It was General Electric practice to fight the Westinghouse high speeds. There was a good reason for this; the General Electric vertical-type units became increasingly difficult to construct and operate as the speeds were increased, and, consequently, when the Westinghouse large-capacity turbo-generators were pushed to the ultimate limit of two poles, it was too much for the General Electric type, and this had to be changed from the vertical to the horizontal. It is amusing now to look back over the criticism of Westinghouse practice. It was pointed out that nobody else, either in Europe or in America, advocated such high speeds as Westinghouse and, therefore, Westinghouse must be wrong. However, these speeds are now standard practice all over the world.

It is difficult to exaggerate the effects of the turbo-alternator on the electrical industry of today. It is hard to see how the situation could have been met by the engine-type alternator, especially in view of the 20,000- to 40,000-kilowatt (53,000-horsepower) turbo units of today. The saving in space required has been of immense value, especially in large cities. The fuel economy of the huge turbo-generators is of vital importance. The great generator units and generating plants have driven out of business many of the small isolated plants and even some of the larger individual plants. The central station with its turbo units can manufacture and sell power at a rate which tends to kill off all competition, and its growth is most interesting. Cities which a few years ago bought units of 2000 kilowatts now buy generating units of 20,000 kilowatts, and larger cities, which a few years ago bought units of 5000 kilowatts, or even 10,000 kilowatts, now are buying units of from 30,000 to 60,000 kilowatts. It is hard to see that this could be, without the turbo-generator.

The development of the turbo-generator required the highest analytical engineering. Take a high-speed alternator, for instance, one of 3600 revolutions per minute. This cannot be designed by cut and try, for there must be no undue experimental elements in the construction, at the terrific speed at which these machines run; namely, at about 25,000 feet peripheral speed per minute. The same is true of the turbine, for here even higher speeds may be attained. The designers of the turbo-generator sets have, in many cases, worked far ahead of any available data, and, accordingly, have had to depend mostly upon analysis. Considering the difficulties of the problem, the record has been good. True, difficulties have arisen from time to time, which analysis did not cover. For instance, protection against the effect of short circuits in the larger machines had to be worked out largely by actual test. The 20,000-kilowatt turbo-alternator may give momentarily ten to fifteen times its rated current on short circuit, corresponding to 200,000 to 300,000-kilowatt load, as far as distorting forces are concerned. The effects of such short circuits are so enormous that in some of the earlier large units, the end windings "twisted up like a wet towel," as one customer explained. One large generator, after a short circuit, ran melted iron down through itself for several minutes. With increased experience, engineers have been able to meet this situation, until now generating powers of enormous capacities can be tied together in one system without undue danger. A few years ago it was suggested that 50,000 kilowatts was the greatest capacity which it was safe to tie to one bus-bar system, but now they talk about five to ten times this.

Another problem which has been; to a large extent, the outgrowth of the turbo-generator is that of switching such large powers. As said above, a 20,000-kilowatt unit may give ten to fifteen times the rated current on short circuit. With a number of such units tied together, obviously the problem of rupturing a short circuit on any kind of a switch is a tremendous one. The oil breaker of the present time is an attempt to do this, and the problem of the successful oil breaker has been considered as solved from time to time. However, with the growth of the turbo-generator units and the growth in the size of the stations, with more and more units tied together, the oil breaker has had increasing difficulty in keeping up with the situation, and it may be said that the race between the generating station and the breaker is still on.

To see one of these great stations equipped with huge turbo-generating units, one would get the impression that the generating unit, in itself, is really a minor part of the plant, so great is the amount of auxiliaries necessary, in the form of switchboards, breakers, and protective devices. The boiler plant is not a secondary element either. Moreover, ventilation has become serious in such stations. The amount of air required to cool a large alternator is such that each unit puts through itself practically its own weight of air in from forty to sixty minutes, and these machines are no toys either. A station of 200,000 kilowatts would require approximately 600,000 cubic feet of air per minute for ventilation alone. If this air is discharged directly into the generator room, provision must be made for discharging from the room. This may mean replacing the entire amount of air in the room every ten or fifteen minutes.

The turbo-generator has brought with it many problems, which are not those of the turbo-generator itself, but which have to do with the manufacture of power in enormous amounts. In fact, here we are dealing with something in the nature of high explosives. For instance, a little short circuit in an instrument transformer, in one of the great New York power houses, blew the windows out of the building. A short circuit in one of the generators itself is often in the nature of a real disaster, as has been told above. Strange means have been devised for suppressing fires which sometimes occur in these highly ventilated machines. Live steam in large quantities has been used to put out such fires. Here we are dealing with huge powers, the dangers are huge, and the preventive and protective means must be correspondingly huge. The turbo-generator has brought its own troubles and sometimes one is tempted to wish that the thing had never been heard of. Then he may take some comfort in the saying of a philosopher, that progress has been by a series of catastrophes.

Chapter Twelve - Signaling and Interlocking

AT the outset of a consideration of the work of George Westinghouse in railroad signaling and interlocking, it seems desirable to say a few words by way of definition which to many readers will seem elementary, but which to many more readers are necessary to an understanding of the nature and the importance of the art.

The function of signals is not merely, perhaps not principally, to stop trains. An important function is to keep trains moving - to keep them moving with such frequency, such regularity, and at such speeds as will get the best economic results, in service and in cost, under the conditions which control a given situation. These conditions differ widely, from the single-track, cross-country road with half a dozen daily trains, to the city transit road with four tracks and trains following each other at intervals of 108 seconds. Signals tell a train when to reduce speed, when to stop, when to start, when to proceed under control, and when to go ahead at speed. Such information is highly important when different kinds of trains, fast and slow, local and express, freight and passenger, are moving on the same track. It is absolutely necessary to getting the maximum service out of a dollar invested in track.

Block signals seek to preserve an absolute interval of space between trains. The length of this space interval must vary with the grades and curves and with the kind of traffic and the maximum speed of trains working over a given piece of track. In a paper prepared by Westinghouse in 1913, and never published, are some figures of train stops which show the difference in block-signal spacing demanded for different speeds. A train of ten cars, hauled by two locomotives, was fitted with the most perfect brake equipment. Stops were made from 90 miles an hour in 2900 feet; from 60 miles an hour in 1100 feet; from 20 miles an hour in 120 feet. These were under ideal conditions. Under the conditions of good every-day practice stops were made from 90 miles an hour in 4450 feet, and from 60 miles an hour in 1750 feet. Obviously fast traffic demands longer blocks than slow traffic; but, on the other hand, the longer the blocks the fewer the trains that can be passed over the road. Signal engineering is a complicated art and worth the attention of a man of even Westinghouse's ability.

Interlocking provides for such control and operation of switches and signals that they must move in certain sequences, and that it shall be mechanically impossible for them to move in any other order. Switches are interlocked with other switches and with the signals that govern movement through them, and the signals are so interlocked as to make conflicting signals impossible. The levers which move the switches and signals are assembled in one machine and there interlocked. If a man were blindfold and pulled the levers at random he could stop traffic but he could not produce a collision. As many as 215 electropneumatic levers have been assembled in one machine. The possible combinations of these are many millions, the safe combinations some hundreds, and as interlocked only the safe combinations can be made.

When Westinghouse became interested in interlocking and block signaling those arts were well developed in Great Britain, but were almost unknown in the United States.

Block signaling began in England about 1846 and interlocking began in 1856. By 1890 all British railways doing passenger business were thoroughly signaled and interlocked. The first interlocking machine seen in the United States was an English machine brought over in 1876 for the Centennial Exposition. By 1900 many big railroad yards, junctions and crossings were interlocked, but many more were still unprotected. Block signaling had begun on a few railway systems, but hardly more than begun. Even yet we have not reached the completeness of protection of the British railways, but in mechanical methods of signaling and interlocking we have gone far beyond the rest of the world, and this is due in great degree to the impulse and direction that Westinghouse gave to the art.

When Westinghouse entered this field in 1880, he found it entirely unoccupied here. He had not only to design and make apparatus, but he had to create his market, and the market grew very slowly. For twenty years the company which he organized, the Union Switch and Signal Company, struggled along in the tedious process of educating the buyers of its product, and then it came into great prosperity. Westinghouse had supported it through these lean years by his personal credit, and he laid the foundations of its success by his perception of the future course of the art and by his own contributions to its technical growth.

A basic contribution by Westinghouse to the signaling and interlocking art was the development of the use of power. He was not the first inventor to take out patents in power interlocking and signaling; probably he was not the first to conceive the idea. He was, however, the first inventor to conceive and develop methods and apparatus that went into actual and lasting use, that laid the foundations of general practice, and that are still in use substantially as he first worked them out and installed them in the railroads. In actual priority of patented invention he was close to the first. In priority of conception he may have been the first. That no man can tell. Westinghouse was not the first man to invent an air brake. James Watt was not the first man to invent a steam engine with a piston and cylinder. But they invented mechanisms that worked, and they made revolutions in economic life, and mankind is quite satisfied to remember them, while Papin, Newcommen, and Nehemiah Hodge are names known only to inquiring students.

To understand the meaning of Westinghouse's work in invention and design in the signal and interlocking field from 1880 until his death, a few general facts should be known that indicate the means available at the various periods of his inventions, and also explain the sentiment then existing toward what were and what were not permissible methods in switch and signal control and operation.

Prior to 1880 the air brake was substantially the only application of compressed air to railway working. The telegraph was the only well-established institution employing electricity in the service. To some extent, but in a crude way, electricity had been adapted to the operation of certain forms of block signals and to the various indicators, locks, bells, and annunciators then used in both the block and interlocking field. Electric lighting was confined to the series-arc method almost exclusively, and electric motors applied to locomotion and to power purposes in general were practically unknown, and very imperfectly developed.

Hydraulic pressure had long been recognized as a flexible medium of great possibilities in many capacities, and especially as affording means whereby a relatively feeble energy applied over considerable time might produce great mechanical effects, as in hydraulic lifts, jacks, etc. Consequently, attempts had been made to apply this force to switch and signal operation, and with some success at the period of Westinghouse's entry into this field. Naturally, he began with the belief that in the hydraulic principle lay the quickest, if not the surest, road to success, and, hence, his first patents use hydraulic pressure rather than pneumatic pressure, though "fluid pressure," as he designates it, covers both elements. He was quick to see, however, the difficulties inherent in the use of a liquid, not alone because it must be non-freezing and, hence, more or less expensive to maintain; but also, because not being compressible, it did not lend itself to the rapid action of impacting devices (such as the art then included) for setting it in motion without the development of excessive pressures within its conductors due to its inertia. These and many minor reasons precluded the successful adaptation of hydraulic pressure to the automatic operation of block signals by treadle devices actuated by train wheels, as embraced in one of his early patents. With his prior experience in airbrake operation, it was but natural that he drifted away from hydraulic and to pneumatic developments.

Though early conceiving the great advantages of electricity as a medium for the control of compressed air, automatically or otherwise, from a distance, in the application of that pressure to switch and signal mechanisms, he shared, at the time, with railway men in general, the aversion to the use of electrical devices in close proximity to, if not actually upon, the railway tracks. Consequently, though having contrived an extremely simple, efficient, and remarkably practicable electropneumatic device for the operation of signals - a device free from track vibrations and well shielded from adverse weather influences in service - he hesitated to apply its principles to practical switch operation until as late as 1890, and preferred to use hydraulic pressure to apply power and pneumatic pressure to set it in operation for handling switches, in his early interlocking efforts.

For ten years this policy was followed in the numerous large terminal interlockings that were equipped with his system. The signals of the system, as well as the many that were installed during that period as automatic block signals, employed the electromagnet, however, controlled from a machine lever or a rail circuit, or both, as a means for admitting and discharging the air pressure to and from the signal-operating mechanism.

In 1890, when the control of pneumatically operated switches was finally recognized as also wholly practicable by electromagnets under the influence of the tower operator, the hydraulic control was abandoned in its favor, and the truly electropneumatic interlocking was commercially born.

During these ten years great strides had been made, not only in the general education of the world in electric matters, but in the enlightenment of railway men in particular concerning the possibilities of the use of electricity in many applications that in 1880 could not have been served electrically. Electric generators, chemical and mechanical, had reached high perfection; insulated wire, conduits, motors, and various other electrical appliances had been introduced in all branches of industry, and the education that followed removed the barrier that for ten years had prevented the use of the electropneumatic principle in switch operation.

With these facts in mind one may readily follow, from the successive patents granted to Westinghouse for signal and interlocking devices the processes of the gradual evolution of the electropneumatic system from the more or less impracticable hydraulic system that held the stage when he came upon it - a stage illuminated by the tallow candle and the kerosene lamp. A complete list of the eighteen patents that he took out in signaling and interlocking is given in an appendix. Here we shall consider only those inventions which changed the art.

In early practice, switches and signals were moved by man power. Handling a busy interlocking cabin with switches 1000 feet away (more or less) was heavy work. In 1887 a British writer said that in the London Bridge Station, North Cabin, 280 levers were assembled in one frame. Six hundred trains passed in a day and ninety trains in two busy hours. These figures do not include the many switching movements. This plant was worked by gangs of four men in eight-hour shifts, and it took a husky man to pull over some of the levers. In power interlocking, a girl can move the little levers, and combination of functions reduces the number of levers. One plant of 215 electropneumatic levers built in St. Louis by the Union Switch and Signal Company does the work of 696 levers of the London type. There are 403 units, switches, and signals operated from this machine.

Westinghouse having decided to add railroad signaling to his many other activities, it was inevitable in his character that he should proceed with energy. In one year he took out six patents in signaling and interlocking, ten brake patents and five in other arts. On February 1, 1881, he received a patent for moving a switch by compressed air, using a principle employed in his brake devices; "the switch movement is effected by changing from one direction to another the balance or excess of two pressures which act simultaneously in two directions." In April came a patent for operating the signals in a block-signal system by the movement of the train. This was entirely automatic. Manpower was required only for inspection and maintenance. Compressed air is "the motive power...and a hydraulic column or line is the means of transmitting and applying the power." The mechanism is brought into operation by the wheels of a passing train striking a treadle or other track instrument. This scheme does not appear to have been put to actual use. On the same day a patent was issued for Westinghouse's first interlocking machine. The movement of the switches and signals was by "putting in motion a closed hydraulic column," from the interlocking machine to the operating cylinders. A movement of a small lever admitted a puff of compressed air to one side of a flexible diaphragm and set in motion the hydraulic column, which, in turn, actuated pistons in the working cylinders, however distant they might be. Twenty-one machines of this kind were installed between 1883 and 1891, but they were all replaced in time by electropneumatic plants.

The conception was ingenious and the mechanical details were worked out with great skill and thoroughness, but the first cost was large and maintenance was expensive and difficult. Leakage in long lines of pipe under pressure was serious, and the white salts deposited from the leaking of the non-freezing solution were unsightly. Westinghouse foresaw these objections to his "pneumatic-hydraulic" devices, and from the first looked forward to the electropneumatic system. In that system the work is done by compressed air, conveyed in a common line pipe and fed by a short branch to each cylinder. Air is admitted to the piston chamber and exhausted by an electromagnetic valve which is energized by an electric impulse sent out from the interlocking machines in the signal cabin. This simple and elegant device was first used in signaling and interlocking by Westinghouse and is still standard practice. His application for a pneumatic-hydraulic system was filed January 8, 1881; two days earlier he had filed an application for his first electropneumatic patent, showing a switch moved by compressed air, controlled by an electromagnetic valve. This was a complete and workable design, thoroughly developed in detail. In May he applied for a patent showing the same system for operating signals, and incidentally showing its use in a system of block signals automatically controlled by track circuits. Thus, at the beginning of his activities in signaling and interlocking he foresaw the principles and laid down the fundamental elements of all the later developments in the art.

The first power interlocking put into service in America and, so far as we have discovered, the first in the world, was installed at East St. Louis by the Union Switch and Signal Company in 1882. This was built under the patents of Guerber and Tilden, which had been bought by the Union Company. It worked entirely by hydrostatic pressure secured and maintained by a pump and accumulator. The switch cylinders were double-acting, pressure acting on both sides of a piston to move a switch in both directions. The signal cylinders were single-acting, the signal being moved one way by hydrostatic pressure and the other way by gravity. Alcohol was used as a precaution against freezing, and, although it was returned from the cylinder to the pump after each operation, there was leakage and waste, and the cost of operation was serious. The system had other inherent defects that could not be corrected easily, if at all. The plant was eventually overhauled to work by compressed air. This seems to have been the beginning, in actual practice, of power interlocking.

In the years when power interlocking was getting born the operation of signals by power and their automatic control by track circuit began to interest American inventors. Here again Westinghouse was amongst the pioneers. Other inventors preceded him in the use of a weight to be wound up and released by an escapement controlled by a magnet and also in the use of hydrostatic pressure; but both of these means of applying power were impracticable for extensive use and were short-lived. So far as we have discovered Westinghouse was the first to use compressed air to move signals and switches, and in the dawn of the art of power signaling he invented, designed, and patented mechanisms which are in very wide use and have been but little changed.

Other inventors also anticipated Westinghouse in track-circuit control, but here again he promptly took the lead in devising systems which went into large and lasting use. It was another of those situations which arose often in his career when the combination of comprehensive vision, mechanical insight and contrivance, thoroughness in detail, determination and driving power carried him on to great and lasting accomplishment when others failed. In brief, it was a case of the difference of mental stature.

So the signal business was launched in the United States. The education of railroad officers and of the public went on slowly. The education of those who dictated the financial policy of the railroads was perhaps still slower. There was little demand for the product of the Signal Company, and Westinghouse gave the greater part of his time and thought to matters which promised quicker returns and greater results. The Machine Company was organized in 1880 and called for much attention. The natural-gas development began in 1884 and a new art was to be created.

In two years, 1884 and 1885, Westinghouse brought out twenty-eight patents in this art. The Westinghouse Electric Company was formed in 1886. Shortly before this Westinghouse began one of the most important efforts of his life, the introduction and development of the alternating current for the distribution and use of electric energy. This called for absorbing thought and labor. In 1888 came the most critical and dramatic episode in the history of the air brake which brought out a swift and brilliant display of Westinghouse's temperament and genius.

Notwithstanding such demands, Westinghouse filed in 1888 an application for his most elaborate and his most important patent in interlocking, and the patent was issued in February 1891. This invention was developed in collaboration with Mr. J. G. Schreuder, afterward Chief Engineer and one of the vice-presidents of the Union Switch and Signal Company, whose name appears in the patent specification as a co-inventor. This was the basis of an important and profitable business, which still endures. Many of the greatest railroad yards in the country are handled by the electropneumatic interlocking, and it has gone into considerable use abroad. It was the culmination of ten years of study and experience, and the specifications of this great patent were worked out with such unsparing labor and such comprehensive skill that but few changes in detail have been made from the original designs.

One must regret that the plan of this book does not permit adequate mention of several excellent engineers who helped Westinghouse in working out electropneumatic signaling and interlocking, but the story would be incomplete without the name of John Pressley Coleman. He has been with the Union Switch and Signal Company from very early days, and has been a prolific and judicious inventor and designer. In the special field of operating switches and signals by electropneumatic means he has long been a high authority - perhaps for twenty years the highest authority.

The development of the power brake was one of the greatest events in the evolution of the art of land transportation, second only to the invention of the tubular boiler and of the Bessemer process for making steel; but the development of power signaling and interlocking was necessary to the full effects of the brake. One was the complement of the other. So, too, the development of the uses of alternating electric current for the transmission and application of power was one of the greatest events in the evolution of the art of manufacturing power. These two arts are at the base of the structure of modern society. As we go on in our study we become more and more clearly aware of the place of George Westinghouse in the evolution of these two fundamental arts. In this chapter the aim has been to show something of his part in railway signaling and interlocking.

Chapter Thirteen - Natural Gas

WESTINGHOUSE was not the first man to bring natural gas into Pittsburgh. At least two companies were operating there for a year or two before he became actively concerned in the matter; but their operations were narrow in conception and scope and crude in execution. Westinghouse saw the situation in a large way and he saw it as an engineer, and he changed it abruptly and fundamentally. One of his associates in this development, a Pittsburgh man, writes: "Mr. Westinghouse was the only man of all those engaged in the natural-gas business who sized up the situation and was willing to spend money to meet the wants of the people in Pittsburgh and Allegheny City and the vicinity." He organized the Philadelphia Company with sufficient capital, and bought land in possible gas fields and secured gas rights by lease on a royalty basis. The large sums paid annually to the farmers in western Pennsylvania for the rent of gas wells were an important addition to the wealth of the region.

He organized the transportation of gas over considerable distances on a new plan. Gas was then piped in and distributed in six-inch and eight-inch mains. Westinghouse started at the wells with an eight-inch line. After four or five miles this was stepped up to ten inches; then to twelve, twenty, twenty-four, and thirty inches. Later, thirty-six inch pipe was, and is still, in use. At the points where the gage of pipe changed there were safety valves, and men were constantly on duty to watch the valves. Perhaps it is superfluous to tell the reader that this is an expedient for reducing friction and pressure, well known and obvious to engineers. Westinghouse had the courage and sagacity to apply it to a new and experimental situation.

Westinghouse seems to have had no active interest in the use of natural gas until late in 1883. By midsummer of 1884 he was in full swing. His company was organized and financing was well under way; a broad charter and adequate city ordinances had been procured; and a copious stream of invention began to flow. Thirty-eight patents in this art were taken out by Westinghouse. Of these, twenty-eight were applied for in 1884 and 1885. His great experience in using compressed air at high pressures gave him a good foundation.

Serious inconveniences and more serious dangers had developed in the early distribution and use of natural gas in the Pittsburgh district. Breaks in supply and service lines left mills without power and houses without heat. This was bad, but in dwellings worse things followed. When the supply was cut off or pressure fell, fires went out in grates and ranges. When the supply came on again, if the cocks had not been shut, rooms were filled with unburned gas and asphyxiation or explosions and fires followed. This danger was increased by a common practice of letting gas fires burn continuously, windows being opened to cool the rooms. This was in the days before gas was metered, and while it was looked upon as inexhaustible, and sold to the user at so much per opening. Natural gas has little odor, and leaks may go on unnoticed until dangerous quantities have accumulated and explosive mixtures have formed. It happened in the early days that leakage from street mains crept into houses and the houses were wrecked by explosions.

Westinghouse devised a system of escape pipes which paralleled the street mains, and by which leakage was carried off through corner lamp posts. He invented meters for household and factory use, the latter, the Westinghouse proportional gas meter, having a capacity of 500,000 cubic feet per hour. His most important safety device was the automatic cut-off regulator. When the gas pressure drops below four ounces (the working pressure for household use) the supply is automatically cut off, and the consumer cannot light a jet until all the valves in the house have been closed. Then the supply can be restored by pressing a button on the regulator. This provides against such accidents as have been described above. In brief, he created the technique of a new art.

The direct personal activity of Westinghouse in natural gas ended in December 1899, when he resigned as president and as a director of the Philadelphia Company. Meantime, there had been a great development of the business in western Pennsylvania. Eleven and three-quarter billion cubic feet of gas was sold in 1898. There were 395 producing wells, 962 miles of pipe line, 318 miles of telephone lines, and 114,471 acres of gas and oil lands.

The waste was prodigal, and it was the constant effort of the officers of the Philadelphia Company to get its customers to use gas economically. The gradual establishment of meters corrected what one of the old officers calls "a crying shame." As the near-by wells were exhausted and the distance from which the supply must be drawn increased, the cost to the consumer rose, and the use of gas in the mills fell off, but it is the chief domestic fuel in the district, and is still much used in the industries.

A minor but picturesque event which happened at the outset of Westinghouse's natural-gas experience has often been described. It made great excitement in Pittsburgh and some uneasiness amongst those who were already bringing in gas in a small way. This was the sinking of a well in the grounds of "Solitude," his home at Pittsburgh. Having decided to prospect for gas in his own back yard, a contract for drilling was made, December 29, 1883, and about the end of February a small vein of gas sand was tapped, with a moderate yield. Mr. Gillespie, who was drilling the well, remembers Westinghouse saying that "he would prefer a well of this size to a larger one, as he had enough gas for his house and for some of his friends in the neighborhood. This feeling lasted only a few days, and he was keen to go on." Of course he was. There were unexplored possibilities in the earth beneath and in the water under the earth. At 1500 feet another vein was struck, with a good yield, and the drillers wished to stop for fear of getting salt water and spoiling the well. But Westinghouse "had a new thing to play with, spending his evenings at the well, scheming new drilling tools and improvements in ways of prospecting." Why stop? A little deeper "we struck such a volume of gas that it blew the tools out and ripped off the casing head with such a roar and racket that nobody could hear his own ears, within a block." The gas was set alight, and for weeks the neighborhood was lit up by this roaring torch, a hundred feet high. It was fun for Westinghouse, but rather disturbing to the peace of a handsome residential section. The well was got under control and capped, and Westinghouse went into the natural-gas business.

The administrative and executive machinery for this enterprise was provided by the creation of the Philadelphia Company. This company exists and works under an old charter, one of four or five "omnibus" charters granted by the Pennsylvania legislature about 1870, and carrying very broad powers. The discovery and purchase of this charter by Westinghouse and his officers and agents secured to the new company an asset of great value. The company has for years owned and operated the street railways of Pittsburgh and San Francisco, and it produces and distributes electric current for light and power for Pittsburgh and the near-by suburbs.

Westinghouse eventually withdrew from the Philadelphia Company and from the natural-gas business. The developing and pioneering period had come to an end and he had but mild interest in accomplished activities. Meantime, he had created an enterprise of great public service. It gave to a large region a new fuel clean, convenient, and relatively cheap. This fuel was distinctly superior in the heating furnaces of the varied iron and steel industries, and especially superior in making glass, and for a time it was much used for making steam.

However long these conditions may or may not continue, certain permanent results followed from the natural-gas development. Early in our Colonial history Pittsburgh was seen to be a strategic point, in trade and in war. Later it took on new importance as a convenient place to assemble iron ore, and coal, and all the world knows what followed, for Pittsburgh is as famous as Westphalia. The discovery and development of the Lake Superior iron mines led to the establishment at lake ports of new iron and steel works and the enlargement of old ones. There was some alarm in the Pittsburgh district, but the supply of natural gas on a large scale came in the nick of time and stopped much of the threatened diversion of this industry. Pittsburgh is more than an iron and steel city. In that vicinity more glass is made than in all the rest of the United States, and about half of our total output of cork products comes from that district. In some degree these and many other industries were held or stimulated by natural gas. It would be idle, though interesting, to speculate upon what would have happened if natural gas had not been brought into Pittsburgh just at the critical moment, and developed swiftly and on a great scale; but we know what did happen. George Westinghouse came on the field at the tactical instant in an industrial battle.

For a few years Pittsburgh had blue skies. People again saw its beautiful hills and valleys. Its smoke-stained buildings came out into the sunlight and seemed suddenly to have grown old. This lasted but a few years; the black and red clouds again rolled up from the valleys, and clear skies again became a sign of adversity. Westinghouse loved Pittsburgh in all its aspects. In the short period of sunshine and in its normal gloom, to him it was beautiful. Standing before the electric works at East Pittsburgh, looking down the Turtle Creek valley to the impenetrable clouds hanging over the Carnegie Works and Homestead, looking up the valley to the black columns rising over the Air Brake works, looking across to the bare and blasted hillside and the naked oaks, smothered by soot and gases, he made a sweeping gesture and said: "Isn't it beautiful?" Ruskin could not have understood the emotion, but Carlyle would.

FUEL GAS

There came a time when two serious considerations forced themselves upon the minds of engineers and investors. One was that if the natural gas gave out, there would be a large idle investment in the plant for distributing, controlling and using gas. The other was that if electric lighting became general there would be another idle investment in plant for making and distributing illuminating gas. To Westinghouse, and to various other engineers, came the notion of making fuel gas for heat and power. This would fill the natural-gas pipes and save that loss. It was further proposed to use the existing illuminating-gas plants to make fuel gas and save another loss of invested capital. In the mind of Westinghouse this group of ideas grew, as was always the case. He foresaw gas producers, established at suitable places, making gas to run gas engines; these engines to drive electric generators, producing lighting current. Then, as the art advanced, he foresaw the production of power current in the same way. His imagination saw the railroads of the United States lined with electro-gas plants, the trains to be hauled and the shops to be run by power thus produced and transmitted short distances. This was before the possibility of long-distance transmission by alternating current was demonstrated. There was no visible limit to the extension of this general idea.

In 1887 the Fuel Gas and Electric Engineering Company was organized and experiments were begun in making fuel gas. Westinghouse enlisted some able engineers and spent money and energy with his habitual courage, not to say prodigality. Mr. Emerson McMillin seems to have proposed rearranging and using existing gas works and was retained as consulting engineer of the new company. Mr. Samuel Wellman (past-president, The American Society Mechanical Engineers) designed the general arrangement of a very complete experimental producer plant, and was active in the enterprise and passed upon all plans before the work was begun. Mr. Alex M. Gow, now of the Oliver Iron Mining Company, was one of the engineers employed. An adequate laboratory was provided for the constant analysis of the gas. The engineer who reads this will know the competence of the men engaged in this bold and instructive experiment, and he will not fail to understand the lavish completeness of the apparatus provided. This is not the place to go into the technical details, interesting and informing as they are. The result was one of Westinghouse's great contributions to the scrap-heap and the further education of a few men who have been important in engineering and industrial history.

The obvious and familiar suggestion is made that the controlling factors in the scheme might have been tested by detached experiments on a small scale. Mr. Gow writes: "The answer is, Mr. Westinghouse rarely did things that way. He was an 'incorrigible optimist.' He experimented on a full-size scale and backed the faith that was in him to the limit. Once having put his hand to the plough - and he was usually driving at least a dozen furrows at a time - he never looked back, never was discouraged, and never had any regrets over past failures. This work consumed months of time and many car loads of coal, and the stand-pipe of the holder blazed like a gas well. A few explosions and a few fires added zest to the experiment. It was hard to say what a day would or would not bring forth; but no day brought forth fuel gas on a commercial basis." It is interesting to recall that while the fuel-gas furrow was being ploughed, the quick-action brake was getting born and the alternating-current projects were coming into being.

The costly and interesting fuel-gas experiments were a commercial failure, but the matter was never entirely given up. For many years Westinghouse had great hopes in the gas engine as a prime mover and he caused gas producers to be designed, developed, and made as a part of the product of the Westinghouse Machine Company. The swift and great development of the steam turbine and the turbo-generator gradually crowded gas engines into the background and the producer went with them. These are now but a very small element in the activities of the Company.

Chapter Fourteen - Various Interests and Activities

LAMPS

THE earliest great use of electricity was in lighting, first arc lighting and next incandescent lighting. The situation as to invention and patents when Westinghouse entered the field of incandescent lighting is briefly explained elsewhere. Several able and ingenious men had well begun the line of invention which led up to the established art as it is now practised. Fundamental and controlling patents were under way in various stages. It was late for Westinghouse to begin invention in lamps, but he watched the field and made some interesting excursions into it.

The story of the stopper lamp is told in the chapter on the Chicago World's Fair. It was a useful but passing contrivance. It could not long compete with

Mr. Edison's simple and clever little invention of the one-piece globe. In the course of years and after great research the tungsten lamp came - a very important event in electric lighting. Westinghouse realized what had happened and bought a company in Vienna which was making tungsten lamps and which owned patents in several countries, including the United States. He at once established metal-filament lamp companies in France and England. The patents then bought were of little relative value. The controlling patents are now owned by the General Electric Company, with licenses to the Westinghouse Company; but the enterprise brought technical knowledge and a commercial position, which helped to build up the Westinghouse Lamp Company into a prosperous institution with sales of about $12,000,000 a year. The Westinghouse Metallfaden Glühlampenfabrik Gesellschaft, M. B. H., of Vienna, still lives in the shadow of the Great War. It has lately been sold to Germans and the name changed.

The incandescent-lighting system is about the most inefficient contrivance used by man. Of the potential energy in the coal, about 10 per cent gets to the lamp, and the carbon lamp, using three or four watts per candlepower, gave an efficiency, from the coal pile to useful energy in the light, of from one-fourth to one-half of one per cent. The best metal-filament lamp of today is five or six times as efficient as the old carbon lamp; but to get back three per cent of your coal in the shape of light energy is not a result that engineers can be really proud of or satisfied with.

In 1897, long before the tungsten lamp arrived, Mr. Henry Noel Potter brought to Westinghouse's attention a crude form of incandescent lamp invented by a German physicist, Doctor Walter Nernst. The illuminant of this lamp is a small porcelain-like rod made of so-called "rare earths," such as magnesia, thoria, and ytria. When connected in an electric circuit like the ordinary incandescent lamp, no current will flow through the rod until it is heated by outside means. Then it becomes conductive. The heat generated by the current flow thereafter keeps the rod in its conductive condition and it emits a beautiful soft light, the spectrum of which more nearly corresponds to that of sunlight than any other artificial light. Another interesting feature of the Nernst lamp is its capability of being used, "burned," in the open air, thus avoiding the necessity of using an evacuated globe.

Westinghouse at once became intensely interested in this lamp and bought the American rights. He organized the Nernst Lamp Company and employed a force of engineers to develop the lamp to commercial form. Many ingenious devices were invented for automatically applying the starting heat and for controlling the current flow through the conducting rod, or "glower," as it was called. The electrical efficiency of the Nernst lamp was found to be one and one-half watts per candlepower, twice that of the best form of ordinary incandescent electric lamp then known. This fact and the superior quality of the light justified Westinghouse in his belief that it would be a successful competitor in the incandescent-lighting field.

The sales of the company grew fast and the, Nernst Lamp Company gave promise of great success. At the height of its prosperity, however, something happened which doubtless Westinghouse as well as others engaged in this kind of enterprise expected would happen sooner or later; namely, the production of the tungsten filament, which far surpassed the carbon filament in electrical efficiency, and was more efficient than the Nernst lamp. It soon became apparent that the Nernst lamp could not successfully compete with the tungsten lamp of higher efficiency, particularly as the Nernst lamp was inherently complicated and expensive, as compared with the exceedingly simple form of the evacuated tungsten lamp. The color qualities of the Nernst lamp, although desirable, were not of sufficient commercial value to outweigh the disadvantages of its complexity when confronted by the higher efficiency and the simplicity of the tungsten-filament lamp. Realizing this, Westinghouse promptly arranged for the discontinuance of the manufacture of the Nernst lamp except upon a very small scale.

Perhaps the greatest benefit to the public from the work of Westinghouse in promoting the Nernst lamp is hi the education in proper light distribution. This subject the engineers of the company were compelled to study carefully because of the peculiar structure of the Nernst lamp, which led to placing it above the normal line of vision. The rules governing the location of lamps established by the Nernst Company are essentially those now followed in placing incandescent lamps. From an aesthetic view-point it is greatly to be regretted that the Nernst lamp could not have kept a commercial position, since no other artificial illuminant has yet been discovered with so nearly a daylight spectrum as that of the glowing rods of rare earths.

Soon after the Nernst lamp came the Cooper Hewitt lamp, which still lives and in fact is in increasing use. For years unsuccessful attempts had been made to produce a commercially successful lamp in which an enclosed gas traversed by an electric current would serve as the illuminant. Late in 1899, Mr. L. F. H. Betts, a patent lawyer in New York, asked Terry whether Westinghouse would be interested in a new form of electric light invented by Peter Cooper Hewitt, (Hewitt died in August 1921.) with the result that Betts arranged for Terry to meet Hewitt at his laboratory in the Madison Square Garden Tower. The lamp shown by Hewitt was startling. For a long time Hewitt had been seeking to get efficient light by transmitting high-potential, high-frequency currents through tubes containing a gas or vapor, somewhat along the lines of the familiar Geissler tubes. One day he chanced to connect the tubes in circuit with a direct-current source while the high-frequency current was also flowing. Suddenly the rather faint Geissler glow burst into a brilliant greenish-white light. Hewitt's assistant sitting in a chair nearby was so startled that he fell over backward, but Hewitt himself, who had been expecting some such result, calmly proceeded to analyze the causes, with the result that he had soon developed the lamp which bears his name. This was the first effective gas or vapor lamp ever devised. Terry lost no time in bringing the invention to the attention of Westinghouse, who was intensely interested. Negotiations, at once begun, resulted in an agreement dated March 7, 1900, between Westinghouse and Hewitt, whereby Westinghouse was to finance the enterprise and organize a company to exploit the lamp. He personally supplied the money to carry on this work until 1902, when the Cooper Hewitt Electric Company was formed with Westinghouse and Hewitt as its principal stockholders, the patent rights and business being taken over by this company.

The lamp was of very high efficiency as compared with the best incandescent lamp. From an aesthetic point of view it had a great drawback: the light lacked red and violet rays and was over-rich in green rays. This gave to illuminated objects an unnatural, indeed a ghastly, appearance. The "native hue" of one who sat under it was "sicklied o'er with the pale cast" of dirty green. But Westinghouse's gift of intense and enthusiastic interest made each thing absorbing and delightful, if not beautiful, while he was at it, and when one is writing of his relations to any one matter there is temptation to exaggerate its place in his mind. We can only get a proper perspective when we remember that there were half a dozen such absorbing things in every twenty-four hours. The Cooper Hewitt lamp appealed to him by its originality and by the technical ingenuity displayed. He not only pushed it commercially but he played with it. One was flooded with its ghastly green rays in the most unexpected places. The ladies would not tolerate it in the drawing rooms, but he put it in his own offices. When Charles Francis Adams got back to Boston from a meeting in New York he wrote to Westinghouse: "I was shocked by your appearance. You really ought to take a vacation." Westinghouse answered: "I wish you could see how you looked." The absence of the red and violet rays made the light far less tiring to the eye than that of other artificial illuminants, and it found large use in machine shops, drafting rooms, printing establishments, government buildings, and other large places where good and cheap light is more important than true color effects. Hewitt later devised an ingenious means for transforming some of the rays into red rays and blending these with the others, thus producing an excellent imitation of daylight where such result was important.

An interesting characteristic of the Cooper Hewitt lamp is that the current flow must be initiated by overcoming what Hewitt aptly termed a "negative electrode reluctance." This was accomplished automatically, and once the current flow is established, this reluctance, or resistance, remains in abeyance so long as the flow is in a given direction, and it is prohibitive to current flow in the reverse direction. This peculiar characteristic made the lamp inoperative on a single-phase alternating-current circuit, for the lamp would "go out" at the cessation of each positive impulse, or several thousand times a minute. To overcome this difficulty Hewitt made a lamp with three positive electrodes acting in conjunction with a single negative electrode. When these positive electrodes were connected with the three conductors of a three-phase alternating source, current would flow at all times into the negative from one or more of the positive electrodes, thus keeping the negative continuously "alive." Various means were later devised adapting the lamp to two phases derived from a single-phase current, and it thus became a commercial device for single-phase alternating circuits also.

The fact that the flow of the current through the conductor connected with the negative electrode was always in a given direction gave Hewitt the idea of utilizing this characteristic for rectifying alternating current for use as direct current. This led to the development of the Cooper Hewitt rectifier. The commercial value of this rectifier promised to be great, and as the original agreement between Westinghouse and Hewitt related only to the lamp, a supplemental agreement was made in 1902 to include the rectifier. This device consists essentially of an exhausted glass globe containing multiple positive electrodes and a single negative. The principle of operation is the same as that of the alternating-current lamp, but the construction is such that very little energy is absorbed in the production of light. The rectifier soon became a standard product of the Cooper Hewitt Company.

In 1913 license agreements were entered into between the Cooper Hewitt Company and the Westinghouse Company, and between the latter and the General Electric Company, whereby these two companies secured licenses to manufacture and exploit the rectifier, paying suitable royalties to the Cooper Hewitt Company. An agreement was also made between the Cooper Hewitt Company and the General Electric Company providing for the exchange of licenses on the lamps, the latter company having meanwhile secured a number of patents of value in that field. These arrangements still continue, although since the death of Westinghouse the General Electric Company has bought the control of the capital stock of the Cooper Hewitt Company. So the manufacture of the lamp and the rectifier goes on in growing volume. Westinghouse, as an incident in his work, or as a by-product, had founded another enterprise.

MULTIPLE-UNIT CONTROL

It is elementary in the art of land transportation that when the volume of traffic is large enough there is gain in massing the cars into trains. This situation began to appear quite early in electric transportation in and about the large cities. Very little thought makes clear the advantages of having a motor under each car, and with electric traction that is possible. When every wheel in a train is a driving wheel great tractive power is secured without concentration of weight destructive to the track. In city and suburban traffic, where stops must be frequent, this is especially important, for it makes it possible to get up to speed quickly. Obviously it is essential that all of the motors in a train should be controlled from the head of the train, and these conditions were met by the invention and development by Mr. Frank J. Sprague of a fundamentally new system of electric train make-up and operation which he called the "multiple-unit system."

This provided for the individual equipment of cars and locomotives with motors, and main controllers therefor, and a train line, with coupler and master controllers, in such fashion that any number of wholly or partly equipped units could be assembled in any order or sequence, and then controlled by like movements, relative to the track, of the master controller from the head of any car. This made it possible to get the maximum of train and track capacity.

Mr. Sprague had the foresight and ability as an engineer and inventor to not only devise means for the practical application of the principles involved but to see the possibilities of its influence upon a comprehensive system of electric traction.

The system was first used on the South Side Elevated Railroad in Chicago in 1897, and its success led to the ultimate adoption of this general method of control, modified in details, on all electric roads where two or more motor units are operated under a single control.

Westinghouse saw clearly what was coming in the great, new field of electric traction, and the advantages to the electric companies, to the inventor, and to the public of participation by both the Westinghouse and the General Electric Companies in the inventions of Mr. Sprague. The great cost of duplication in invention and development might thus be avoided, and the companies would still compete hi manufacture and sale, while the product would not be loaded with an unnecessary charge. He suggested a plan of participation which was not acceptable. Westinghouse did not take his troubles lying down, and while retaining the essential principles of the multiple-unit system, he proceeded to develop the application of electrically controlled pneumatic equipment as an alternative to the all-electric Sprague apparatus.

In 1898, a few months after the failure of diplomacy to save waste, the electropneumatic control was in service on the Brooklyn Elevated Railway, and it is still there, working well. The long and exacting experience of Westinghouse in electropneumatic work, particularly in handling switches and signals, had prepared him for this situation, and he had already developed the essential elements, but there were new features of extraordinary ingenuity.

A few years later came the necessity of devising a controller for the subway equipment in New York. Larger volumes of current were to be handled here than in any existing installation, and the subway engineers thought that the "drum" type was inadequate. With this the Westinghouse engineers did not agree and proposed to adequately change the electropneumatic drum-controller. The General Electric Company brought out a new design which they called the "plunker" type, and it soon became pretty clear that the drum-controller would not be accepted. Westinghouse was suddenly face to face with the sort of situation which he most enjoyed a radical change of tactics in the face of the enemy. The writer of these lines had the privilege of getting a glimpse of the beginnings of this change of tactics. It was in a night ride from New York to Pittsburgh in Westinghouse's car. For a large part of the night he worked, drawing and erasing, brooding and drawing. In the morning he had a set of sketches ready for the shops at the air brake works. This was the birth of the "turret control." In a few weeks the equipment for a train was built and tested, and it was a working apparatus. As an example of speed, resource, skill, and success, the incident was as interesting as the classic episode of the quick-action brake, although of nothing like the same importance.

The first order for the subway controller equipment went to the General Electric Company, but a great many electropneumatic controllers have since been supplied to the heavy traffic electric systems in and about New York. Both types persist, but the preponderating opinion seems to favor the electropneumatic type.

CAR, AIR, AND ELECTRIC COUPLER - COMBINED

The conditions of heavy subway traffic led to the invention of an automatic combined coupler. The object is thus told in the patent specification:

My present invention relates to couplings for the connection of railroad vehicles; and its object is to provide an appliance for automatically coupling railroad vehicles for the purpose of draft, with which there may be combined means for coincidently and automatically coupling lines of fluid-pressure pipes for the operation of brake and steam-heating apparatus, etc., or for coupling electric conductors for the conveyance of electricity for light, power, and braking purposes and for signaling, or both of such means.

In the coupler heads, passages are introduced to carry air from one car to another, and electric conductors are also introduced. When the cars are coupled the necessary connections and contacts are made automatically between these passages and conductors. By the use of this coupling device all manual operations hi uniting cars of the train are dispensed with, the air connections and electric circuits being automatically established when the car-coupling is effected. One can imagine some of the mechanical difficulties involved in an apparatus so complicated and doing automatically such a variety of things. Obviously they must be done reliably and precisely. There must be no leakage of the air under pressure and no failure to make the electrical contacts. These are vital elements in such train operation. Westinghouse perfected the details of this invention with his customary thoroughness and energy and satisfied himself that it solved the problem by tests made upon a few cars that were operated by the Westinghouse Electric Company. The customer, however, was not yet ready for it, so it was held in reserve for a demand that was sure to come. When the length of trains on the Interborough Subway service was increased from eight to ten cars, better car couplings were required, and the Westinghouse coupling with air connections was the form selected and has operated successfully for many years. This coupling is also used on the Brooklyn system, including the electric as well as the air connections.

The advantages resulting from its employment are: Greatly reduced risk to employees because of automatic coupling of the air and electric connections;

greater facility and speed in coupling and uncoupling trains; and freedom from accidental stoppages due to broken electric circuits or burst air hose. These advantages are of commanding importance in the conduct of transportation of the character required in congested subway traffic.

RESEARCH

Perhaps most of us, however intelligent and well informed, have no adequate notion of the present place of research work in industrial development. All great concerns now have research laboratories and staffs of highly educated and trained investigators who have no direct relations with production and sales. They are part of the "overhead." They cost much money and the results of the expenditure are often obscure. They are essentially modern. In old-time British foundries and machine works it used to be said "where there's muck there's money." Individual skill, ingenuity, and driving power contrived the things to be made and the ways and means of making them, and pushed production. Chemistry, physics, and sanitation had about as much place in the process as differential equations; but all these enter now into the manufacture of complicated engineering product and some of them enter into refining oil and packing pork.

George Westinghouse saw pretty early the value of pure research, and from the first days of the Electric Company it has gone deeply into what used to be called experimental work but has later taken the more accurate name of research. This is true also in principle but less in degree of his other companies. Many years ago the writer ventured to suggest to Westinghouse that if he would get out of active work and devote himself to research, humanity would be the gainer in the long run and he would be happy. He had already gathered fame and ample fortune. He said: "Perhaps so, but think of the many men to whom I give employment. I can't stop now." No doubt he realized, too, his handicap in his lack of higher mathematics and physics. But his gift of seeing into things went a long way to make up for what he had missed in education. He always gave impetus and encouragement to the research work of the Electric Company, and they have spent very great sums in that field; probably no more than several other companies, perhaps not so much as some, but they have spent liberally for the advancement of the electric science and art, which means the progress of man.

We have said that it was in 1883 that Westinghouse began serious work in the electrical field. Already an important science of electricity had been built up. Indeed, it is held that the science had been founded three hundred years before; but the applied art was still insignificant. Many laws and principles had been established, but many more remained to be discovered, and this was particularly true of the possible applications of the alternating current to practical uses. The phenomena of alternating current had to be observed and worked into principles by experiment, and that experiment was mostly in connection with active manufacturing orders. Each piece of apparatus brought through the shops gave experimental data for later designs. Mathematical analysis, now greatly used, and often with brilliant effect, was almost unknown, and necessarily so for lack of facts, observed and recorded. The literature of the art had mostly yet to be written, and each investigator had to depend pretty much on his own limited experience. The farmer in Nebraska who sits on the fence and thinks out a brand-new system of government or religion while he whittles does not really need history. But if one is dealing with steam, electricity, friction, and gravity, experimental facts are necessary, and if they are not on record he must dig them out of his own experience. This was the situation in the early days of the Electric Company, and through the stages of practical experiment, pure research, and mathematical analysis the art was built up. It was an extraordinary privilege for Westinghouse and his young engineers to live in the dawn of an art and to be an essential part of its development.

The reader may be interested in a few words about some specific research work. When the Westinghouse Company began to build alternating-current machines and apparatus a potential of 1000 volts was used, and the problem of insulation at once became acute. For thirty-five years that problem has been insistent, if not always acute; and for thirty-five years to come it will give occupation for the learned and ingenious specialist. That is in the nature of things. As voltages increase insulation must be improved; as insulation is improved voltages increase. It is the old situation of guns and armor. The story of electricity is a story of increasing voltages, and thus the whole story of electrical development is tied up with insulation. And yet the function of insulation is negative - to keep something from happening.

In a piece of machinery electric currents must be confined, but the heat developed by the currents must be dissipated. A poor conductor of electricity is a poor conductor of heat also, and insulation that prevents destruction of apparatus by wandering currents may promote its destruction by confined heat. A compromise must be made, and this is one of the functions of research. Many different materials are used for insulations - cloth, paper, fiber, mica, varnish, gums, enamels, oil, paints, oxides, rubber, and so on in great variety - and all have their own peculiar properties. These must be determined and weighed by research and experiment. The study never ends, as the requirements ever increase, and perhaps the problem of insulation is as severe now as it ever was; but it is believed that the Westinghouse engineers have gone further in insulation research than have the engineers of any other electrical concern in the world.

A beautiful example of the combination of mathematical analysis and experimental research was the development of a fundamental method of calculating electrical machinery. Crude methods were in existence as early as 1890, but they were empirical and of very limited application. In 1893 research investigations were made while laying out the generators for Niagara Falls. Templates were made representing sections of the armature and field and a picture was obtained of the distribution of the magnetic flux, by the arrangement into which fine iron filings fell on paraffined paper laid over these templates when current was passed through. Study of this picture suggested an attempt to reproduce the representation of the flux distribution by calculation. This suggested the calculation of the electromotive-force wave form of the machine and this, in turn, pointed to the possibility of a fundamental method of calculation of electrical machinery. For three or four years the study went on, by mathematical analysis and by experiment, and finally a fundamental method was developed which is the basis of the methods of calculation in use by the company today. The essential characteristics of a complicated and costly machine can be determined by calculation, in detail, before the working drawings are begun. It is quite obvious that by such scientific procedure time and money are saved, as compared with the cut and try methods, which were used when apparatus was built by experiment and not by analysis. So far has the scientific method been established that in modern practice calculation is relied upon entirely in the design of electrical machinery, and contracts for the electrical equipment of power stations, railways and industrial plants are taken based entirely on calculated designs. No error in proportions or characteristics is permissible in the calculations, for no check can be had upon their operating characteristics until the work has gone so far that important modifications in the design are not permissible. Preliminary trial machines cannot be built, except in rare cases, for there is not time, the huge apparatus of today often requiring considerably more than a year to construct. Thus the accuracy in calculation, based on research data, is one of the marvels of the electrical art.

TELEPHONE

In October 1879, Westinghouse filed an application for a telephone patent. This was followed in the next year by three other patents designed to extend and perfect the invention shown in the first patent. He proposed to save wire by a system of auxiliary telephone exchanges. The wires from a group of subscribers were carried into a local, auxiliary exchange, and from there communication was made with the central exchange by one common wire. The underlying idea was to connect groups of country users with the central exchange in a city some distance away, but it was thought that it might be advantageous to use such auxiliary exchanges in cities also by grouping subscribers in districts. These local exchanges were automatic and thus, while wire was saved, the cost of attendance was not increased. The specifications were worked out in great detail, and a "mechanic skilled in the art," having the specifications before him, could have constructed an operative system complete to the last contact and set screw. This is characteristic of Westinghouse's patents. It is also characteristic that he should have found time and energy to interject into the midst of his crowding activities a subject so foreign, and to carry it out with such minute elaboration. These inventions were something for him to play with a little while, and then drop for some other kind of diversion. They did, however, dimly forecast machine switching. A high authority in telephony says they "apparently disclose a rudimentary form of a semi-mechanical system." So far they are interesting.

In the annual report of the American Telephone and Telegraph Company for 1919 it is said that "amongst possible improvements in economy and efficiency, the most important is the machine-switching system which has been the subject of constant study and experimentation by the Department of Development and Research over a period of more than ten years. During the past year the Engineering Department has been engaged in planning and directing the introduction of .machine switching or automatic switchboards into the Bell system. It is our plan to study each improvement in apparatus to determine how it can most economically be made a part of the plant. Such studies show that in the large cities machine-switching equipment should be employed for extensions necessary to provide for growth and for reconstruction to replace worn-out equipment."

We may see in this book other cases where it took a good while for the growth of an art or the evolution of social conditions to catch up with George Westinghouse, but forty years is the longest interval that we have discovered. In this case, the delay was merely a consequence of the reluctance of evolution, and with that the judicious will not quarrel. It was not at all a consequence of dullness or unreasonable conservatism on the part of those who have developed the telephone in America. They have put into it costly research, engineering skill, commercial sense, and imagination to a degree not known to, or even guessed by, those who are not specially informed. In this splendid episode of our history George Westinghouse would have shone if he had dropped half a dozen other interests and diligently followed telephony. He would have speeded up the evolution of the art; but after a brief excursion he dropped telephony for good and all.

BOARD OF PATENT CONTROL

The wide and varied business of the Westinghouse Companies was making and selling engineering material. Most of this business was carried on under patents, and it was inevitable that there should have been a great deal of litigation in attack and defense. Westinghouse was a good fighter - bold, resourceful, and stubborn. He enjoyed fighting and would have made a great general; but he was big enough not to fight for the sake of fighting. He deprecated the waste of money and the diversion of energy. He preferred to protect the interests of his companies by agreement when that was possible. We say the interests of his companies, not his own interests. His interests were always subordinate to those of his companies. In fact, his private fortune was almost entirely invested in the stock of his companies - not even in their bonds, except now and then to help some plan of financing.

A famous agreement was that made with the General Electric Company in 1896. It is told elsewhere that when the General Electric Company won the suit in the case of the Vanderpoel underrunning trolley, Westinghouse said: "That's good; now there is a basis for a trade." The trade was made forthwith, for both parties welcomed a patent truce. It was agreed that each company should extend to the other a license under the patents controlled by it, to the extent that each might sell an agreed percentage of the aggregate amount of business of the two companies without payment of royalty, but if either exceeded such percentage, a suitable royalty should be paid on the excess. To carry out this plan there was created a Board of Patent Control comprising four members, four alternates, and a fifth member and his alternate.

The appointees on the part of the Westinghouse Company were: members, George Westinghouse and Paul D. Cravath; alternates, Charles A. Terry and B. H. Warren, the latter being later succeeded by F. H. Taylor and later by E. M. Herr.

The General Electric Company appointed as members C. A. Coffin and F. P. Fish, and as alternates Robert Treat Payne and Gordon Abbott, the former succeeded by Eugene Griffin and later by Anson W. Burchard, while Abbott was succeeded by Charles Neave. The fifth member was E. B. Thomas; alternate, Samuel Spencer.

So well did this plan work that the fifth member, whose function it was to act as an arbitrator in case of dispute, was called upon in but two instances, and his alternate not at all, during the term of the agreement. After the Board had been in existence some thirteen years or so its operations were made the subject of investigation by a representative of the Department of Justice, for the purpose of determining whether the Sherman Anti-Trust Law was in any way being violated, and it was greatly to the credit of both companies that the Department after exhaustive examination found no occasion to interfere with its operations. Westinghouse used always to say that he would like to have this agreement hung on the walls of his office, so sure was he of its fairness to both parties and to the public. While none of those concerned doubted its legality, perhaps there were those who questioned the expediency of such publicity in the actual state of feeling about agreements between corporations. The agreement continued to govern the patent relations until the end of its stated term of fifteen years, which expired in May 1911.

AIR SPRING

The air brake, the alternating current, and the steam turbine are, no doubt, of somewhat remote interest to a good many people to whom the air spring for automobile pleasure cars is a thing of immediate and daily interest. In the life of Westinghouse it was a very minor matter, but he put into it the same qualities of energy, enthusiasm, and thoroughness that he put into major matters. For these reasons a few words about it will be illustrative and may be interesting, and we cannot do better than to quote literally a letter on the subject from Mr. H. T. Herr, a vice-president of the Electric Company. The letter was not written for publication and is all the better for that. It gives an intimate view of Westinghouse at work.

In the spring of 1910 I went into Mr. Westinghouse's office in New York to keep an appointment with him in reference to some important gear matters. A spirited dispute was on between Admiral Melville and Mr. MacAlpine in which Mr. Westinghouse and I were involved in bringing about a settlement of the Melville-MacAlpine gear contract, with George Westinghouse as trustee. On this particular morning we spent a half-hour going over different matters. I always tried to be as concise as possible with him, and when finished I would generally say: "Now, Mr. Westinghouse, I know you are very busy, and I won't take any more of your time." He generally replied, "Well, I'll call you again tomorrow or this evening," or he would say, as he did many times: "Mr. Herr, I have a good deal on my mind, but I like to talk to you about these mechanical things. They relieve me."

This day he asked me to pull up my chair, and taking a block of cross-section paper said: "Some little time ago I saw a device which had interested my chauffeur at Lenox. This device was made by a couple of men up in the country and applied to an automobile to reduce the road shocks. I have been interested in it somewhat and it has some merit. It needs changing to make it successful."

He then made a sketch of two telescoping cylinders with a leather packing on one which slid into the other. The ends of the cylinders were closed and a certain amount of oil was kept in the interior over the packing to make an airtight joint. "Now," said Mr. Westinghouse, "this won't stand up on account of the oil leaking out past the leatherpacked piston, but I will put a pump on the inside (illustrating by a sketch) operated by a flapper, which, as the air spring collapses and extends, will automatically pump back into the inside any oil that leaks by the packing leather." He was as usual very enthusiastic and very clear in his description and sketches, and after he had finished his explanation he sat back in his chair and said to me: "What do you think of it?" I told him I thought it would work if the plunger pump would function. He said that the pump would work all right and asked me if I could build one at the Machine Company, to which I replied that we could make anything. He said: "Take the sketch with you and show it to Green (patent attorney of the Machine Company) and have one made," adding that he would have Liebau (one of the inventors) come to Pittsburgh with the drawings, etc.

I took the sketch with me to Pittsburgh and the second day after the conference Mr. Westinghouse arrived at the works with Liebau. In the meantime I had started the development of the first springs built at the Machine Company, which incorporated the pump device. There followed a year's experimental work on the best method of mounting the springs, the first set being placed on a car at Homewood that Mr. Westinghouse owned, and the second set on my own car in Pittsburgh. These air springs were applied by the complete removal of the steel springs, and made a wonderful difference in the riding qualities of the car. The wear of the guides proved abnormal, and this method of suspension was subsequently abandoned, there being substituted therefor the application of the air springs as an adjunct to the steel springs, as they are now applied.

Mr. Westinghouse was a great mechanician. He had a wonderful knowledge of and intuition for the proportions of a device of this kind, and could with little calculation, simply by good judgment of these proportions, have a splendid design produced. The fact that the present air springs have had practically no change since he announced them ready for commercial work is a good example of his ability in this direction, I presume a great deal of this came by experience in the air brake art for a device such as the air spring.

The introduction of a pump into the air spring made the operation feasible and also broadly patentable. With this arrangement many people have for long periods been sceptical about the ability of the air spring to maintain air under pressure in such small volumes, but the fact that the oil seal prevents any leakage of air and that leakage of oil is taken care of by automatically pumping it back by the plunger, makes the spring a practical device. We made a great many experiments on proportions and operations of springs, and a number of different sizes, also a great many schemes for the suspension of the chassis of the automobile.

Mr. Westinghouse was always enthusiastic about the outlook for this project, as it affected transportation, one of the greatest industries in the world, and he often said to me that the spring was not limited in its application to automobiles, but that he expected to apply it to railway cars as well.

In the midst of the air-spring development Mr. Westinghouse became interested in other devices and arrangements which might affect the riding qualities of automobiles, and we began a very comprehensive series of developments and experiments in spring wheels, cushion tires, etc., and all sorts of appliances were tried, not only as built by our company, but whenever a new device of this order appeared on the market Mr. Westinghouse immediately had it investigated, either through the Machine Company or personally. Some very ingenious spring-wheel arrangements were designed, constructed, and reduced to practice. Mr. Westinghouse never believed in a paper design, but insisted on its application, which very often showed the impracticability of devices, which on paper appeared most promising. It was by these practical demonstrations that his judgment was almost always strengthened for future developments. He was extremely quick to see a situation and to judge of the possible merits of any device.

During this development period of the air spring we were also carrying on a very exhaustive line of experiments and development work in turbines for marine purposes and for the commercialization of the reduction gear; and coming in addition to the regular business of the company, it brought a large demand on the time and energies of the shop, the experimental division, and some of the engineers. Mr. Westinghouse relied on me personally to be able to tell him about any of these developments and I found it necessary to keep in the closest touch with them, which, while quite confining, was intensely interesting and gave me an association with him and a training which I would not have missed for anything.

He had said to me many times that he thought the air spring was one of the best things he had done. I feel quite convinced that if he had lived its application would have been more widely extended and its introduction into automobile work would have been accelerated quite materially.

THE STEEL CAR

In the decade before the Great War the people of the United States saw the beginning of the steel passenger car on railroads, and they saw its use extend quickly from the tunnels of New York out over all the great lines of railroad. Westinghouse was one of a very small group of men who initiated and brought about this event. No doubt others had speculated about it in a more or less academic way, but it is possible, and indeed probable, that the first man of authority and influence, having actual responsibility for immediate construction, to suggest and urge steel cars was Mr. George Gibbs. Whether Gibbs first suggested this to Westinghouse, or whether Westinghouse first suggested it to Gibbs, does not seem to be a matter of prime importance. They worked together, and Westinghouse threw into the scale strong conviction and his influence and force. Another powerful man soon joined the movement, Mr. Cassatt, then president of the Pennsylvania Railroad.

The Rapid Transit Subway Construction Company had been formed to build the first subway railroad in New York. Mr. Gibbs was appointed consulting engineer in charge of the designing and installation of the mechanical equipment, which included road-bed, track, signals, and cars. Mr, L. B. Stillwell was consulting engineer in charge of the electrical equipment. They were set to do pioneer work. They were faced with a set of conditions that had never been brought together before. They had to consider and largely to contrive methods and materials to meet these conditions. Heavy and fast trains were to be run at short intervals, calling for volumes and potentials of electric current never before used in railway working, and this was to be done in tunnels just large enough to take the four tracks. Only an engineer, and not every engineer, has the background to enable him to realize the complications of the situation.

Before the mind of Mr. Gibbs arose the danger of fire with wooden cars, in case of a wreck or a short circuit. He talked often with Westinghouse about the danger and the possible precautions. Westinghouse asked why steel cars should not be used. At that time there were no railroad passenger cars built entirely of steel, and no one had seriously proposed them. Mr. Gibbs replied that he thought that a practicable steel car could be built, but the tunnel construction was well advanced and the time was short in which to design a car from the ground up and get it built, in quantity, for the opening. A great number of details must be worked out to get a car of acceptable weight, cost, appearance, and performance, going back to shapes not then made by the mills and involving new dies, rolls, and patterns. He had designed a wooden car, metal-sheathed outside and sheathed underneath with fireproof material. He proposed to install all wiring hi fireproof conduits and to suspend all apparatus below and out of contact with the underfloor. It was recognized that this did not fully meet the case, but it did diminish the fire risk.

Westinghouse was urgent and ready to help, and Mr. Gibbs undertook to design a sample steel car. He talked with Mr. Cassatt, who faced the same problem in the project for electrical operation of the tunnels into New York. Mr. Cassatt at once fell in with the plan and offered to have the car built at cost in the Altoona shops of the Pennsylvania. The car was designed and built. To save time, commercial shapes were used. Consequently, the car was not handsome, and it was too heavy to be finally acceptable; but it was the basis of a redesign. There was strong opposition to the innovation, not only amongst the subway people but in the shops where the car was built; but the hearty indorsement and reliable cheerfulness of Westinghouse were always sustaining, and the practical support of Mr. Cassatt was a great help. The interest of two of the most important car-building companies was aroused. They consented to make propositions to build 300 steel cars and to guarantee their delivery within a certain date at a reasonable price - about 10 per cent more than a wooden car.

Thus assured, Gibbs recommended that the first equipment of the subway should be all-steel cars. Of course there was a fight, and a hard one. Those who believed in the present expediency, if not the final superiority of fireproofed wooden cars, were many and strong and well intrenched. The matter got into the daily newspapers, and one great journal pointed out the appalling prospect of dreadful electric shocks to passengers imprisoned in a steel car charged with high-tension current. But the steel car won. Gibbs says: "Without Mr. Westinghouse's confidence and encouragement, and his insistence upon the safest possible construction for cars used in tunnels, and Mr. Cassatt's progressive policy in the same direction, it is evident that steel cars might not have been in general use today. Credit should be given also to Mr. Belmont (President of the Subway Construction Company) for his willingness to undertake what must have seemed to him to be an expensive experiment for the sake of providing the safest possible equipment."

COPPER

It seemed to Westinghouse that it would be an excellent thing if the Westinghouse interests could have their own supply of copper, or, at any rate, a supply. When the yearly output of a concern making electrical machinery runs into scores of millions of dollars, the item of copper bought is big. Obviously, with mines of its own the manufacturing company can have some control over prices, or at least share in the profits of high prices. When Westinghouse ventured into copper-mining, as in many other cases, he did not ask the Electric Company to risk company money; he risked his own. Naturally, a part of his venture was in search of new methods of reducing lean or refractory ores. That was inevitable with his temperament. Furthermore, to buy developed mines and to work them by familiar and customary methods would take too much capital, and would leave too small a margin of profit over interest charges, if any. To look for great unknown deposits of rich ore was a slow and uncertain way of attacking the situation; but there was always the chance of finding new ways of handling ore now unprofitable. In the same spirit Edison spent millions in trying to win the iron from the lean ore of the old mines of New Jersey by an elaborate and costly scheme of magnetic separation.

Westinghouse bought heavily in remote copper fields in southern Arizona where the ore was refractory, the haul to a railroad was long and hard, and water was scarce; consequently the purchase price was relatively low. In the plant at Pittsburgh which had been built for his fuel-gas experiments he began experiments with a new process for reducing copper ore, and he spent much money there, his own money, not the company's. He bought an old copper mine in Vermont as a convenient source of ore for experiment.

The net result is summed up in a cablegram which is a classic in the Westinghouse traditions. His multitudinous foreign enterprises, British and Continental, required the help of many strong financiers, and the Rothschilds had some part in them. This led to pleasant personal relations with several members of the family. When dining with Lord Rothschild at Newcourt, Westinghouse told of the process for reducing copper ore which he was working out at Pittsburgh. Lord Rothschild was particularly interested in this, and asked to be kept informed of the results of the experiments. A story was told at this dinner of a Chicago gentleman given to exaggeration and somewhat conscious of its perils. It was related that at another dinner party a man had described the hothouses of the Duke of Portland at Welbeck. The gentleman from Chicago said they could not compare in size with those of his cousin. One of these was 400 feet long, 300 feet high, and (then a friend kicked him under the table) - and two feet wide. Westinghouse went back to America. Months later his associate in London, Lukach, who was in relations with Lord Rothschild, and who had told the hothouse story, received this cable: "Process two feet wide. Westinghouse." All the code books in the office were searched in vain, but finally Lukach remembered that Westinghouse had promised to cable the result of the copper process.

Failing the development of a magic process for reducing refractory ore, the Arizona mine has not been profitable except during the short period of war prices for copper, but it is not without value, and is a part of the Westinghouse estate.

Chapter Fifteen - European Enterprises

WESTINGHOUSE'S plans for commercial expansion included the world. These vast plans must have become somewhat definite pretty early in his career. We have seen that three years after the air brake was started in America he was in England, and that within another year a Pennsylvania company was formed to handle export business. Nine years later the first English company was organized. This was soon followed by German, French, and Russian brake companies, and later by the brake companies of Italy and Australasia. As the electric field opened up, another group of Westinghouse companies spread over Europe. We find listed some twenty-two foreign companies, including a Hungarian automobile company.

Westinghouse wrote: "I have never had much difficulty in working out plans, but my greatest difficulty seems to have been in finding enough men to carry out such plans." It will be recalled that young Napoleon could not find a man in Italy, and the Pharaohs had to import ability from Asia. This difficulty in finding men is common to the human race. Lord Fisher said "the secret of efficiency is favoritism," which, being interpreted, is "when you find capacity grab it and push it forward, regardless of age or rank." This principle appealed to Westinghouse's practical common sense, and he acted on it often. Yet he was loyal to his men and had a punctilious sense of justice. He kept some men too long in high places, and he injected into the organizations some men who had later to be ejected - he being human.

In 1896 Westinghouse wrote a letter to an officer of the Westinghouse Electric Company, Limited (called the London Company), setting forth in some detail his idea of a vast scheme of foreign companies. At that time there existed, besides the London Company, the Westinghouse Brake Company, Limited, in England, and the Westinghouse Bremsen Gesellschaft, in Germany, all having broad territorial rights. The London Company was registered in 1889. The Westinghouse Electric Company (American) transferred to it all its patent rights for the whole world outside of North and South America. This was a trading and constructing company. It did not manufacture, but did install machinery on contract. The three brake companies, American, English, and German, covered the world, trading within their defined territories. The 1896 plan contemplated the formation of new companies - British, French, Belgian, German, Russian, and Austrian (to include the Balkan States). Norway, Sweden, and Switzerland, "should probably be reserved for the Westinghouse Company (British) as part of its territory." Italy is not mentioned in this letter but an Italian brake company was formed in 1906, and an electric company in 1907. These European companies and the parent companies in America were to take care of the habitable globe.

Trade relations within the companies were provided for. It might be advantageous for one company to sell or construct in the territory of another. This might be done on payment of a stipulated percentage fee. Patent rights were to be exchanged, as were drawings, plans, specifications, and engineering and manufacturing information. The shops and equipment of the Westinghouse Electric & Manufacturing Company and the Machine Company at East Pittsburgh were designed for the manufacture, not only of electrical material but of locomotives, steam and electric, and of stationary engines, steam and gas. The companies were prepared to contract for complete installations of shops and city railways. It was proposed to put the capacities and experience of the American companies at the service of the European companies. In short, it was proposed to provide for the most complete cooperation that jealous and narrow-minded men and broad and generous men are capable of.

Any man could dream such a dream, but not many men have the courage to try to make it come true, and the mental and moral forces to effectively back their courage. Westinghouse lived to see most of this dream become a solid reality.

In the plan of 1896 Canada was not included. In October 1896, the Westinghouse Air Brake Company (United States) began the purchase of land, buildings, and machinery in Hamilton, Ontario, with a view to the manufacture of brakes, and in the January following the Westinghouse Manufacturing Company, Ltd., was incorporated under the laws of Canada. In July 1903, the Canadian Westinghouse Company, Ltd. was chartered, and took over all the Westinghouse interests and operations in Canada - electrical, steam engineering, and air brake. This company still exists, strong and prosperous.

The British Westinghouse Electric & Manufacturing Company was organized in 1899. It built great and famous shops at Manchester, and became an important producer. It is counted amongst Westinghouse's mistakes. It was never successful financially and was a heavy burden upon the home company and upon Westinghouse personally. Nevertheless, it was a striking example of his prescience. Mr. Paul D. Cravath, who for many years was closely associated with Westinghouse, speaking to a gathering of the veterans of the Air Brake Company, said:

I am sure none of us has ever known a man who combined faith, imagination, and courage as they were combined in George Westinghouse. Those who are familiar with his enterprises are constantly finding new evidence of these qualities. A very interesting, almost dramatic, instance came to my attention in London during the last year of the war. I presume that most men would look upon the British Westinghouse Company enterprise as one of Mr. Westinghouse's failures. In one sense it was a failure. Yet the conception out of which that enterprise grew was the conception of a great man, although a man whose vision, imagination and courage carried him beyond the limits of prudence and business discretion. About two years ago perhaps the strongest group of industrial leaders in Great Britain made up their minds to enter the electrical field. They bought the British Westinghouse Company. One day during the last year of the war one of these men asked me to spend an evening with him and four or five of his associates and give them such information as I could about the early history of the British Westinghouse Company. Their leader asked me to explain to them the reasons that prompted Mr. Westinghouse to organize the British Westinghouse Company and build the great works at Manchester which until the outbreak of the war were larger than the business that the company had been able to secure would justify. I tried to give them Mr. Westinghouse's conceptions as I remember them: that the alternating current was sure to become the foundation of all central-station development; that England was an ideal field for the extensive use and distribution of electricity; that on a large proportion of the railroads the traffic was so dense that they were practically suburban roads according to American standards; that the most economical method of providing electric power for the United Kingdom was by great generating stations near the coal mines so that instead of distributing coal, electricity would be distributed; that instead of many central stations scattered all over the country there should be few; that as the financial structure of the railroad enterprises of Great Britain was such that they would find it difficult to raise new capital there should be separate organizations, separately financed, for developing the electrical power and selling it to the railroads. When I had finished my story the leader of the group to whom I was talking turned to his associates and said with real emotion: "This is most remarkable. The vision of Mr. Westinghouse is almost word for word our vision. The plans that he had formed are identical with the plans that we have formed and that we propose to carry through," and then he turned to me and said: "Mr. Westinghouse's conception of what should have been done was faultless. It was his misfortune that he was a quarter of a century ahead of the times. If Great Britain had accepted his advice countless millions of waste would have been saved. It will now be necessary to scrap enormous investments in un-economical plants to make way for the carrying out of Mr. Westinghouse's plan." He added that, "so conservative, so slow to adopt new ideas are the British people that even today the government will be compelled to apply the spur of legislation to compel the British nation to adopt the measures which were proposed by Mr. Westinghouse a quarter of a century ago, and which we are urging today." When he finished I said: "You must agree, gentlemen, that while Mr. Westinghouse may not have always been a prudent man, he was a great man." "Yes," said their leader, "Mr. Westinghouse was a great man."

What the newspapers of the time called the "Invasion of England" was a mistake, but it was the kind of mistake inevitable in the temperament of the man, the sort of mistake common in the history of the pioneering of civilization. Huxley said: "The advance of mankind has everywhere depended on the production of men of genius."

Two years after the formation of the British Company a Securities Company was organized to aid in the flotation of the securities of electric and power installations contracting with the British Company. Amongst other enterprises this company took over the electrification of the Mersey Railway, and the development of a power company in the Clyde Valley in which company Bonar Law was sometime Chairman of the Board. The Clyde Valley enterprise is so good an example of the working out of the central-station thought dominant in the mind of Westinghouse for many years that we are fortunate to be able to give the following account of it furnished by the present Secretary of the Clyde Valley Electrical Power Company:

The development of the electric power supply in Great Britain by power companies operating on a large scale over considerable territory, both industrial and rural, was the direct outcome of the greater freedom from restrictive measures granted by the Electric Lighting (Clauses) Act of 1899. Among the companies formed for this purpose was the Clyde Valley Electrical Power Company, which obtained from Parliament a franchise or act in August 1901, confirming to the company, the exclusive right for electrical power supply over the highly important industrial area formed in the valley and on the banks of the river Clyde in Scotland, and extending about 735 square miles. This area with its shipyards, steel works, blast furnaces, engineering establishments, collieries, etc., is a highly industrialized center of activity and an ideal one in which the advantages to the general community of electrical power generation and distribution on a large scale can be attained and demonstrated along the lines successfully adopted by the great American power undertakings. Such being the case it followed as a matter of sound policy that the work of carrying out, in its initial stages, this large enterprise should be intrusted to a company possessed of the necessary experience in similar work all over the world. The contract for preliminary work, which involved the construction of two large generating stations at Motherwell and Yoker with 8000 kilowatts of turbo-alternator plant and a comprehensive system of 11,000-volt mains with substations, radiating therefrom, was accordingly placed with the British Westinghouse Electric & Manufacturing Company, Ltd., Trafford Park Works, Manchester, then a branch works of the parent company in Pittsburgh, U. S. A. Work was commenced in 1902, and the installation was handed over to the operating company late in 1905, the cost running to 480,000.

Mr. Westinghouse took a deep and personal interest in the whole scheme, and was visiting the works shortly before the opening of Yoker Power Station in 1905. He was in regular touch with the company's progress, from its inception onward, being a firm believer in, and indeed one of the strongest exponents of, what is now the accepted practice of progressive countries, viz., the large, well-situated, central electric-power generating station with high-voltage transmission lines to industrial centers. The Power Company, which is, apart from municipal undertakings, the only one operating in the West of Scotland, is now a very large concern with three power stations, having 72,500 kilowatts of generating plant in use or under construction, 193 substations and switch houses, 285 miles of extra high-tension lines and cables, and 45 miles of low-tension lines and cables, and 45 miles of low-tension distribution cables. The Electricity (Supply) Bill, 1919, is a still further confirmation of the soundness of Mr. Westinghouse's views as to central generating stations, these stations, under the aegis of the electricity commissioners, as appointed under the act, being proposed at numerous favorable sites in Great Britain with every prospect of success.

An interesting side fact is that the cost of operation of the Clyde Valley Company is twenty-five per cent less than that of the Glasgow Corporation (Municipal) for the same kind of service.

Westinghouse began work in France early. In 1879, he established a little shop in Paris to make brakes. This was ten years after the beginning of the first brake company in America, and seven years after the first British brake company. This French enterprise was under the English company, but the installation and first manufacture were directed by an American from Pittsburgh as chief foreman. Operations began with orders from five French railroad companies, and in twelve years it was necessary to find room for growth outside of the city. Land was bought from the Duke of Orleans in the forest of Bondy, a mile from the nearest town and about thirty miles from Paris, and here was built a little town which they called Freinville (Braketown) in the Commune of Sevran. The works are on the Canal de l'Ourcq, with easy rail connections with the Northern and the Eastern Railways. This French enterprise has always prospered. Until March 1915, it was a dependency of one of the other companies; then it became independent as the Compagnie des Freins Westinghouse. Its war work was varied and much appreciated, especially the work of precision in range-finders and mountain guns. The works have lately been greatly enlarged to take care of important orders for switch and signal apparatus.

The French Company (Société Anonyme Westinghouse) was organized in 1901. This company took over from older companies the electric business and the brake business in France, Belgium, Spain, Portugal, Italy, and Holland. This is the most important foreign company after the British Westinghouse and the Westinghouse Brake Company. It was long unprofitable and a burden on the home company, but after eight years or so it turned the corner and it is now making money. It was another case of building in advance of the market.

The Società Italiana Westinghouse was organized in 1907 to execute contracts taken by the French company, a stipulation being that the machinery and apparatus should be built in Italy. The contracts included generating machinery and fifteen locomotives for the Giovi line, a state railway. A later order was for twenty-five locomotives, part of them for the Savona-San Giuseppe line. Works were built at Vado, thirty miles from Genoa, on a fine harbor. The managing director, the manager of works, and the commercial manager were Italians, and had been in the employ of Ganz & Company in the electrification of the Valtellina line. The success is partly due to this fact. The French and Italian companies were closely affiliated with the British Westinghouse Company, and control of them recently went into the hands of the British owners, the Metropolitan-Vickers Company.

The Russian Brake Company was started in 1898 to manufacture in St. Petersburg. An engineer who went from Freinville to help at the start writes: "The shops were ready to commence work. We had to choose a patron saint and erect a small permanent altar in the shops, after which the priest came and blessed the works, sprinkling holy water on each floor and machine. The saint chosen was St. George and the icon represented St. George and the Dragon." In spite of the high patronage of George of Cappadocia (Emerson might have said it was a logical consequence) the life of this Russian company was not always smooth but, on the whole, it prospered until the Russian Revolution - paid good dividends and strengthened its financial condition. Then began troubles which even St. George could not avert. Shop management by the workmen was demanded, and the project for general nationalization of industries soon came. Long negotiations followed, and they must have been ably managed by the local officials, for the company escaped both evils. A workman was put on the managing board and the chief engineer of the company was made a member of the Commissariat of Ways and Communications. When the decree was issued for nationalizing the large enterprises, "works manufacturing brake apparatus" were excepted. It soon became impossible to carry on the business in Petrograd for want of fuel and raw material, and arrangements were made to remove the works to Yaroslaff, on the Volga, and then the curtain fell. At the moment of writing nothing is known of the personnel or the works. [1]

From time to time various other European companies were started: the Westinghouse Electricitats Gesellschaft, the Société Electrique Westinghouse de Russie, the Westinghouse Cooper Hewitt Company, Limited, the Compagnie pour les Applications des Rayons Ultra-Violet in France, and another in Belgium; the Westinghouse Metallfaden Gluhlampen Fabrik Gesellschaft, Vienna; the Westinghouse Metal Filament Lamp Company, Limited, London; the Compagnie des Lampes a Filaments Métalliques, France, and still others.

It does not seem desirable to consider in further detail the various European companies. The plan of 1895 was always in mind and was pretty well carried out, but often with disappointing financial results. Writing in 1909, to the directors of the Electric Company, Westinghouse said: "The extraordinary growth of your business in America required the whole time of your best officials, so that neither they nor I had adequate time to effectively carry out the plans outlined. Nevertheless, there was established a strongly favorable financial situation which existed for several years, and a manufacturing record was created in Europe which has made the name a real power in business." These words were written two years after the panic of 1907 and the receiverships of several Westinghouse Companies. The triumphant and audacious note of the past years is not heard; but the old lion was still struggling to save for his stockholders what might be saved. Large equities were saved. All of the important companies except the Russian Electric Company are still operating.

The results of the world plan cannot be estimated for years to come. They will not be developed for years. It is not at all probable that they will ever develop, as Westinghouse hoped, into a great system of allied companies co-operating closely under one central management. It is not certain that such a development was ever practicable or desirable. But those bold and varied enterprises carried the air brake into Europe and Australasia, and so helped on the evolution of transportation. They made familiar to British and Continental engineers and financiers the distribution of energy by the alternating current, and that spread abroad the fundamental idea of the central power station. Thus they stimulated and advanced the manufacture of power and pushed along the industrial revolution, the most important phenomenon of the nineteenth and twentieth centuries.

[1] A gentleman who saw the works in July 1921, writes (Sept. 20) that about 200 men were at work. "They produce some air brakes, carts for the army, and farm implements which they use to exchange with the peasants for their wheat, etc." The manager received 300,000 rubles a month, plus rations of bread, butter, a little sugar, etc. He was bartering away his clothing and other things to live.

Chapter Sixteen - Financial Methods, Reorganization, Equitable-Life Episode

THE enterprises founded and organized by Westinghouse are using not far from a quarter of a billion dollars of capital. Their financial structures are of his building. The capital was raised by him almost unaided, often in the face of opposition. Those companies now stand as his financial monument, and yet when some of his companies were in rough and deep financial waters one sometimes heard it said: "Westinghouse is a great inventor but he is no financier." It is a common error to try to separate the qualities of a man into pigeonholes. It is just as reasonable to say that a man has moral courage but not physical courage, which is, perhaps, a distinction without a difference. They are not separate qualities but two manifestations of one quality. To finance Westinghouse brought the same qualities that he brought to the organization of his enterprises and to mechanical and electrical invention. He looked out upon his world with imagination, courage, hope, enthusiasm, and determination. He brought to bear upon his projects a gift for analysis; capacity for concentrated, sustained, and powerful thought; broad and fertile inventiveness and quick resourcefulness. All of these qualities and faculties we have seen exercised, over and over again, in other fields of his activities; they are to be seen also in his financial plans. But, like all strong men, he had the defects of his qualities.

To do great things one must be self-reliant. That is a commonplace. George Westinghouse was often too self-reliant in mechanical things; perhaps, he was oftener so in financial things. It is related that the board of directors of one of his European companies once rejected his proposition. When he insisted that it was for the good of the company and should be adopted, the chairman said that it was the privilege of the board to determine the policy of the company. Westinghouse replied that this was quite true, but it was his privilege to say who should sit in the board. He voted a majority of the stock. In 1890 a group of bankers offered to lend money to the Electric Company if they could name the general manager. Their offer was rejected without discussion.

These little incidents show the fundamental difference which often stood between Westinghouse and the bankers. They would not be responsible for financing his enterprises unless they could have a strong, if not controlling, voice in the organization and administration. He would not give up control to any man or group of men. There were elements of right on both sides. Bankers are responsible for the money of their clients. Their obligations as trustees are more compelling than their strictly legal obligations, if the two can be separated. On the other hand, Westinghouse saw the weaknesses of divided control, in plans and in execution. He saw that which folks call the timidity of capital. Napoleon said: "There is no greater coward than I when I am drawing up a plan of campaign. I magnify every danger, every disadvantage that can be conceived. When once my decision is made, however, I forget all except what may carry it through to success." Perhaps Westinghouse had not enough of Napoleon's kind of timidity in planning; certainly he had Napoleon's audacity in execution. He threw everything into the attack with perfect confidence in the quickness and resourcefulness of his own tactics. The bankers said that he did not think enough about his reserves.

It is said elsewhere in this book that Westinghouse valued consultation; that was one of the reasons why he was so well served. This is precisely true. He consulted philosophers and bankers, administrators and machinists, and then he made up his own mind, and nothing milder than an earthquake could budge him. We have seen him sitting like a rock, serene, gentle, and unmoved when every member of the board of directors was against him. Whether he was determined or just obstinate depends upon your point of view. The result of such fundamental differences of opinion was that Westinghouse usually had to do his own financing. He did it with great ability and ingenuity, but it may have been unfortunate that he tried to do it at all. It absorbed a prodigious amount of time and energy in doing what could have been as well done by specialists, leaving him free to do things that they could not do.

For the reasons just given, Westinghouse's enterprises, especially during the early periods of development, were not financed through groups of strong bankers and syndicates, which is the customary way of financing large enterprises. He secured capital for his enterprises by personal appeals, largely to his friends and to his stockholders. In this way enormous sums of money were invested in his enterprises by persons who relied on their faith in Westinghouse. He had such an impelling personality and such a remarkable power for effectively presenting his case that he frequently secured large sums of money from men of wealth. [1]

Westinghouse also showed his faith in his enterprises by investing his own money with the greatest liberality. Many of his new enterprises were financed at the beginning with his own funds, which he procured by selling, or borrowing upon, his holdings of the securities of the seasoned enterprises which had already become successful and established. He several times imperilled his fortune and his credit by investing practically his entire fortune in his enterprises when others lacked the faith to invest. The result was that more than once he was personally financially embarrassed when his enterprises were able to take care of themselves. They were solvent, although temporarily their shares of stock, in which Westinghouse had invested, had so declined as to affect their availability as collateral for the personal loans that he had incurred to finance his enterprises.

Westinghouse's procedure necessarily involved very heavy borrowings both by himself and by his companies and brought periods of embarrassment; but the fact that the enterprises were essentially sound enabled them to pass successfully through every period of financial stress. At no time did Westinghouse show his faith, courage, and resourcefulness more than in two or three periods of financial crisis when almost all of his associates and financial advisers had lost their faith. The result of this policy was that although Westinghouse died with but a moderate fortune, he left all of his enterprises sound and prosperous. On the strength of the foundations he had laid, after his death his principal enterprises, and more especially the Electric Company, were able to make very large flotations of securities simply because the foundations were sound. It is part of the tragedy of his life that he did not live to see the complete fruition of his plans.

The more one thinks about the Westinghouse doings in finance as well as in science and in commerce, the more must he feel the power of a personality, and of an idealistic personality. It would be hard to find an organization in which personality has such a place as it had, and still has, in the Westinghouse companies. All the American companies have their veterans' associations made up of men who have been twenty years or twenty-one years in the service. The association of Electric and Machine Company veterans has over 1300 members. In Japan is an organization of over eighty men who had more or less training in Westinghouse companies in America. (There are about 400 such men in Japan.) These include admirals in the navy, officers of the imperial railways, and other men in high position. In London is another organization of old Westinghouse men. When these men meet for a dinner the important toast is "Our Founder." They are never tired of hearing about him. Adequate reasons for this feeling will be apparent to any one who has the patience to read this book, but we venture to point out one reason which may not be immediately apparent. Westinghouse was always working for ideals. He was always trying to produce a perfect air brake, and this is true of everything else that he touched. Of course the commercial result was in his mind, but that was only incidental. Commercial success was bound to come automatically, and so were other desirable results, like the prosperity of his employees; but the present thought was always to do larger and better things. Such a spirit at the head, incarnate in a man of such charm and force, was sure to pass down through the ranks.

While Westinghouse's head was in the stars, his substantial feet were on the ground. The idealist stood, foursquare and solid, before his facts. This situation is always interesting but it is sometimes awkward. Here is an instance: A project was up for electrifying a little piece of steam railroad with dense traffic. It was in the beginning of that kind of use of electricity. Direct current had been settled upon for the good reason that the methods and apparatus were much more developed than for alternating current. The General Superintendent of the railroad was present at a little dinner-party at which Westinghouse talked freely, and even ardently, of the advantages of alternating current. As the party was breaking up, the General Superintendent seized the writer and said: "Look here, Mr. Westinghouse scares me to death. Are we making such an awful mistake in using direct current?" The commercial men were scared, too, but they took the contract. In principle Westinghouse was right, in its immediate application he was a little indiscreet. But the blazing indiscretions of a bold and honest man are amongst the things that make us like him and follow him. Nelson was indiscreet when he went into action with his stars shining on his breast. When his officers remonstrated, he said, "In honor I gained them; in honor I will die with them" and he was killed by a sharpshooter in the enemy's tops. He was not prudent or logical, but his stars and his spirit shone through his fleets and saved England. High spirit flowed down through the Westinghouse companies and left enduring love, loyalty, and enthusiasm. A corporation can have a soul.

In considering the financial operations of George Westinghouse it should be remembered that they were always for his companies first, for himself second if at all. He never speculated. He made almost no investments except in the securities of his own companies. He repeatedly bought their stocks and bonds to help in their financial plans. His identity with his companies was complete. He did not try to get rich except as an incidental result of their prosperity. One recalls the matter of certain options. He sold one of his smaller companies, having first got options from the other stockholders at a definite figure. He sold at a price higher than the agreed option price. He did not pocket the difference, but distributed it amongst the stockholders whose options he held. If he had retired at forty-five and given the rest of his life to careful investment and to scientific research and invention, he would have had ease and comfort, and have done a great deal for the advancement of civilization. Probably he would have been alive and active today, for he died of overwork. But we might as well speculate on what would have happened if a glacier had not moved. Westinghouse did what his nature compelled him to do, and his financial methods, like all his other doings, were an expression of that nature.

THE REORGANIZATION OF 1908

The organic risks of the Westinghouse method of finance, as described above, culminated in the disaster of 1907. The Westinghouse enterprises had spread over the civilized world. Their requirements for working capital were immense. Westinghouse paper was scattered amongst comparatively small holders, as has been told, and when the severe and wide-spread money crisis of 1907 came his loans were called. He was protected by no powerful group of bankers. The consequence was receivership of three of his companies - the Electric Company, the Machine Company, and the Security Investment Company. The Electric Company was very much the largest of these. Its debt, funded and floating, was $43,000,000 and, including its outstanding stock, its total liabilities were over $70,000,000. A careful student of finance and economics has written that this was "the most considerable mercantile failure that America has ever witnessed." The Air Brake Company and the Union Switch and Signal Company had no debts and ample cash, and the Canadian Westinghouse Company was in a sound condition.

It took fourteen months to put into effect the plan by which the Electric Company was taken out of receivership and returned to the stockholders, and in the meantime other plans, contrived by able financiers and lawyers, had failed. Westinghouse, more than any other man, worked out the simple and novel plan which succeeded, and high authority has said that nobody but George Westinghouse could have carried it out. The plan was called the Merchandise Creditors' plan, and the committee of these creditors cooperated ably and loyally and with rare perception and foresight in preparing the plan and in carrying it out. By the plan the merchandise creditors took stock in settlement of their claims, and so ran more risk than any other class of creditors. Their courage and vision were gratefully recognized.

Mr. Cravath, whose broad experience in corporation affairs is well known, says: "In at least two great financial crises, when the financiers had given up the task as hopeless, Mr. Westinghouse, by his faith, by his untiring energy, and by the exercise of his power to influence men, which I have never seen equalled, was able to weather the financial storm, raise enormous sums of money, and restore his enterprises to a sound financial position when his critics and most of his friends were certain that he had suffered a crushing defeat. It was inevitable that a man of his boldness should have financial setbacks, but he never suffered financial defeat."

The outcome of the reorganization of 1908 is thus told by Mr. Arthur S. Dewing: "The debt of the company was actually decreased from $43,000,000 to $29,000,000 and the interest charges were cut from $2,600,000 to $1,600,000. The capital stock was increased from $28,000,000 to $41,000,000. A large debt rapidly maturing and carrying heavy charges was changed into a stock liability with no fixed charges. This, in brief, was the actual accomplishment of the Westinghouse reorganization."

One element of this plan was a subscription to $6,000,000 new stock to get working capital. Of this, Westinghouse himself subscribed $1,500,000 and over 5000 of his employees subscribed $611,250, a fine testimony to the spirit of loyalty and confidence amongst the men who had worked with him for years.

When the plan went into effect a new board of directors was elected, of which more than half represented the bank and merchandise creditors. A proxy committee was formed to insure the permanence of the new management. Westinghouse remained as president, but with powers considerably limited. In 1911 he gave up definitely any effort to recover his former controlling position and his official relations with the Electric Company ceased, but his name remains as one of its great assets. The immediate force of his prodigious ability and of his inspiration was in a measure lost to the company, but he had built the structure on solid foundations and it is still illuminated by his spirit.

THE EQUITABLE-LIFE EPISODE

Westinghouse always had the confidence of his stockholders and of the public. He stood before the nation as a high-minded, sincere, unselfish citizen, who was seeking to do his duty and to be honest and fair to the public and to the investors in his enterprises. The reputation he had thus earned was responsible for his choice to fill a very important public post, to which he gave his best qualities of mind and character.

All remember the bitter controversy regarding the management of the Equitable Life Assurance Society, which culminated early in 1905, which made and unmade several reputations, and which launched Mr. Charles E. Hughes on his distinguished public career. It transpired that the absolute control of the management of that society was vested in a young man, the only son of the founder, Henry B. Hyde. The father was a man of colossal ability and enterprise. It was charged that the son was using his power over the company with its $400,000,000 of assets, representing the savings of over 6,000,000 individuals without full regard to the interests of the policyholders. The leader of the opposition to the management was James W. Alexander, the president of the society. The two factions rivalled one another in charges and counter-charges, with the result that the safety of the great institution, and indeed the position of the life-insurance companies generally, was in peril. At that juncture, in June 1905, Mr. Thomas F. Ryan stepped into the arena, and bought the majority of the stock of the Equitable Society, having a par value of only a little over $50,000 and entitled to earn only 10 per cent dividends. Mr. Ryan paid for this stock $2,500,000 and publicly stated that his purpose in making the purchase was to save the Equitable Life Assurance Society from the disaster which threatened to cause untold injury to the policyholders. In order to demonstrate and carry out his excellent purpose, Mr. Ryan determined to turn over the voting power of his stock to three trustees whose honesty and disinterestedness and intelligence should be so conspicuous that no one could question their motives. He chose as the three trustees Grover Cleveland, in many ways the foremost American citizen, Morgan J. O'Brien, the presiding judge of the Appellate Division of the Supreme Court of New York, and George Westinghouse. George Westinghouse had no personal relations with Mr. Ryan, and was chosen solely because of his reputation for honesty, fair dealing, and unselfishness, which was of course true of the others. The appointment of these gentlemen was broached in an identical letter dated June 9, 1905, addressed to Messrs. Cleveland, O'Brien, and Westinghouse, an extract from which follows:

I have purchased this block of stock and propose to put it into the hands of a board of trustees having no connection with Wall Street, with power to vote it for the election of directors, as to twenty-eight of the fifty-two directors in accordance with the instructions of the policyholders of the Society, and as to the remaining twenty-four directors in accordance with the uncontrolled judgment of the trustees. This division of twenty-eight and twenty-four is in accordance with a plan of giving substantial control to policyholders already approved by the Superintendent of Insurance.

I beg you to act as one of this board with other gentlemen, who shall be of a character entirely satisfactory to you.

I would not venture to ask this of you on any personal grounds; but to restore this great trust, affecting so many people of slender means, to soundness and public confidence would certainly be a great public service, and this view emboldens me to make the request.

Mr. Cleveland's answer so well expresses the feeling of the three trustees that an extract from it is given:

After a little reflection I have determined I ought to accept this service. I assume this duty upon the express condition that, so far as the trustees are to be vested with discretion in the selection of directors, they are to be absolutely free and undisturbed in the exercise of their judgment, and that, so far as they are to act formally in voting for the directors conceded to policyholders, a fair and undoubted expression of policy-holding choice will be forthcoming.

The very general anxiety aroused by the recent unhappy dissensions in the management of the Equitable Society furnishes proof of the near relationship of our people to life insurance. These dissensions have not only injured the fair fame of the company immediately affected, but have impaired popular faith and confidence in the security of life insurance itself as a provision for those who in thousands of cases would be otherwise helpless against the afflictive visitations of fate.

The character of this business is such that those who manage and direct it are charged with a grave trust for those who, necessarily, must rely upon their fidelity. In those circumstances they have no right to regard the places they hold as ornamental, but rather as positions of work and duty and watchfulness. Above all things, they have no right to deal with the interests intrusted to them in such a way as to subserve or to become confused or complicated with their personal transactions or ventures.

The Board of Trustees was organized with Mr. Cleveland as chairman, and Mr. Ryan put before them this statement:

I am the sole owner of the 502 shares of the stock of the Equitable Society which I purchased from Mr. Hyde, and no other person or interest has contributed, or has the right to contribute, a single dollar toward the purchase of the stock. The policyholders with whom I conferred in making the purchase have had no connection with the management of the Equitable Society and their connection with the transaction was entirely advisory. I am under no obligation to any living man with respect to my action as the owner of this stock.

A deed of trust, prepared by Elihu Root and Paul D. Cravath, was signed by Mr. Ryan and the three Trustees on June 15, 1905. This deed transferred to the Trustees the 502 shares of the Equitable stock owned by Mr. Ryan (the total was 1000 shares) "for the purpose of vesting in the trustees the right to vote" the stock in such a way that out of fifty-two directors twenty-eight shall be policyholders and selected by the policyholders, and twenty-four shall be selected by the Trustees "in their sole discretion." The Trustees were also authorized to take any action necessary to carry out the plan for mutualization of the Society. The Trustees were empowered to fill vacancies in their own board, and the agreement was to continue in force five years and "thereafter so long as the Trustees shall deem advisable."

The Trustees then proceeded to follow out the spirit of the preferences of the policyholders and to elect as a majority of the Board of Directors of the Society policyholders chosen by the body of policyholders. It goes without saying that the Trustees acted in the broadest spirit without in any way seeking to advance the interests of Mr. Ryan or any other interests than those of the Society. In this way the mutualization of the Society, that is, the transferring of control to the policyholders, was accomplished indirectly, although under the then state of the law it could not be accomplished directly. The foundations were laid for the ultimate legal mutualization of the Society, which did not occur until about ten years later. The result of the action of Mr. Ryan and the Trustees was to end the scandal in the Equitable Life Assurance Society, to regain for it the confidence of the public and the policyholders, to install a sound management, approved and supported by the policyholders, with the result that the Society entered upon a new period of confidence and prosperity, which continues to exist. Indeed, the Equitable episode has worked out to the great good of life insurance in general, and every one knows what an important business that is.

[1] Amongst his assistants in this personal financing should be especially mentioned his financial secretary, Mr. Walter D. Uptegraff.

Chapter Seventeen - The Personality of George Westinghouse

RELATIONS WITH HIS MEN

AFTER reading the record of the activities of George Westinghouse, some notion of the man must remain in the mind as a by-product. Now, let us look at him a little closer, and we shall first consider his relations to those who worked for him. Those relations were so close, so natural and sincere, that they are revealing.

The attitude of Westinghouse toward the men in his employ was not that of "uplift." It was not the outcome of any theory of sociology or economics. It was not conscious and deliberate altruism. It was just man-to-man comradeship and good feeling - the most natural thing in the world. He respected the men and liked them because it was his nature to. He was kind to them because he was kind. He was just to them because he was just. They were not a different kind of men from bankers, lawyers, doctors, ministers, and engineers. They were men and he had lived amongst them in the friendliest relations since he was bora. Such was the foundation of his simple policy toward labor and of his welfare schemes. When the beautiful Welfare House of the Air Brake Company was opened at Wilmerding, the writer was asked to speak for the directors before a considerable audience of workmen. He thought that it was rather clever to point out that this was no philanthropic enterprise that the directors realized that it was good business to make the men and their wives and daughters more comfortable, and to help to improve the physical and mental and moral situation. Westinghouse showed signs of uneasiness, but the speaker went on with that complacency which sometimes attacks sensible men when they get a chance to make a speech. When the time came Westinghouse popped up and said that the directors recognized their obligation to the men who were helping to carry on the job. The men enjoyed the situation more than the orator did. Thereafter he, like Mr. Pliable, "sate sneaking among them."

It was logical that Westinghouse should spend money to keep the men at work through hard times. An old employee says: "Mr. Westinghouse was very thoughtful about his men. During the panic in the early nineties, and others following, he always told our foreman to find us something to do. During my service I was never laid off." A foreman of those days says: "During the panic of 1892 many men were laid off at the Electric Company. I laid off some of our men, but Mr. Westinghouse said: Get those men back to work; I am not hard up. He was away about three months. The first thing he asked me on his return was: 'Did you and your men get your pay?'" Of course this policy is common amongst intelligent employers for several excellent reasons, and Westinghouse was too acute" not to see all those reasons and feel their force, but it is doubtful if they much affected his conduct. His men were part of his family, and his attitude toward them was mostly a matter of instinct.

One phase of the family feeling is shown in this statement from a man who was appointed acting general superintendent of the Electric Works in 1888, still the days of small things in the Electric Company. "After I had been on the job a week or two, Mr. Westinghouse startled me somewhat by informing me that he had so many personal experiments under way at the works that he reserved the right to go direct to any superintendent or foreman in the shop to give instructions and confer on their work without speaking to me about it. I objected strenuously to such an arrangement, and tried to make it clear that I could not maintain discipline when the president of the company went over my head to my assistants with orders and instructions which would take precedence over my own; but, of course, it was no use. Mr. Westinghouse had his way, and I had my troubles."

An old hand says: "Mr. Miller, our foreman, informed eight of us men that we had to work the following day, it being New Year's. Mr. Westinghouse put in a full day at the works, and I can assure you we put in a busy one, with no stop for dinner. So we finished our day's work about five o'clock. Mr. Westinghouse said: 'Miller, those men have worked hard today, and have not had any lunch.' So he gave us a fifty-dollar bill to get lunch with, which sum was mighty big in those days."

Westinghouse was just by instinct, by inheritance, and by family tradition. In practice, his average of justice was high. Sometimes he did not try very hard. He had wholesome prejudices and greatly enjoyed them. Doctor Johnson said that one good prejudice is worth a thousand reasons, and Huxley said: "I love my friends and hate my enemies - which may not be in accordance with the Gospel, but I have found it a good working creed for honest men." Westinghouse did not formulate for himself any such rules of conduct. He never bothered himself to analyze his own emotions; but he did not always go far out of his way to be reasonable, although he took pride in being a reasonable man. He closed a debate about two men against whom he was much prejudiced with the question: "Why do you always stick up for crooks?" The lack of discrimination would have shocked an "intellectual," but it was final.

It would be a waste of time to try to assess the relative value of policy and feeling in Westinghouse's attitude toward his men, but feeling was a big part of it. He was fond of young folks; he liked clean men; he enjoyed courage, candor, and courtesy. To an executive vice-president he said: "I want you to employ none but gentlemen." After going through the works a visitor asked: "Where are your old men?" Westinghouse answered, "We have no old men; I believe in young men for a new business," and looking back now one realizes how young they were. With this spirit as a foundation, there was built up a splendid corps of energetic, enthusiastic, and able young men, with a fine feeling of cooperation. Amongst these young men there soon grew up an institution famous in the annals of the Electric Company - the Amber Club. This club Westinghouse helped with money until the members told him that it could stand alone, and he always helped it with personal interest. He used sometimes to spend a part of a Sunday afternoon at the club with his "boys." The roll of this club bears many names since become eminent, amongst them the names of four presidents of the American Institute of Electrical Engineers - Scott, Mershon, Lincoln, and Townley. All of those men think now with pleasure and gratitude of the inspiration which they drew from contact with the great and generous personality of their chief. This contact had qualities which must be rare in combination. It seemed close and genial. It seemed so simple that it was almost intimate. But there was a border-line of dignity and of deep respect that was never passed; never even closely approached.

It is pleasant to look back through the years and see the ethical effect upon those young men of close association with George Westinghouse. It was like being with a good father. The talk was never didactic; it was conversation. It was always about worth-while things; never about mean things. If gossip became too personal, he would say: "Well have no backbiting." An old officer of one of the companies was presiding at an informal dinner at which Mr.

Westinghouse was not present. A youngster told a risky story. "Boy," said the chairman, "you know Mr. Westinghouse would not like that." The youngster sat humiliated and ashamed. There soaked into the mind of those young men, unconsciously, not only lasting contempt for what was off color but deep disdain for cunning and craft, and for dishonesty, moral or intellectual. They learned, too, to be careful not to boast. Westinghouse had a fine fund of irony and sarcasm which he poured out on the braggart with especial joy. The writer told one evening of an adventure with Indians in the Rocky Mountains in which he thought that he had shown unusual courage and quickness of mind. Westinghouse said: "Did you ever think that perhaps the Indians were having fun with you?" Poor vanity! How it curled up in his presence! AJI English barrister once said to the writer: "English justice comes high, but it is prime." This seemed sometimes to be true of education by Westinghouse. The process was not always agreeable, but the result was prime. In the early days of the electrical companies they had to put into responsible places men just out of college, for the work required knowledge of kinds of mathematics and physics that the older engineers did not have. Even the language was unknown to the older engineers. To such a group of young engineers the Westinghouse Electric Company was a postgraduate school with George Westinghouse as dean. They were lucky fellows to come under a dean who gave them an ethical start, not by precept but by practice.

Feeling often entered more than was judicious into his selection of men, and, like the late J. Pierpont Morgan, he liked to have handsome men around him, although he did not have Morgan's unusual aesthetic sense. One day out of a clear sky Westinghouse asked the writer: "Do I make many mistakes choosing men?" It was a hard question to plump at a hired man in that abrupt way. We all knew that he had made many such mistakes, and a few serious ones, and a careless answer might call for specifications. He probably would say: "I suppose I made a mistake in hiring you." The answer was: "With your qualities and experience, you ought to make none, but you are often quick on the trigger." He mused a few minutes. At such times it was interesting to watch his face, and try to guess what was going on. Presently he said: "Yes, there was So-and-so, whom I thought of for the head of such a company. I asked him to stay with me a couple of weeks, and I found that he had no business in him." Nothing more was said. So-and-so was a man of distinguished social position and of some achievement, but his selection for one of the most important places that Westinghouse had to give would have been unfortunate, perhaps disastrous.

Of course he had parasites, sycophants, and flatterers. What man of place and power ever escaped them? He was not always entirely immune to them, he having some trace of human vanity, but we think of no case where their influence lasted long or did much harm. He used to say that he saw well when the lights were out. We knew that he sometimes put incompetent men into high positions, and that his instinctive loyalty sometimes kept men long after their unfitness had become notorious. But this was not altogether damaging to the organizations. It is fundamental that loyalty in an organization must begin at the top. If an administrator expects loyalty in his staff he must be loyal to the staff. Few leaders can have had greater loyalty from his followers. "Once a Westinghouse man, always a Westinghouse man," was the motto of his associates; and few were the instances where one who had enjoyed his friendship and confidence failed him. As one of his lieutenants who took exception to certain of his plans said after an interview which had promised to be stormy: "When the old man looks at you with that smile of his, there is nothing you will not do for him."

With his soft voice, his kind eyes, and his gentle smile, he could charm a bird out of a tree. It is related that in a knotty negotiation it was suggested to the late Jacob H. Schiff, then the head of a great banking-house, that he should meet Westinghouse. "No," said the astute old Jew, "I do not wish to see Mr. Westinghouse; he would persuade me." His gentle and always ready humor was a help even hi the process of persuading or charming bankers. But it was not always gentle. In one of his British enterprises he decided to accept the help of the X Company. He told Lord Blank, with whom he had been negotiating in the same matter, and was warned that the X Company were greedy people who demanded exorbitant terms for their financial support. Westinghouse said that he quite agreed that they were greedy, for they were asking nearly as much as Lord Blank himself wanted.

Lord Cromer said: "I should term most of the leading British officials in Egypt humanitarians under any reasonable interpretation of that term, but the responsible nature of their position naturally obliges them to look at the questions with which they have to deal from many and not from merely one point of view." He stated a broad principle, applicable indeed to all responsible men, with the exceptions inevitable to all general principles. At the moment we may apply the principle to great industries in general and to the Westinghouse Companies and George Westinghouse in particular. We take the Air Brake Company as the oldest and always the closest to his heart. As the dealings of Westinghouse with his men, from vice-presidents to sweepers, rested on the solid foundation of his own nature, they were simple and consistent, generous and broad. These dealings, like all of the other doings of this self-reliant man, flowed naturally from his own character.

From the organization of the Air Brake Company in 1869 to this day, there has been a steady policy in all of the Westinghouse Companies of cooperation with the men, for the spirit of George Westinghouse still abides there. The "open shop" has been maintained in all of the Westinghouse organizations. It has often cost money and trouble, of course, but there has been no departure from the principle. And the shop has been really open. No man has been discriminated against because he was a union man or a non-union man. Even I. W. W. agitators and organizers have been treated with uniform tolerance. Presumably, an arrogant or narrow-minded foreman or superintendent has cropped up here and there; but the writer, having a broad and intimate knowledge of the companies, has no doubt of the scrupulous fairness with which the open-shop principle has been followed.

It is generally accepted that Westinghouse started the Saturday half-holiday in large works in the United States, having seen its operation in England. Whether or not that is exactly true, he was the pioneer in the Pittsburgh district. On June 1, 1881, he announced the Saturday half-holiday in the Air Brake Works, and it was an established custom in all his other plants as they came along. To us now, the chief interest is that the innovation is an example of the feeling of the innovator.

Westinghouse had no gift for abstract speculation, and it did not interest him. His thoughts on welfare were always in concrete terms. A veteran officer of the Air Brake Company writes: "Mr. Westinghouse said that in his judgment one of the most serious problems in the development of the country along right lines was the proper housing of the masses that were flocking to our industrial centers. He intimated that he had given the question much thought, and, if his affairs permitted, would be glad to attempt its solution along business lines, and yet in the spirit of the highest and most practical philanthropy." In 1889 the Brake Works were moved from Allegheny (now part of Pittsburgh) to a site about fourteen miles east of the city, on the Pennsylvania Railroad, in the Turtle Creek Valley. There the town of Wilmerding was built around the new shops. It is as distinctly a brake town as Crewe is a London & Northwestern Railway town, or Essen a Krupp town. The company still owns more than half the houses after selling many to employees on monthly instalments. It has helped generously in town matters in building and supporting schools, churches, and parks, but it has refrained carefully from attempts to influence town politics. Radical socialistic influences have sometimes prevailed, and troublesome men have been elected to office, but the company has gone serenely on, and let the radicals dig their own graves.

When the plant went to what became Wilmerding, there was but one building on the site of the town to be. A building plan was made, having in mind topography, water supply, sanitary disposal of sewage, and roads. Good houses were built, and practically all of those houses still stand - stanch and serviceable. They have gas, water, electricity, and baths, and a large proportion of them have lawns and gardens. Barracks and monotonous rows of operatives' houses were not built. Many years ago the company established lawn and garden contests, with cash prizes for lawns, flower culture, vegetable gardens, window and porch boxes, and for the best-kept grounds as a whole. A committee of five award the prizes. Three members of this committee are elected by the competitors, one is the company's gardener, and the fifth is a non-resident landscape gardener. Thus the little town has become a focus of taste in a commonplace and even dreary region. Conditions did not lend themselves to such enterprises at any other of the American works, but at East Pittsburgh the Westinghouse Electric and Manufacturing Company is pushing forward an excellent housing plan, a little out of the town.

The enlightened employer of labor long ago learned to take good care of the men in the shops. That has become so customary in large establishments as to be commonplace, and yet the means are always interesting. Westinghouse thought much of safety and sanitation in his shops. Standards and methods have changed radically since he began to build, but his shops, built in the eighties, are still modern in heating, lighting, ventilation, water-supply, and drainage. As one walks about in them, he often thinks that the men at work are a good deal better off than in their own homes. One finds there, too, little emergency hospitals, with operating room and pharmacy, all complete and modern, and with surgeon and nurse. Prompt treatment of a wound often saves long disability or the loss of an arm, or perhaps a life. It adds to the well-being of the man and to the wealth of the nation, and the employer knows that it is money in his own pocket, so his altruism rests on a solid base.

Benefit associations have always existed in the Westinghouse shops - that goes without saying. Ordinarily, they are financially quite independent of the company, which, however, bears the expense of administration and medical examinations. There, except for moral support, the company's part ends. Monthly assessments of 50 cents to $1.50, graduated by wages, have, in the case of the Brake Company, built up a surplus of over $86,000 in seventeen years. Originally, both sick and accident benefits were paid to members, but two years before the passage of the Workmen's Compensation Act in Pennsylvania, the Air Brake Company established a Workmen's Compensation Fund provided solely by the company, out of which disability arising through accident received compensation upon a much more liberal basis than that established by the act subsequently enacted and, later, amended. Relief payments are larger, and begin on the day that the accident occurs. The law requires no payment for the first ten days of disability. The company pays all hospital and surgical expenses; the law sets a maximum limit, beyond which the employer is not liable. This fund is supported entirely by the company, without cost to the workmen.

It is obvious that the cheapest and best way to take care of factory injuries is to prevent them. The Westinghouse Companies have been diligent and enterprising in developing the art of mill safety, and, in this, the old Air Brake Company has been a leader. The result is shown by the fact that now, with a personnel of approximately 5000 employees, serious accidents are almost unknown. Safety matters are under a chief inspector and a committee of eight employees, with, also, the plant fire chief. Each committeeman has his own territory, but at irregular intervals he invades the territory of other committeemen. This plan of cross-inspection brings to light risks that an eye grown accustomed to them might not see. The committeemen are concerned with safety, sanitation, and comfort. They have regular weekly meetings, and get extra pay. The chief inspector has authority to act immediately in an emergency. It is not suggested here that such things are peculiar to the Air Brake Company or to the Westinghouse group. They have become commonplace with all enlightened employers of labor. Anyone who has been in touch for many years with the great industrial corporations knows that in the last quarter of a century they have had well in mind the humanitarian and economic bearings of safety.

The most comprehensive and beneficent relief institution of the Brake Company is the pension system, established in 1906, eight years before the death of Westinghouse. The employee pays no premium; service alone entitles him to a pension. He is retired at seventy, and may be retired at sixty-five, in certain circumstances. After retirement he is pensioned. The pension is continued to his dependents after his death. Further, and of much greater import, if any employee, after having been a member of the relief department for two years, dies before reaching the age of retirement, and while still in active service, his dependents are pensioned. The scheme was worked out with the help of an eminent actuary, and provision has been made for the payment of all pension obligations, even if the Brake Company should become insolvent or go out of business. A plan so liberal and so unusual could only be put in force by a prosperous company.

This very excellent pension system did not originate with Westinghouse, but was worked out with his active and indispensable support. For its origin and development, Mr. John F. Miller, then Secretary of the Company, and later its President, is more responsible than any one man, and its establishment simply carries forward the Westinghouse spirit, which is the large thing for us to have in mind now.

About the time of the organization of the pension system in the Brake Company, the Union Switch and Signal Company put in force a plan for the sale of its stock to employees. This was successful and popular amongst the men, and had excellent results in at least two ways. The men who became stockholders took a new attitude toward the company, and the habit of saving spread and grew. This was soon seen in the neighboring savings-banks. This, again, like the pension system, could only be done safely by a prosperous company. In later years, the Westinghouse Electric and Manufacturing Company introduced a comprehensive and liberal plan of group insurance.

In 1907 a "Welfare Building" was put up by the Brake Company at Wilmerding, and, about the same time, a small but adequate building was erected nearby, for women. The Welfare Building is admirably complete, with auditorium, gymnasium, swimming pool, classrooms, and reading rooms. The operation of the building was handed over to the Young Men's Christian Association, and the Young Women's Christian Association took the management of the women's building. Thus the buildings became of general use to the people of the valley. One result is that the Wilmerding Y. M. C. A. has become the second in size in Pennsylvania - larger than the Pittsburgh Y. M. C. A. Here, general classes are carried on in a variety of subjects, and lectures are given by specialists from all over the country. Besides these, there are technical classes for the apprentices in the shops. The boys put in eight hours a week for nine months in the year. They are paid their hourly shop rate while attending classes. Many of the graduates from these classes now hold high executive positions. A similar but much larger school has long been carried on by the Electric Company the Casino Night School. Very much of the same sort of work, educational and social, is done for the girls and young women of the works and the neighborhood.

PERSONAL CHARACTERISTICS

Westinghouse had a considerable advantage over his fellow mortals in his physical stature. He had a greater advantage in his mental stature. Both were the gift of the gods, and, if one is to do eminent things, he must start with the favor of the gods. We often hear of the "masters of fate." Alfred the Great and Julius Caesar are said to have been epileptics (which we may doubt), and Alexander Pope is known to have been a crooked and fragile invalid; but in all such cases we find uncommon energy of will and power of mind. It is a pretty safe general proposition that success is a constitutional trait, and "for performances of great mark, it needs extraordinary health." This Westinghouse had in a splendid body, and in that body was housed a powerful mind which worked swiftly, and without heat or friction. He stood well over six feet and was strongly built. When he raised his great right hand, palm toward you and fingers a little spread, and said in a gentle voice and with a hint of a smile, "But you don't understand," it was quite plain to the dullest mind that the sooner he understood the better for him.

His commanding presence was not merely a matter of size and proportion; he had the subtle quality of distinction. If he sat in a box at the opera or walked through a crowded waiting-room, the stranger would think: "Who is that distinguished man?" As the years went on, and his face was softened by gray hair and ennobled by the habit of responsibility and power, the air of distinction grew.

He had dignity which protected him from familiarity, but he was simple, unaffected, and instinctively cordial in his manner - what we like to call democratic, but might better call aristocratic. His manners and his language were exactly the same with princes and with machinists, and with his old negro butler, which seems to be the height of good breeding. He respected the workman and the prince, the justice of the Supreme Court and his butler, just as he respected himself, and on that basis rested his intercourse with his fellow men. Along with this basic self-respect and respect for others, went a natural kindness. It hurt him to hurt the feelings of another. This was the foundation of his unfailing courtesy. Being human, he was sometimes impatient, but he remembered and regretted impatient speeches that a smaller man would not have thought twice about. His self-control was such that his closest associates find it hard to recall any show of anger, but he did often disarm his antagonist by the genial smile which reflected the kindness of his heart.

In the few hours of ease which he gave himself in a life of prodigious toil, he was a charming companion, genial, courteous, and sympathetic. Unfortunately for his friends, and unfortunately for the world, he did not give himself enough hours of ease. His life long, Westinghouse was temperate in everything but work. He never smoked. Until middle life he hardly knew the taste of wine or spirits. In later years he took a glass or two of wine with his dinner, and perhaps a glass of brandy or liqueur with his coffee after dinner, but that was all. His table was bountiful and handsome as became a man of wealth and position, but he chose simple food and ate moderately.

Hospitality was his greatest diversion, and in this he was ably assisted by Mrs. Westinghouse. It was their normal life to have several guests in the house, and to have a dinner-party every night. The varied company included distinguished men of many lands. One recalls having met there, not merely as dinner guests, but as house guests, Bonar Law, Baron Takahira, Earl Grey, an eminent Russian general, and Lord Kelvin, to say nothing of Americans of the highest position. This may be taken literally, for at least one President of the United States was his guest as far as affairs and conventionalities permitted. For many years such people frequented his home, drawn partly by matters of specific business or scientific interest and partly by the combination of dignified thought, broad outlook, wise judgment, brilliant speculation, and gracious manner which they found there.

It is no very uncommon thing to see American country boys from the farms and the small shops rise to high positions and become the companions and friends of the great of the earth. We become familiar with such careers in the land of opportunity. It has been said that "there is no magician like the enlightened human will," and we might add, "when it works in the mental and moral stimulus of freedom." So we like to think of Westinghouse as the normal result of our institutions.

Westinghouse did not work for wealth. Money to him was merely stored energy, to be used to extend industry and to do good. He recognized the duty of producing proper returns to those who invested in his enterprises, but his own dividends were constantly reinvested in the further development of those enterprises. He might have retired in middle life a comfortably rich man, but he chose to spend his life in gigantic toil. He enjoyed power; but that was only an incident in his career, not an end. Like all noble minds, he enjoyed the approbation of the discriminating, and he was always solicitous that no reproach should attach to the name Westinghouse; but he did not work for glory. He had honorary degrees, but no one ever heard him called doctor; he had decorations, but no one ever knew it from him, and his medals were not displayed in his houses.

One underlying motive actuating his life was perhaps best expressed to an intimate friend while subject to the solemn influence of a walk through Arlington Cemetery, where now his body rests beside that of Mrs. Westinghouse. The friend, solicitous as to the health of Westinghouse, urged him to rest from the work which threatened to break down even his robust constitution, adding that he had already accomplished vastly more than other men and possessed all the wealth that he could require. In a thoughtful manner Westinghouse replied: "No, I do not feel that it would be right for me to stop now; I feel that I have been given certain powers to create and develop enterprises in which other men can find useful and profitable employment, and so long as I am able, it is my duty to continue to exercise those powers." The great spirit within him could tolerate no ease but drove him forward remorselessly. Morley says of Cromwell's wish to withdraw from public life: "The inspiring daimon of the mind prevented it."

We have seen in technical detail, the things that George Westinghouse did as an engineer and an inventor. We have seen something of his doings in organization, administration, finance, and trade. We have considered his relations to those who worked with him and we have looked at him physically and socially. Let us now try to estimate some of the qualities of mind and soul which enabled him to do what he did. Emerson said, "there is not yet any inventory of a man's faculties." Far be it from us to try to inventory George Westinghouse, but we may pick out a trait here and there.

Perhaps his most important faculty was imagination. This was of the creative rank, like that of the empire builders, like, for instance, Clive and Cecil Rhodes, or like that of great poets and painters. This is not to make comparison in degree, but in kind. He was not introspective. He bothered himself little about his own gifts, and he was perhaps unconsciousness of the power and quality of his own imagination. Talking one evening, about young men to hire and train, he said: "Get boys with physique and memory, and you can make men of them." The reply was, that he had overlooked the most important quality. "What's that?" asked Westinghouse. "Imagination," said his friend. For some minutes he did not answer, and when he did, it seemed as if this was an element that he had not thought much about. Some one said that Daniel Webster was a steam engine in breeches. George Westinghouse was an imagination in breeches, walking about over the face of the earth, and doing things that changed the face of society, just as birds sing. But although not a bit introspective he was not unconscious of the meaning of his work. He saw in a large way the consequences of his inventions and activities. He knew perfectly well that he was building for nations and not for parishes. It was often hard for his subordinates and associates to follow him in his estimate of consequences, and in detail he was often mistaken, but in the broad results his vision and his faith were splendidly justified.

Next in rank we may put fortitude, which is courage in adversity, and which is one of the noblest attributes of man. There were black moments in the life of Westinghouse. There were times when his bravest associates thought that his enterprise must go on the rocks; but his serene courage was never dismayed. In his saddest reverses, the splendid spirit flamed on, unquenched.

Closely allied with fortitude is audacity, a quality less noble, but useful in execution. Lord Fisher said of Nelson: "The key-notes of his being were imagination, audacity, tenderness." We cannot think of Westinghouse saying, "kiss me, Hardy," as he lay dying. He had tenderness, as we constantly saw, but it was shy and was never expressed in words. He had imagination, as is obvious to the world. His audacity was Nelsonian. He would have "Copenhagened" the Danish fleet, or would have engaged the French fleet at the battle of the Nile, just as gaily as Nelson did - and, in the Nelson philosophy, "the boldest means are the safest." An audacious youngster of twentyseven, Westinghouse invaded England with his still undeveloped brake. Fortitude and audacity won a great victory for the brake, after the Burlington trials. His Chicago World's Fair enterprise was pure audacity, and it was audacious to fight the scientific world at Niagara.

Westinghouse's persistence was proverbial amongst those who were near him his life long. Nothing but fate could tear him loose from his purpose. This was shown somewhat amusingly in an affair to be described shortly, when we take up his education. It will be seen that for thirteen years he persisted in an engineering fallacy against high authority. Many times the quality was costly in time and money, but a ledger account of his doings would show an immense balance to the good.

When Huxley first sailed into the harbor of New York, he was attracted by the tugs as they tore fiercely up and down and across the bay. He looked long at them and finally said: "If I were not a man, I think I should like to be a tug." He saw energy and power combined and compressed. Many of us have been put to inconvenience by Westinghouse's remorseless energy. Unlike the tug, it did not seem restless. It went smoothly on, without effort, but as inevitable as the flowing of a river.

In the first chapter it is told that in a certain eleven years, Westinghouse took out 134 patents, started six important companies which still exist, took the air brake through its one great crisis, and, most important of all, started the alternating current revolution in industrial history. How could mortal man do so much? We have told of his strong body and perfect health, of his powerful mind which worked swiftly, and without heat or friction, and his imagination, persistence, and energy. But his gift of concentration has not been mentioned. He could close his mind suddenly and completely. He took a subject into a water-tight compartment, and there he and the subject were alone five minutes or five hours, until he was ready for another subject. He could handle simultaneously and without confusion or waste of energy a dozen companies in two hemispheres. So, when financial waters were rolling deep, he could find rest in a new kind of blading for a turbine, and another sort of rest in a new friction draft gear. Perhaps things got jumbled in his dreams, but they were kept in their own places when he was awake; and, as he had perfect digestion, it is unlikely that he dreamt much.

It is a commonplace that concentration is a necessary element in effective mental work, and all methodical men try to discipline their minds to concentrate; but Westinghouse never consciously disciplined any of his faculties, for he was the least introspective of men. Nor did he ever have the discipline of systematic education, of which more will be said presently. Along with his unusual concentration went unusual memory, which is a function of concentration - a result. Upon the intensity and singleness of interest must depend the depth of the impression made on the brain cells, and that is memory. It was a proverb amongst Westinghouse men that you must not tell the "old man" anything that you did not wish him to remember ten years from now. Files, and records, and memoranda were little part of the machinery of his life. He never carried a note-book or a pencil. Things stowed themselves automatically in his mind, and they came out when they were wanted. The power of association - a great help to memory - was strong with him. Perhaps Smith, whom he had not seen for a year, came in. "Good-morning, Smith! Has your wife got quite well? You were wrong about the efficiency of that gear. It is 10 per cent better than you thought," and Smith, who had forgotten that his wife was indisposed a year ago and had forgotten what he thought about the gear, would be astonished and flattered.

The prodigious output that has just been mentioned, was made easier by quick and versatile resourcefulness. Mr. Albert Kapteyn of Holland, who had important places in the air brake organization for many years, writes:

It was always a treat to see him at work to solve a problem in the workshop, drawing office, at home, or anywhere else. One could almost see the wheels go round in his brain. His resourcefulness was something marvellous. When one solution did not satisfy him, he had instantly several others ready at hand, as if his brain was a storehouse of original ideas and as if he had only to take them out as wanted. I remember an important interview we had with some chief engineers of the French railways, who had a favorable opinion of his brake, but they pretended that they wanted several additional things. This one wanted the brake to do this, the other, something else, and I had a strong impression that they wanted to test his capacities as an inventor, or perhaps to embarrass him. Instead of avoiding them, Mr. Westinghouse rather enjoyed this game, and said to them: "Gentlemen, I really don't think that you can want such things in daily use, but if you are interested how such questions could be solved, let me show you!" And he proceeded then to give most original and practical solutions of all they had asked, which made them exclaim: "This is a most marvellous man! He will readily invent anything you like!" He always realized so completely the interrelation of cause and effect that it seemed as if, to him, the apparatus was made of glass, and he worked with the greatest ease, as if playing.

It should not be overlooked that this resourcefulness was not limited to mechanical matters. It was shown, time and again, in company organization, in trading and in finance. Andrew Carnegie, who was a pretty good judge of men, said: "George Westinghouse is a genius who can't be downed."

Westinghouse attacked with energy and audacity, and he held on with tenacity and fortitude, and he was completely self-reliant. People who did not know him very well are apt to think of him as imperious and self-sufficient. Nothing could be further from the fact. He was self-reliant, not self-sufficient.

Morley says that "Cromwell had that mark of greatness in a ruler that he was well served. No prince had ever abler or more faithful agents...Nobody knew better the value of consultation." This mark of greatness Westinghouse had too, in kind; we need not try to estimate the degree. One is tempted to follow further the likenesses of these two iron men - so dominant and compelling; so tender, loving, and loyal, so wise and modest - but such a comparison might seem extravagant. We may be content to see that "one star differeth from another star in glory," and admire both stars. The point in mind now is, that Westinghouse, like Cromwell, knew the value of consultation, from which flowed the fact that he was well served. He communicated to his staff the sacred fire. They came to have a respect for him. They served him not only as a duty, but with devotion and esteem. It is true that the other man did not always know that he was being consulted. Westinghouse never revealed his whole mind - not from craft, but partly from inborn reticence, partly from incurable shyness, partly because his mental process was so swift that the man who was being talked to, or consulted, could not keep up. One was often reminded of something Huxley said about Darwin: "Exposition is not his forte (and his English is sometimes wonderful). But there is a marvellous dumb sagacity about him, like that of a sort of miraculous dog, and he gets to the truth by ways that are dark" - dark to the slower mind. Those of us who have read a little mathematics have often met the phrase, "whence it follows," a dozen intermediate steps being omitted; and to us it did not follow at all. Such situations often faced the man who was "consulted" by George Westinghouse. He sometimes rejected advice and opinion to his own serious Joss, as the greatest men have done - being human. Napoleon's ruinous mistake, Russia, was made "against the remonstrances of the men whom he consulted. In brief, Westinghouse sought freely and respectfully the opinion of those about him. He put that opinion through the mill of his mind, and made his own decisions. He had one of the attributes of genius the capacity to withdraw into the loneliness of his own soul, and there to conceive and meditate, and then to act. After all, can really great things be done in any other way? Whether the result is good or bad, must depend on the qualities of the soul. He had this attribute of genius and many others. It is easy to say that a man is a genius. The term is so vague that it fits almost any large and unusual combination of endowments. We have tried to show that Westinghouse was a good deal more than a genius. He was a man of balanced character, which a genius may or may not be. He had high and simple standards to which he was consistent. He was strong and he was gentle. He was acute and he was sincere. Carnegie was quite safe in saying that he was a genius and Kelvin was quite right in saying that he was great in character.

EDUCATION

It will be remembered that Westinghouse enlisted before he was seventeen, was mustered out at the end of the Civil War, still under nineteen, and that he went to college three months, and then went back to the machine shop. There his formal education ended. All of his schooling after he was thirteen was about a year and a half. His life gave him an ample education in the Henry Adams sense, but of systematic and disciplined education he had little; but from his speech and writing no one would have suspected that he was not university bred. This is evidence not only of his own taste, but of the sound English that he heard in the home of his childhood - the Bible English brought over by the colonists and still spoken by country folks in the old colonies.

Some of us who knew Westinghouse well, have often speculated whether or not he would have been a greater man if he had had a formal and conventional education. Gibbon says in one of those sweeping generalizations in which he delights: "The power of instruction is seldom of much efficacy except in those happy dispositions where it is almost superfluous." Westinghouse was one of those "happy dispositions." The education of the schools seemed "almost superfluous." With the power and quality of his mind he could easily have been eminent in physics and mathematics. Thorough training in those branches of knowledge would have saved him time, money, and energy. It was a tedious and costly process to learn the hard and fast limits of those records of experience which, for convenience, men call laws of nature, by actual demonstration in the metal; but without the knowledge acquired by other men and stored in books, it was a necessary process. The man who could understand and intelligently discuss the deep and subtle speculations of Lord Kelvin was not ignorant of the laws of nature, and Westinghouse had quick, just, and deep perception of the relations and action of natural forces. He did things that the text-books said were against the laws of nature, and, in course of time, the text writers caught up with him. On the other hand, he did things that the text-books said were against the laws of nature, that his engineers protested against, that cost time and money, and that ended on the scrap heap, that great institution of which Mr. Don J. Whittemore, Past President, Am. Soc. C. E., once said: "The scrap heap that inarticulate witness of our blunders, and the sepulchre of our blasted hopes; the best, but most humiliating, legacy we are forced to leave to our successors, has always, to me, been brimful of instruction." Few men have made so copious and so instructive contributions to the scrap heap as Westinghouse. His scrap heap is there, visible to mankind, and when one is in a pedantic mood, he may incline to think that it would be smaller if Westinghouse had possessed more of the stored learning of the ages, or had felt more respect for authority. That is quite possible, although even a pedant is not always safe from mistakes. We have Carlyle's word that Robespierre was a man of strict, painful mind; that he was a logic formula, but he made a horrible scrap heap and eventually scrapped his own life.

The deeper we dig into Westinghouse's scrap heap, and the more we know of the circumstances of its creation, the clearer it appears that it was mostly the result of courage. He had the courage of the habit of success, and he took risks, well knowing that they were risks, confident in the insight, resourcefulness, and persistence that had often carried him through. A considerable exploration of that scrap heap reveals the fact that it grew largely from experiments in which the text-books would have been of no help at all, and the outcome of which no professor of physics could have known by the light of pure reason. Professor Bartlett said: "Mechanics, in the hands of those gifted with the priceless boon of a copious mathematics, is a key to external nature." Granted, but it may be doubted if a committee made up of Archimedes, Newton, Laplace, Kelvin, Rankine, and Bartlett, could have reasoned out the best size for the ports of a brake valve. Westinghouse spent many thousand dollars, and sent much good gray iron back to the cupola to find that out, and he knew all the time that he would find it out.

Early in his career Westinghouse had an encounter with a certain law of nature which may have had something to do with the hardihood of his usual attitude toward those laws. In 1878-1879, the Galton-Westinghouse Brake Tests were carried out in England. They are famous, and have profoundly affected the air brake art. They are described at some length elsewhere in this book. One important discovery made by Westinghouse and Captain (later, Sir Douglas) Galton was that, under the conditions of their experiments, the coefficient of friction rises as the relative speed of motion of two surfaces in contact falls. But in 1781, Coulomb laid down certain laws of friction which were confirmed by Morin in 1830-1834, and became laws of nature. One of these laws is that "friction is independent of the velocity with which the surfaces slide one upon the other." The Galton-Westinghouse tests showed that friction varies inversely as the velocity. They were fully and admirably described in three papers read before the Institution of Mechanical Engineers (British) in 1878 and 1879. Nevertheless, recent text-books on physics say that "friction seems independent of velocity," and that "friction is independent of the rate of motion." The truth seems to be that the Morin "law" still holds for the range of his experimentation and that the Galton-Westinghouse "law" holds for the pressures and speeds of their experiments, and that the custodians of the laws of nature should use due diligence.

Finally, while we may feel sure that Westinghouse would not have been hampered by awe of formulae or respect for authority, the question with which we started, as to the relation of education to greatness, in his case, remains open as an interesting topic for debate.

In reviewing Mr. Leupp's "Biography of Westinghouse," one of the great engineering journals of England said: "Westinghouse was not a trained engineer...apart from his air brake, he is more rightly regarded as a great manufacturer than as a great inventor or a great engineer." Presumably that reviewer would not call Archimedes a trained engineer, or Leonardo da Vinci or Watt or Stephenson. They never heard of Sadi Carnot's "Motive Power of Heat," or of Rankine's "Civil Engineering" or Bartlett's "Analytical Mechanics." They did not go to the Ponts et Chausées, or the "Boston Tech," or pay a thousand guineas to sit five years in the office of an eminent engineer in

Westminster. But they contrived to do famous things in engineering, not to say immortal things. There seem to be several kinds of training.

Westinghouse had one encounter with the laws of nature which illustrates well some of the things that happened to him for lack of training in theory, and the laws won. It illustrates, too, his persistence. It is known only to a small group of engineers. In reading Lord Kelvin's philosophical and mathematical papers, he came upon one written in 1852, which took hold of his imagination. This was upon "The Economy of Heating and Cooling Buildings by Means of Currents of Air." Lord Kelvin (then Professor William Thomson) showed that by the extraction of heat from the atmosphere by suitable apparatus, requiring 0.288 horsepower to drive it, thirty-five times as much air could be raised thirty degrees fahr. in temperature as could be raised to the same degree by the direct expenditure of the heat equivalent of the 0.288 horsepower of energy. That is, if the entire heat energy of one pound of coal were converted into mechanical energy in a perfect thermodynamic engine, that would, by extracting heat from surrounding objects (the atmosphere), raise as much air thirty degrees in temperature as would the perfect combustion of thirty-five pounds of coal. Professor Thomson suggested the essential features of a mechanism to do this.

Westinghouse meditated long on this principle. He concluded that it might be applied practically to heating and cooling buildings and to refrigerating, and that an excess of power might be developed that would be available for other purposes. He speculated deeply on the matter, and designed some of the apparatus, and by much ingenious and subtle reasoning thoroughly convinced himself and more than half convinced some excellent engineers. He drew up preliminary specifications for a patent and sent them to Lord Kelvin. It was his purpose not only to heat or cool buildings, but actually to generate useful power in excess of that required to set the mechanism in motion. Lord Kelvin, being a true and loyal friend and a scrupulous gentleman, cabled back immediately on receipt of the specifications, and the sanguine letter transmitting them: "Heat of atmosphere cannot be utilized to generate power. To prove this, I am writing and sending printed books." He did not intend to let his friend make a mistake, and followed the cable the same day, with a letter, giving references to passages in the books. About the same time, an engineer in the Westinghouse Machine Company wrote to Westinghouse: "I hope it is no intrusion for me to call your attention to a fundamental law of thermodynamics which you appear to have misunderstood after reading Kelvin's paper. I do this not for the purpose of dissuading you from experimenting (as I believe you would probably never feel entirely satisfied without making the experiments) but in the hope that it may enable you to interpret the results which you are likely to obtain," which showed astuteness as well as candor. We all remember that "John P. Robinson he sez they didn't know everythin' down in Judee." Perhaps Westinghouse had some such notion.

Briefly stated, the thermodynamic principles involved are that the heat of the atmosphere may be concentrated by expending power derived from an external source. If the concentration is through a range of only a few degrees a large quantity may be concentrated by expending a small quantity of power. The heat thus concentrated may be used in a heat engine to again produce power by undergoing degradation of temperature; but the power produced by the degradation of this concentrated heat can never, under any conditions, equal the original power from the external source used in concentrating the heat. Westinghouse recognized the authority and the respectability of this dictum, but to him it was not a law, universal and unqualified, until he had seen the proof. He could not "feel entirely satisfied without making the experiments."

Less than a month after his cable, Lord Kelvin wrote in answer to further letters from Westinghouse: "You should indeed think no more of this chimera of utilizing the heat of the atmosphere for motive power." And again, in the same letter: "The thermodynamic activity of the heat you will get must be greatly less than that of the heat supplied to the machine." Westinghouse valued informed and judicious opinion, but he was not awed by the authority of a great name. Only eight years before the letter just quoted, he had met and defeated a group of the most eminent physicists and electricians, led by Lord Kelvin himself, in the discussion over the use of direct current or alternating current in the first Niagara Falls hydroelectric development. He had long ago ceased to shrink from measuring himself with any man - if he had ever had any such shrinking. He writes to Lord Kelvin: "I duly received the books - and read the paper that you thought clearly demonstrated the impossibility of utilizing the heat of the atmosphere for power purposes. After most careful study of the paper, I came to the conclusion that it did not meet the case at all." He adds: "I fear you have come to the conclusion that I have already wasted a good deal of time on this subject, but as my work on the apparatus is, in a measure, a pastime, I shall not lose anything. On the contrary, I find that I have already gained a good deal from this work in connection with other matters." Lord Cromer said of Chinese Gordon: "A man who habitually consults the Prophet Isaiah when in a difficulty, is not apt to obey the orders of any one." The man who faces a difficulty as a form of sport - the greater the difficulty, the greater the sport - will not always be governed by the opinion of philosophers, however eminent.

Westinghouse followed this particular pastime with his usual purpose, to win the game. That which has been told above, took place late in 1900. In November 1901, he put the matter before Professor Dewar of the Royal Institution, London, asking for a report on his patent specifications. In ten days, Professor Dewar answered that "the specification explicitly claims perpetual motion." The reasons are set forth, briefly but adequately, and the report ends with these words: "For these reasons the proposals in the specification will undoubtedly fail to achieve their object; and there is no possibility of any modification of them leading to success." In Colonel Roosevelt's delightful letters to his children, he tells of wrestling three times a week with two Japanese wrestlers. "I am not the age or the build to be whirled lightly over an opponent's head, and batted down on a mattress without damage - my right ankle and my left wrist and one thumb and both great toes are swollen enough to more or less impair their usefulness, and I am well mottled with bruises elsewhere. Still I have made good progress, and they have taught me three new throws that are perfect corkers." Dewar's throw was a perfect corker, but it did not stop the sport. Three years later, Westinghouse asked for a report from a learned and ingenious engineer associated with him in work on reducing gears for marine turbines, MacAlpine. He reports (implicitly) that the heating and cooling principle is theoretically sound, but that the "cumbrous apparatus would consume so much energy by friction that in practice no economy could be realized." The power proposition (no part of Kelvin's project) is "perpetual motion. It violates the second law of thermodynamics, in the form given to it by Professor Thomson (Lord Kelvin)" which law "is not likely to be overthrown by any simple mechanism." Thereafter the matter languished, but it never lost all its interest, for as late as 1913 there are references to it in Westinghouse's letters; but in later years his serious thought was in the direction of heating and cooling, rather than power.

What has just been told is an extreme example of Westinghouse's independence of mind. He was not "entirely satisfied without making the experiments." He accepted nothing on a great name or a great position. But it must not be inferred that he was lightly sceptical. Far from it, he was a reverent man in mind and soul. This was his attitude toward religion, toward the State, toward the courts, toward the family, and toward his father and mother. He respected established things; he revered high and fine things. This was not a matter of reason, but of instinct. When he was a young man he joined a church, and his lifelong he was an orthodox Christian. He was never interested in religious speculation, and he gave little time or attention to religious observances, but to the end of his life there was no sign of any loss of faith.

Chapter Eighteen - The Meaning of George Westinghouse

A PROFESSIONAL biographer says, "the first office of the biographer is to facilitate the proper reaction between biography and history." Perhaps so. The man who undertakes to write the life of George Westinghouse does not need to ask what this wise-sounding saying means, nor does he need to have such a purpose definitely in mind. The life lived by George Westinghouse was history; not a history of wars and politics, but of something greater. As we have lately seen, to our sorrow, war and politics sometimes block the advance of civilization for generations. The Great War, by an appalling destruction of property and a more appalling destruction of the flower of the race, has set the world back by years that cannot even be guessed at. The things that concerned Westinghouse were all, every one of them, fundamental things in the advance of civilization. We have been more or less conscious of this as we have looked at them in detail. Now let us sum up.

Just what did George Westinghouse mean to the world? Few rulers of nations have done so much for mankind, for he was an agent of civilization acting in the new era. He belongs to the generations. All of this will be better understood as the years go on, and as scholars and philosophers analyze the influences at work in the last part of the nineteenth century and the first part of the twentieth century to carry forward the evolution of transportation and the manufacture of power. These are major causes in the progress of the race in that new era into which we have entered within a century and a half.

We shall first consider transportation. It is a famous saying of Macaulay's that, "of all the inventions, the alphabet and the printing press alone excepted, those inventions which abridge distance have done the most for civilization of our species. Every improvement of the means of locomotion benefits mankind morally and intellectually as well as materially." This idea long ago passed into the common intellectual stock of mankind. Nobody questions it.

In 1890, Mr. Abram S. Hewitt was awarded the Bessemer Medal for his distinguished services to society in the development of the iron and steel industry. In receiving that medal, he said:

The Bessemer invention takes its rank with the great events which have changed the face of society since the time of the Middle Ages. The invention of printing, the construction of the magnetic compass, the discovery of America, and the introduction of the steam engine are the only capital events in modern history which belong in the same category with the Bessemer process...The face of society has been transformed by these discoveries and inventions...First, the cost of constructing railways has been so greatly lessened as to permit of their extension into sparsely inhabited regions...Second, the cost of transportation has been reduced to so low a point as to bring into the markets of the world crude products which formerly would not bear removal...I think it is doubtful whether any event in modern times of equal significance has occurred. Sir Henry Bessemer has certainly been the great apostle of democracy.

Through the ages serfdom has been not merely a matter of laws and customs, but also a consequence of the cost of carrying goods, and the cost and difficulty of movement of the individual. Cheap and abundant transportation has released man from his bondage to conditions, and given him his opportunity. Mr. Hewitt spoke in fine and just terms; but there have been other apostles of democracy working in the field of transportation. Amongst them were George Stephenson and George Westinghouse. It is not necessary to try to fix their relative rank; there is glory enough to go around. Westinghouse's best-known and probably his most important work in the field of transportation was in power braking. Close after this come power signaling and switching. Power braking and signaling became automatic almost from the start. Another improvement in the apparatus of transportation, originated and developed by Westinghouse, is the friction draft gear. The importance of this in reducing the cost of transportation is known to railroad men, but the public has never heard of it.

The ultimate effect on the art of transportation of the work of Westinghouse in the field of alternating current especially, and in the electric art generally, cannot yet be estimated, but it may possibly be greater than the effect of any other one of his activities. That will depend upon the direction in which electric traction develops, but it is already very great.

No adequate conception of the immense importance of this group of activities can be had except by considering them all together as part of the great art of land transportation. The weight of trains, the speed of trains, their frequency and regularity of movement, as now seen as a matter of course, would have been impossible without the automatic power brake. But weight, speed, frequency, and regularity are not merely matters of public comfort and convenience; they are elements in the cost of moving passengers and goods. By the combination and adjustment of these elements the greatest use is got out of the units of track, of equipment, and of man power. The humanitarian service of the air brake in saving life and personal injury appeals first to the imagination of the public, but that is the least of its services to mankind. In the reduction of cost of carriage it has helped to "change the face of society."

The same things are true in a less degree of automatic power signaling. Excellent signaling can be done by man power, as is done in the British Islands, but it is costly when wages are high. Automatic power signaling, like power braking, is one of the "improvements in the means of locomotion which benefit mankind morally and intellectually as well as materially."

Let us stand on the platform at a subway station hi New York. Presently a long train comes roaring out of the darkness, running at speed, and one thinks it is not going to stop. Suddenly the speed slackens and directly the train stands, with admirable precision, at its proper place. A few seconds later it roars away again into the darkness, and in another few seconds another train follows, with the same performance. And so on, hour after hour and day after day the procession of trains passes with unerring regularity. It is a most remarkable feat of transportation, and it is one of the sights of the world. To one who has knowledge enough and imagination enough to realize what it means in the use and control of power, and in service to mankind, it is one of the most impressive sights.

Or, let us stand at a wayside station on a great railroad, where there are four tracks, and just beyond a yard with a dozen tracks with all the necessary crossovers and turnouts. Above is a group of brilliant signal lights. A train of a dozen sleeping cars hauled by two locomotives thunders by at sixty miles an hour, shaking the earth, and goes its proper way through the maze of tracks, still at sixty miles an hour.

Only a few years ago such things would have been physically impossible, and they are possible now only through the development of the air brake,

Westinghouse's own invention, and the development of the art of signaling and interlocking, in which he was a bold and fertile pioneer.

These phenomena are part of the movement of passengers. A more important matter is the movement of freight, for the cost of moving freight and its regularity affect every civilized human being every moment of his life. Even the savage hi the wilderness is not entirely free from the effects of this fundamental element of society. The cost of our food, our fuel, our clothes, our building material, and our tools is constantly dependent on the cost of transportation. In the United States freight costs are the lowest in the world, and this is especially important because we are the greatest producers of foodstuffs and of the products of the forest and the mine, and because our hauls from producer to consumer are so long. In the United States, too, the tons of freight moved one mile per head of population is probably the greatest in the world; but a positive statement is a little dangerous because ton-mile statistics are not kept in some of the great nations.

It would be idle and, indeed, invidious to try to apportion the credit for the growth in the United States of the art of carrying freight, but to Westinghouse, to his inventions, his courage, his faith and skill, a splendid part of that credit belongs. Mr. Hewitt was speaking of the reduction of the cost of transportation when he said: "I think it is doubtful whether any event of equal significance has occurred in modern times."

Renan says that the capital event in the history of the world was the establishment of the Christian religion. The capital event, he says. The improvement of the means of transportation was not an event, but an evolution, proceeding through the centuries. This evolution stands with the Christian religion, with the written alphabet, and with the art of printing amongst the major things that have influenced the progress of mankind, since mankind emerged from barbarism into civilization. In the list of men who have done most for this evolution we may put four names at the head - George Stephenson, Robert Fulton, Henry Bessemer, and George Westinghouse.

The contributions of Westinghouse to the development of the modern system of land transportation were only part of his services to "the civilization of our species." It is fairly questionable if they were the most important part. A few years ago an eminent American engineer, Mr. George S. Morison, produced a striking group of addresses which, after his death, were published in a little volume under the title, "The New Epoch as Developed by the Manufacture of Power." Mr. Morison cited the ethnical epochs which have marked the development of the human race, viz., the use of fire, the invention of the bow and arrow, the use of pottery, the domestication of animals, the manufacture of iron and, at last, the invention of the written alphabet. Then came historical civilization and the ethnical periods were considered as closed. But Mr. Morison held that it only needed a new capacity to make an epoch in civilization as distinct as those in primitive society. Such a new capacity was found when men learned to *manufacture power*. That is not to create power, "but to change inert matter from one form to another in such a way as to generate power." Not only does the manufacture of power mark a new epoch in development, but the change is greater than any that preceded it; greater in its influence on the world; greater in the results which are to come. "The manufacture of power means that, wherever needed, we can now produce unlimited power. Whatever the measure of a single machine, that machine can be used to make a greater one...The steam engine is still almost the sole representative of manufactured power, but there is no reason why this should continue. Electricity as a conveyor of power has been developed to an extent which may almost be classed with the manufacture of power."

The manufacture of power, now but about a hundred and fifty years old, has already changed economic and social conditions, particularly in immense addition to the wealth of the world. Sir Auckland Geddes, British Ambassador to the United States, has lately said that "in 1770 a new age was born." James Watt's first steam engine patent was granted in January 1769. From that we may date the New Era of manufactured power. Sir Auckland said that "the industrial revolution is more potent, more far-reaching in its effects than any political revolution has been - a change that has brought, or will bring, happiness or sorrow, but chiefly increased happiness, to millions of men and women and children - a change immeasurably more profound in all its implications than the fall of the Roman Empire." He might have gone further and said, as Morison said, that it is a true ethnical epoch in the history of mankind an epoch more important than any of the six epochs that went before it. That is why we have ventured to say that few rulers of nations have done so much for mankind as George Westinghouse did. This is a tremendous claim, but let us examine its foundations.

In the manufacture of power, as in the development of transportation, George Westinghouse stands amongst the apostles of democracy. He invented and caused other men to invent. He created companies and built factories in many countries. He organized, stimulated, and guided the activities of scores of thousands of men in the manufacture of prime movers and auxiliary machinery and apparatus. His great service to mankind in this field of manufacture of power was in developing the use of the alternating current for the transmission and employment of electrical energy. That was his own work. He did more, far more, for the foundation of that development than any other man who ever lived. Into it entered his imagination, his courage, and his tenacity in greater measure perhaps than into any other of his deeds.

The state of the electric art when Westinghouse first became seriously interested in the possibilities of the alternating current, was like that of the railroad art when Sir Henry Bessemer brought forth his revolutionary invention for making steel. Then the broad and rapid development of the railroads was arrested by a stubborn physical fact. Iron rails could not stand up under the increasing wheel weights and speeds, and the price of iron rails had risen to some four times the price at which steel rails were selling when the Great War came. The cost of maintenance and of new construction deterred investors, and the physical limit set for weights and speeds set a limit to further reduction of transportation costs and to public service. Bessemer came with cheap steel, and the art of land transportation started forward again and has never since been arrested by physical conditions. This is one of the landmarks in the history of civilization.

Something exactly analogous happened in the electric art. When Westinghouse came seriously into the field, the chief use of electric power was in lighting. Direct current was used at low tension. The economical distance to which power could be transmitted was about half a mile. This meant numerous small generating stations. If we were ever to have cheap electric power, it must be produced in large volume, in generating stations so placed that water power could be had, or cheap coal and abundant condensing water, and with the economies possible only in large-scale operations. But it would be folly to establish such generating stations if the current could not be transmitted long distances, and the cost of transmitting low-tension direct current prevented that. So the electric art was faced by limiting physical facts, just as the railroad art had been twenty-five years earlier.

Certain inventions and experiments in alternating current came to Westinghouse's attention, and he had a vision. He saw the limits of direct current and the possibilities of alternating current more clearly perhaps than any other man of his time, certainly more clearly than any other man who had the force, the faith, and the capacity to carry his vision into reality. Even Lord Kelvin, one of the greatest physicists of his generation, and a man of broad mind and audacious temperament, opposed Westinghouse for years in his projects to advance the use of the alternating current. Eventually he acknowledged generously that Westinghouse was right, and to the end of his life he and Westinghouse were close and warm friends, and they were in constant professional association.

Having seen his vision, Westinghouse proceeded, with his own unsurpassed fervor, courage, and determination, and with his great intellectual power, to develop it into physical being. He bought patents. He gathered about him a group of brilliant young engineers, and stimulated and guided them in design, invention, and experiment, and through many and varied tribulations he moved steadily on to triumph. Considering the magnitude of his task, his progress was surprisingly rapid.

The result is known to mankind, but its importance can only be understood by those who are specially informed. The whole structure of the electric art as applied to lighting, industry, and transportation stands on the alternating current. The system of central generating plants, hydraulic and steam, producing enormous quantities of current and transmitting it long distances, would have been economically impossible if alternating-current transmission had not been developed into practice. But it is precisely this sys-' tern of production and distribution that has given the world cheap electric energy. Cheap lighting current not only beautifies the towns, but it adds every day some uncountable millions of hours of work and pleasure to the activities of men. Cheap power current has increased beyond any possible calculation the capacity of mills and factories. It permitted the prodigious development of trolley roads in the country and of electric transportation in the cities. It has brought into being the electrification of steam railroads, which is well begun and which, so far as can now be seen, will be the next great step in land transportation.

This, briefly and inadequately stated, was Westinghouse's relation to one element in human progress which came with the ability to manufacture power. Of all this he says, with characteristic modesty in one of his rare and lucid addresses: "To the part I took in bringing forward, in the eighties of the last century, the alternating-current system of electric generation and distribution I owe much, if not all, of the reputation accorded to me as one of the many pioneers in what is now a great and important industry." The consequent increase in the wealth, the wellbeing, and the happiness of the people will be a fascinating subject for speculation for centuries to come.

We venture to say, with due regard to the meaning of every word, that a thousand years from now, when scholars and philosophers try to measure the influence in the history of the human race of the era of manufactured power, and when they try to name the illustrious men of that era, they will write high in the shining list the name of George Westinghouse.

Appendix A - Patents

THE main purpose in preparing these lists of the patents of George Westinghouse is to relieve the text of a great volume of technical detail and to make that detail available to any one who may wish to go deeper into the various subjects, now or in years to come. Such deeper inquirers will be comparatively few, but then* investigations will be important in the study of certain arts. Presumably the importance of these investigations will grow; certainly they will become more difficult as the years go on.

A chronological list is made and then group lists are given of the most important or interesting patents in the various arts. Under the designation of each patent the essential characteristics are pointed out in a few words, and in the case of a few patents, which had particular influence in their respective arts, a somewhat fuller description is given. It is supposed that this treatment will make the lists useful to the student of the evolution of transportation and to the student of the manufacture of power, and that material for such study will grow in value as time passes.

One immediate interest of the lists is that they show in detail the working of an inventive mind and the fertility which produced a patentable invention every six weeks for forty-eight years. Here and there a man has taken out more patents, but it is not probable that many men ever lived who have taken out so many.

Another thing shown is the versatility, and another, perhaps still more interesting, is that every one of Westinghouse's patents is for something to be made in his own shops or used in his own enterprises; not one was made to sell. A man so imaginative could have produced speculative patents with ease and without limit, but he always thought of himself as part of his companies. He never thought of gain except through their prosperity.

One finds, also, in examining these patents, that the Patent Office drawings were generally made from working drawings, that the drawings and specifications are complete in detail, and that the thing to be done and the ways of doing it are clearly described.

Several men, having special knowledge of the subjects, have taken part in preparing the lists. If their notes seem sometimes to be short and inadequate, it must be remembered that they have tried to keep the lists within reasonable length.

Only the United States patents are listed, as the foreign patents are mostly repetitions of those, with minor variations.

UNITED STATES PATENTS OF GEORGE WESTINGHOUSE

GENERAL LIST

Numbers, dates, and titles.

50,759
Oct. 31, 1865
Rotary Steam Engine.

61,967
Feb. 12, 1867
Car Replacer.

76,365
Apr. 7, 1868
Railway Frog.

3,584 (Reissued)
Aug. 3, 1869
Railway Frog.

5,504 (Reissued)
July 29, 1873
Steam-Power Brake Devices.

88,929
April 13, 1869
Steam-Power Brake.

106,899
Aug. 30, 1870
Improvement in Steam Engine and Pump.

109,695
Nov. 29, 1870
Atmospheric Car-Brake Pipe.

115,667
June 6, 1871
Steam-Power Car-Brake Apparatus.

5,506 (Reissued)
July 29, 1873
Steam-Power Car-Brake Apparatus.

9,478 (Reissued)
Nov. 23, 1880
Steam-Power Car-Brake Apparatus.

115,668
June 6, 1871
Steam-Engine Valves and Ports.

116,655
July 4, 1871
Valve for Air brake Couplings.

117,841
Aug. 8, 1871
Steam-Power Air brake Devices.

5,505 (Reissued)
July 29, 1873
Steam-Power Air brake Devices.

122,544
Jan. 9, 1872
Improvement in Exhaust Valves for Steam and Air Engines.

123,067
Jan. 23, 1872
Improvement in Steam-Power Air Brake.

124,403
March 5, 1872
Improvement in Relief Valves for Steam Air brake Cylinders.

124,404
March 5, 1872
Improvement in Steam-Power Air Brakes and Signals.

124,405
March 5, 1872
Improvement in Steam Air Brakes.

131,380
Sept. 17, 1872
Improvement in Balanced Slide Valves.

131,985
Oct. 8, 1872
Improvement in Rotary Valves.

134,177
Dec. 24, 1872
Steam and Air Brakes.

134,178
Dec. 24, 1872
Steam and Air Brakes.

134,408
Dec. 31, 1872
Steam and Air Brakes.

6,948 (Reissued)
Feb. 22, 1876
Steam and Air Brake.

136,396
March 4, 1873
Steam-Power Brake Couplings.

136,397
March 4, 1873
Hose Couplings.

136,631
March 11, 1873
Steam-Power Brake Couplings.

138,827
May 13, 1873
Valve Devices for Steam and Air Brakes.

138,828
May 13, 1873
Rotary Valves for Steam Engines.

141,685
Aug. 12, 1873
Valve Devices for Fluid Brakes.

144,006
Oct. 28, 1873
Steam and Air Brakes.

144,005
Oct. 28, 1873
Locomotive Air Brakes.

142,600
Sept. 9, 1873
Railroad Car Brakes.

144,582
Nov. 11, 1873
Slack Taking-up Apparatus for Steam and Air Brakes.

147,212
Feb. 3, 1874
Car Brakes.

149,901
April 21, 1874
Valves for Fluid-Brake Pipes.

149,902
April 21, 1874
Car Brakes.

156,322
Oct. 27, 1874
Discharge Valves for Fluid Brakes.

156,323
Oct. 27, 1874
Tripping Apparatus for Air Brakes.

157,951
Dec. 22, 1874
Pipe Couplings.

8,291 (Reissued)
June 18, 1878
Pipe Couplings.

159,533
Feb. 9, 1875
Pneumatic Pump.

159,782
Feb. 16, 1875
Steam-Engine Valve Gear.

160,803
March 16, 1875
Fluid Ejector.

162,782
May 4, 1875
Governor for Steam Engine.

166,489
Aug. 10, 1875
Vacuum-Brake Pipe Coupling.

168,119
Sept. 28, 1875
Ejector Attachment for Vacuum Brakes.

168,359
Oct. 5, 1875
Air Valve for Power Brakes.

172,064
Jan. 11, 1876
Air brake Valve.

173,835
Feb. 22, 1876
Air Compressor.

175,886
April 11, 1876
Locomotive Air Brake.

180,179
July 25, 1876
Air Brake and Signal.

205,710
July 2, 1878
Governor for Marine Engines.

214,335
April 15, 1879
Brake-Pipe Coupling.

214,336
April 15, 1879
Coupling Valve.

214,337
April 15, 1879
Automatic Brake Regulator.

214,602
April 22, 1879
Cocks for Fluid-Pressure Brake.

214,603
April 22, 1879
Railway Air brake Apparatus.

216,545
June 17, 1879
Operating Valve for Steam and Air Brakes.

217,836
July 22, 1879
Fluid-Pressure Brake Apparatus.

217,837
July 22, 1879
Piston Diaphragm for Power Brakes.

217,838
July 22, 1879
Automatic Brake Relief Valve.

218,149
Aug. 5, 1879
Fluid-Pressure Brake Apparatus.

218,150
Aug. 5, 1879
Automatic Brake Attachment.

220,556
Oct. 14, 1879
Regulating Valve for Automatic Brakes.

222,803
Dec. 23, 1879
Operating Cock for Fluid-Pressure Brakes.

223,201
Dec. 30, 1879
Auxiliary Telephone Exchange.

223,202
Dec. 30, 1879
Automatic Telephone Switch for Connecting Local Lines by Means of Main Line.

224,565
Feb. 17, 1880
Telephonic Switches and Connections.

225,898
Mar. 23, 1880
Fluid-Pressure Regulator.

229,346
June 29, 1880
Carburetor.

235,922
Dec. 28, 1880
Fluid-Pressure Brake.

236,388
Jan. 4, 1881
Pipe Coupling.

236,520
Jan. 11, 1881
Apparatus for Regulating Dampers, etc.

237,149
Feb. 1, 1881
Railway Switch Movement.

239,000
March 15, 1881
Feedwater Apparatus.

239,001
March 15, 1881
Steam Trap.

240,062
April 12, 1881
Fluid-Pressure Regulator for Automatic Brakes.

240,628
April 26, 1881
Block Signaling Apparatus.

240,629
April 26, 1881
Switch and Signal Apparatus.

243,415
June 28, 1881
Air brake Apparatus.

243,416
June 28, 1881
Brake Beam.

243,417
June 28, 1881
Fluid-Pressure Brake.

243,822
July 5, 1881
Compound Hose Coupling.

245,108
Aug. 2, 1881
Fluid-Pressure Switch and Signal Apparatus.

245,109
Aug. 2, 1881
Air brake Strainer Attachment.

245,110
Aug. 2, 1881
Air brake Cut-Off and Relief Valve.

245,591
Aug. 9, 1881
Automatic Electric Current Regulator.

245,592
Aug. 9, 1881
Combined Electric and Fluid-Pressure Mechanism.

246,053
Aug. 23, 1881
Interlocking Switch and Signal Apparatus.

249,128
Nov. 1, 1881
Pipe Coupling for Pneumatic Railway Brakes.

251,400
Dec. 27, 1881
Valve Arrangement for Pneumatic Railway Brakes.

251,980
Jan. 3, 1882
Regulating Valve for Railway Brakes.

267,473
Nov. 14, 1882
Hose Protector.

270,527
Jan. 9, 1883
Cock Grinding Machine.

270,528
Jan. 9, 1883
Air brake Pressure Regulator.

270,867
Jan. 16, 1883
Electric Circuit for Railway Signaling.

280,269
June 26, 1883
Fluid-Pressure Regulator.

282,249
July 31, 1883
Track Circuit Connector.

282,250
July 31, 1883
Track Circuit Connector.

287,894
Nov. 6, 1883
Fluid-Pressure Gage Tester.

288,388
Nov. 13, 1883
Connection for Railway Brakes.

290,507
Dec. 18, 1883
Boiler Feeder.

300,543
June 17, 1884
Apparatus for Relieving Pressure in Brake Cylinders.

301,191
July 1, 1884
System for Conveying and Utilizing Gas Under Pressure.

306,566
Oct. 14, 1884
Means for Detecting Leaks in Gas Mains.

10,561 (Reissued)
Feb. 17, 1885
Means for Detecting Leaks in Gas Mains.

307,606
Nov. 4, 1884
Well-Drilling Apparatus for Oil. Gas, or Water.

309,591
Dec. 23, 1884
Regulating Steam Supply to Compound Engines.

309,592
Dec. 23, 1884
Regulating Steam Supply to Engines.

310,347
Jan. 6, 1885
Pressure Regulator.

310,348
Jan. 6, 1885
Pressure Regulator and Relief Valve.

312,541
Feb. 17, 1885
Means for Detecting Leaks in Gas Mains.

312,542
Feb. 17, 1885
Means for Detecting Leaks in Gas Mains.

312,543
Feb. 17, 1885
Pressure Regulator and Cut-Off.

312,777
Feb. 24, 1885
Means for Carrying Off Leakage from Gas Mains.

313,393
March 3, 1885
Connection for Pipe Lines.

314,089
March 17, 1885
System for the Protection of Railroad Tracks and Gas Pipe Lines.

315,363
April 7, 1885
Means for Detecting Leaks in Gas Mains.

318,839
May 26, 1885
Regulator for Gas and Air Supply to Furnaces.

318,840
May 26, 1885
Pipe Coupling for Gas Mains.

318,841
May 26, 1885
Pipe Joint for Gas Mains.

319,364
June 2, 1885
Means for Detecting and Carrying Off Leakage from Gas Mains.

319,365
June 2, 1885
Pipe Line for Gas Supply.

319,765
June 9, 1885
Stop-Valve Box for Pipe Lines.

323,246
July 26, 1885
Pipe Line.

323,840
Aug. 4, 1885
Method of Conveying and Supplying Gas.

324,905
Aug. 25, 1885
Pressure Regulator and Cut-Off.

328,368
Oct. 13, 1885
Means for Conveying and Supplying Gas.

330,179
Nov. 10, 1885
Means for Detecting and Carrying Off Leakage from Gas Mains.

331,595
Dec. 1, 1885
Means for Detecting and Carrying Off Leakage from Gas Mains.

331,596
Dec. 1, 1885
Means for Detecting and Closing Leaks in Gas Mains.

333,800
Jan. 5, 1886
Means for Conveying and Supplying Gas.

340,266
April 20, 1886
Means for Preventing Leakage in Gas Mains.

340,267
April 20, 1886
Pipe Joint for Gas Mains.

340,268
April 20, 1886
Pipe Joint for Gas Mains.

341,295
May 4, 1886
Pressure Regulator and Cut-Off.

342,552
May 25, 1886
System of Electrical Distribution.

342,553
May 25, 1886
Induction Coil.

342,659
May 25, 1886
Pipe Joint for Gas Mains.

344,701
June 29, 1886
Means for Detecting and Carrying Off Leakage from Gas Mains.

345,093
July 6, 1886
Car Brake.

345,820
July 20, 1886
Automatic Brake Regulator.

347,673
Aug. 17, 1886
Proportional Meter.

349,130
Sept. 14, 1886
Dynamometer.

352,382
Nov. 9, 1886
Pressure Regulator and Cut-Off.

352,725
Nov. 16, 1886
Telegraphic Relay.

353,186
Nov. 23, 1886
Thermostat.

357,109
Feb. 1, 1887
Electrical Interlocking Mechanism for Switches and Signals.

357,295
Feb. 8, 1887
Commutator for Dynamo Electric Machines.

357,296
Feb. 8, 1887
Electric Railway Signaling.

358,518
March 1, 1887
Binding Post.

358,519
March 1, 1887
Electropneumatic Interlocking Apparatus.

358,520
March 1, 1887
Electric Fluid-Pressure Engine.

358,521
March 1, 1887
Electrically Actuated Fluid-Pressure Motor.

358,713
March 1, 1887
Electrically Actuated Fluid-Pressure Motor and Circuits Therefor.

359,303
March 15, 1887
Fluid-Pressure Motor.

360,070
March 29, 1887
Fluid-Pressure Automatic Brake Mechanism.

360,638
April 5, 1887
Railway Electric Signaling Apparatus.

365,454
June 28, 1887
Long-Distance Gas Distribution.

366,361
July 12, 1887
Electric Conductor.

366,362
July 12, 1887
Electrical Converter.

366,544
July 12, 1887
Electrical Converter.

370,510
Sept. 27, 1887
Gas Supply System.

373,035
Nov. 8, 1887
System of Electrical Distribution.

373,036
Nov. 8, 1887
Automatic Circuit Controlling Apparatus for Systems of Electrical Distribution.

373,037
Nov. 8, 1887
System of Electrical Distribution.

373,038
Nov. 8, 1887
Converter Box.

373,706
Nov. 22, 1887
Locomotive Driver Brake.

374,858
Dec. 13, 1887
Dynamo Electric Machine.

376,837
Jan. 24, 1888
Fluid-Pressure Automatic Brake Mechanism.

382,920
May 15, 1888
Nut Lock.

383,678
May 29, 1888
Electric Meter.

383,679
May 29, 1888
Mounting Armatures of Dynamos.

383,680
May 29, 1888
Electric Meter.

388,163
Aug. 21, 1888
System of Gas Distribution.

389,032
Sept. 4, 1888
Pressure Regulator and Cut-Off.

390,930
Oct. 9, 1888
Synchronizing Electric Generators.

391,997
Oct. 30, 1888
Buffing Apparatus.

393,596
Nov. 27, 1888
Electric Fluid-Pressure Engine.

399,103
March 5, 1889
Brake Shoe.

399,639
March 12, 1889
System of Electrical Distribution.

400,420
March 26, 1889
Fluid Meter.

400,532
April 2, 1889
Service Pipe Connection for Gas Mains.

401,915
April 23, 1889
Automatic Pump Governor for Brake Mechanisms.

401,916
April 23, 1889
Engineer's Brake Valve.

404,139
May 28, 1889
System of Electrical Distribution.

405,812
June 25, 1889
Compound Engine.

415,595
Nov. 19, 1889
Brake Apparatus for Six-Wheeled Trucks.

420,132
Jan. 28, 1890
Steam-Heating Apparatus for Railway Cars.

425,059
April 8, 1890
Fluid-Pressure Automatic Brake Mechanism.

427,489
May 6, 1890
Alternating-Current Electric Meter.

428,435
May 20, 1890
Alternating-Current Arc Lamp.

432,715
July 22, 1890
Brake Cylinder Head.

434,165
Aug. 12, 1890
Subway for Electric Conductors.

436,200
Sept. 9, 1890
Electric Converter.

437,740
Oct. 7, 1890
Fluid-Pressure Automatic Brake.

440,082
Nov. 4, 1890
Automatic Brake Regulator.

441,209
Nov. 25, 1890
Compound Pumping Engine.

446,159
Feb. 10, 1891
Switch and Signal Apparatus.

448,827
March 24, 1891
Air Brake.

450,652
April 21, 1891
Electric Locomotor.

454,129
June 16, 1891
Pipe Coupling.

455,028
June 30, 1891
Rotary Engine.

455,029
June 30, 1891
Piston.

466,590
Jan. 5, 1892
Apparatus for Heating Cars.

493,881
March 21, 1893
Rotary Water Meter.

497,394
May 16, 1893
Conduit Electric Railway.

497,436
May 16, 1893
Sectional Contact Conductor for Electric Railways.

499,335
June 13, 1893
Buffing Mechanism for Cars.

499,336
June 13, 1893
Draw-Gear Apparatus for Cars.

520,975
June 5, 1894
Converter System for Electric Railways.

524,749
Aug. 21, 1894
System of Electrical Distribution.

538,001
April 23, 1895
Quick Action Valve for Air Brakes.

543,280
July 23, 1895
Incandescent Electric Lamp.

543,915
Aug. 6, 1895
Draw Gear and Buffing Apparatus.

545,994
Sept. 10, 1895
Draw Gear and Buffing Apparatus.

550,359
Nov. 26, 1895
Exhaust Pump.

550,465
Nov. 26, 1895
Electric Railway.

550,466
Nov. 26, 1895
Rotary Pumping and Motor Apparatus.

550,467
Nov. 26, 1895
Electric and Fluid Locomotor.

550,468
Nov. 26, 1895
Ventilating Means for Electrical Apparatus.

556,602
March 17, 1896
Underground Conductor for Electric Railways.

557,463
March 31, 1896
Engineer's Brake Valve.

560,452
May 19, 1896
Electric Railway System.

573,066
Dec. 15, 1896
Electric Railway Construction.

573,190
Dec. 15, 1896
Fluid-Pressure Automatic Brake.

576,492
Feb. 2, 1897
Truck.

579,506
March 23, 1897
Current-Collecting Device for Railway Vehicles.

579,525
March 23, 1897
System of Circuits and Apparatus for Electric Railways.

579,526
March 23, 1897
Electropneumatic Locomotive.

579,527
March 23, 1897
Electric Railway System.

682,494
May 11, 1897
Core for Electrical Machine.

583,584
June 1, 1897
Gas Engine.

583,585
June 1, 1897
Means for Controlling and Regulating Operation of Gas Engines.

583,586
June 1, 1897
Electric Igniter for Gas Engines.

584,911
June 22, 1897
Electric Railway System.

591,314
Oct. 5, 1897
Electric Railway System.

593,710
Nov. 16, 1897
Quick-Action Triple Valve.

593,711
Nov. 16, 1897
Quick-Action Triple Valve.

595,007
Dec. 7, 1897
Elevator.

595,008
Dec. 7, 1897
Electric Railway.

595,027
Dec. 7, 1897
Hydraulic Pumping and Motor Apparatus.

606,828
July 5, 1898
Travelling Contact Device for Electric Railways.

609,484
Aug. 23, 1898
Fluid-Pressure Automatic Brake.

615,118
Nov. 29, 1898
Center Sill for Railroad Cars.

624,277
May 2, 1899
Electropneumatic Controlling System.

629,943
Aug. 1, 1899
Draw Gear and Buffing Apparatus.

645,612
Mar. 20, 1900
Method of Distributing Energy.

645,613
Mar. 20, 1900
Apparatus for Distributing Energy.

649,187
May 8, 1900
Draw Gear and Buffing Apparatus.

672,112
April 16, 1901
Draft Appliances for Railroad Cars.

672,113
April 16, 1901
Car Coupling.

672,114
April 16, 1901
Draft Appliance for Railway Cars.

672,115
April 16, 1901
Air Brake.

672,116
April 16, 1901
Draw Gear and Buffing Apparatus.

672,117
April 16, 1901
Draw Gear and Buffing Apparatus.

672,970
April 30, 1901
Rotary Motor or Pump.

672,971
April 30, 1901
Rotary Pump.

676,108
June 11, 1901
Electric Railway System.

680,824
Aug. 20, 1901
Contact Device for Electric Railways.

680,825
Aug. 20, 1901
Speed-Changing Gearing.

680,826
Aug. 20, 1901
Means for Utilizing Gaseous Products of Combustion.

680,827
Aug. 20, 1901
Gas Producer.

680,828
Aug. 20, 1901
Gas Producer.

687,467
Nov. 26, 1901
Draft Appliance for Railway Cars.

687,468
Nov. 26, 1901
Draw Gear and Buffing Apparatus.

699,267
May 6, 1902
Automatic Fluid-Pressure Brake Apparatus.

708,107
Sept. 2, 1902
Furnace.

708,747
Sept. 9, 1902
Car Coupling.

710,385
Sept. 30, 1902
Gas Engine.

712,626
Nov. 4, 1902
Rotary Engine.

722,787
March 17, 1903
Gas Engine.

727,039
May 5, 1903
Automatic Fluid-Pressure Brake Apparatus.

727,040
May 5, 1903
Automatic Fluid-Pressure Brake Apparatus.

731,726
June 23, 1903
Method of and Means for Driving Electric Motors.

739,367
Sept. 22, 1903
Gas Producing System.

745,703
Dec. 1, 1903
Gas Engine.

745,704
Dec. 1, 1903
Gas Engine.

749,708
Jan. 12, 1904
Friction-Spring Mechanism.

750,010
Jan. 19, 1904
Air Brake.

751,587
Feb. 9, 1904
Rotary Fluid Motor.

751,588
Feb. 9, 1904
Gearing.

751,589
Feb. 9, 1904
Fluid-Pressure Turbine.

754,400
March 8, 1904
Vertical Fluid-Pressure Turbine.

767,367
Aug. 9, 1904
Turbine Blade.

772,852
Oct. 18, 1904
Fluid-Pressure Brake.

773,832
Nov. 1, 1904
Controlling System for Electric Motors.

773,833
Nov. 1, 1904
Controlling System for Electric Motors.

787,485
April 18, 1905
Fluid-Pressure Turbine.

794,761
July 18, 1905
Friction Device.

799,698
Sept. 19, 1905
Friction Draft Gear.

807,003
Dec. 12, 1905
Elastic Fluid Turbine.

807,145
Dec. 12, 1905
Elastic Fluid Turbine.

807,146
Dec. 12, 1905
Elastic Fluid Turbine.

814,339
March 6, 1906
Supporting Structure for Trolley Conductors.

816,516
March 27, 1906
Fluid-Pressure Turbine.

833,273
Oct. 16, 1906
Metallic Packing.

866,171
Sept. 17, 1907
Elastic Fluid Turbine.

869,606
Oct. 29, 1907
Fluid-Pressure Brake.

880,847
March 3, 1908
Elastic Fluid Turbine.

883,155
March 24, 1908
Shaft Packing.

890,951
June 16, 1908
Gas Producer.

894,927
Aug. 4, 1908
Fluid-Pressure Turbine.

906,177
Dec. 8, 1908
Internal Combustion Engine.

922,827
May 25, 1909
Gearing.

930,906
Aug. 10, 1909
Nozzle Control for Elastic Fluid Turbines.

930,907
Aug. 10, 1909
Turbine Blade and Vane.

930,908
Aug. 10, 1909
Elastic Fluid Turbine.

935,286
Sept. 28, 1909
Elastic Fluid Turbine.

935,343
Sept. 28, 1909
Rotary Engine.

935,438
Sept. 28, 1909
Fluid-Pressure Turbine.

935,567
Sept. 28, 1909
Elastic Fluid Turbine.

935,568
Sept. 28, 1909
Elastic Fluid Turbine.

935,569
Sept. 28, 1909
Elastic Fluid Turbine.

941,395
Nov. 30, 1909
Elastic Fluid Turbine.

941,396
Nov. 30, 1909
Marine Turbine.

946,749
Jan. 18, 1910
Elastic Fluid Turbine.

953,567
March 29, 1910
Elastic Fluid Turbine.

953,568
March 29, 1910
Turbine Blade and Vane.

953,674
March 29, 1910
Elastic Fluid Turbine.

968,823
Aug. 30, 1910
Propelling Device.

969,821
Sept. 13, 1910
Re-entrant Turbine.

972,421
Oct. 11, 1910
Turbine.

976,418
Nov. 22, 1910
Turbine Blade.

976,966
Nov. 29, 1910
Method of Heating Air.

976,967
Nov. 29, 1910
Apparatus for Heating Air.

990,321
Apr. 25, 1911
Turbine Blading.

994,810
June 13, 1911
Electrical Apparatus.

995,508
June 20, 1911
Elastic Fluid Turbine.

998,820
July 25, 1911
Turbine Blading.

998,821
July 25, 1911
Condensing Turbine.

1,014,683
Jan. 16, 1912
Turbine Blade.

1,031,757
July 9, 1912
Re-entrant Turbine.

1,031,758
July 9, 1912
Reduction Gearing.

1,031,759
July 9, 1912
Vehicle Supporting Device.

1,036,043
Aug. 20, 1912
Fluid-Pressure Device.

1,050,186
Jan. 14, 1913
Dynamometer.

1,050,187
Jan. 14, 1913
Blade Mounting.

1,061,648
May 13, 1913
Blades.

1,061,792
May 13, 1913
Elastic Fluid Turbine.

1,073,197
Sept. 16, 1913
Cooling Means for Internal Combustion Engines.

1,088,387
Feb. 24, 1914
Transmission Gearing.

1,136,072
Apr. 20, 1915
Reduction Gearing.

1,136,189
Apr. 20, 1915
Reduction Gearing.

1,142,069
June 8, 1915
Marine Turbine.

1,148,206
July 27, 1915
Combustion Engine.

1,149,881
Aug. 10, 1915
Transmission Gearing.

1,161,095
Nov. 23, 1915
Internal Combustion Engine.

1,185,608
May 30, 1916
Automobile Air Spring.

1,187,212
June 13, 1916
Gland Packing.

1,194,687
Aug. 15, 1916
Multistage Compressor.

1,195,119
Aug. 15, 1916
Reduction Gearing.

1,205,130
Nov. 14, 1916
Turbine Valve Mechanism.

1,208,252
Dec. 12, 1916
Coupling.

1,209,917
Dec. 26, 1916
Engine Starter.

1,209,918
Dec. 26, 1916
Marine Turbine.

1,284,006
Nov. 5, 1918
Automatic Train Control.

Appendix B - *Group Lists Comments on Selected Patents*

As is explained above, the patents selected for brief comment are the most important or interesting. They are such as went into general use, or contained early suggestions of valuable ideas, or otherwise affected their several arts.

AIR BRAKE

STRAIGHT AIR

No. 88,929, April 13, 1869. Steam-Power Brake. - This was the first patent issued to Westinghouse for an air brake, as described in the Air brake chapter. It formed a firm foundation for the air brake structure that was built upon it, and its chief characteristics will be found stated in the opinion of Justice Swayne and Judge Walker, of the United States Court, in litigation between the Westinghouse Air Brake Company and the Gardner and Ransom Brake Company. The conclusions of the court will be found in the Air brake chapter.

No. 115,667, June 6, 1871. Steam-Power Brake Apparatus. - This patent proposed a device to produce a vacuum on the non-pressure side of the brake cylinder piston for the purpose of quickening the release of brakes to remedy a defect of the straight-air system. It was not used in practice, but was one of the earliest disclosures of the vacuum-brake system, as by reissue 5506, under date of July 29, 1873, a claim was allowed for the operation of power brakes by atmospheric pressure.

No. 122,544, January 9, 1872. Improvement in Exhaust Valves for Steam and Air Engines. - This patent is for a valve device, to be used in connection with the straight-air system to provide an escape of pressure directly from the brake cylinder to the atmosphere when it is desired to release brakes so that the time of release will be reduced as compared with that required to permit the air to escape through the train pipe and out of the engineer's valve on the locomotive. But few of them were put in service.

AUTOMATIC

Nos. 124,404 and 124,405, March 5, 1872. Improvement in Steam-Power Air Brakes and Signals. - These patents for the first time reveal the basic invention of the *automatic* brake and also the system of train signaling that subsequently became standard on passenger trains of this country. The following extract from specification of Patent No. 124,404 clearly shows the inventor's conception of the problem and indicates the means proposed for its solution. "In the steam-power air brake apparatus heretofore in use a single line of pipe conveys the compressed air from the main reservoir on the locomotive to each brake cylinder. If this pipe becomes accidentally broken at any point it is, of course, useless for braking purposes from that point to the rear end of the train. For this and other reasons I have devised an apparatus consisting in part of a double line of brake pipes, which may be cooperative or independently operative in braking at the pleasure of the engineer, and which as a separate device I have included in a separate application. The improvement herein described relates to the same class of apparatus, and consists in the features of construction and combination substantially as hereinafter claimed, by which, first, an air reservoir, auxiliary to or independent of the main reservoir, is combined on each car with the brake cylinder; second, by means of a cock or cocks, with suitable ports, such additional reservoir, when used as an auxiliary reservoir, is charged with compressed air from one brake pipe, and the brake cylinder from the other, such pipes in such use being interchangeable or not, at pleasure; third, and by means of a single cock with suitable ports either brake pipe may be used for charging the reservoir and the other for operating the brakes; fourth, when a car becomes disconnected from the train by accident or otherwise, a port or ports will thereby be opened in a communicating pipe or pipes, by which the air from such auxiliary reservoir will be admitted freely to the brake cylinder, so as automatically to apply the brakes; and, fifth, the conductor and engineer may communicate signals or orders to each other by the use of the brake pipes and the compressed air."

No. 138,827, May 13, 1873. Valve Devices for Steam and Air Brakes. - Describes the first form of triple valve experimentally tried in road service, but as it could not graduate the brake pressure it was not introduced into general service.

No. 141,685, August 12, 1873. Valve Devices for Fluid Brakes. - Describes a triple valve capable of graduating the brake-cylinder pressure, and was the first form supplied for service use.

No. 149,901, April 21, 1874. Valves for Fluid-Brake Pipes. Improvement on Patent No. 141,685. - Valves constructed of the design shown in this patent succeeded those of Patent No. 141,685 and were largely used in service.

No. 156,322, October 27, 1874. Discharge Valves for Fluid Brakes. The device shown in this patent was intended to provide for the automatic application of the brakes in case of a derailment of the car. It was included among the devices furnished with the automatic brake when it was first introduced, but as a result of experience its use was discontinued because of its undesired operation, due to its being operated by flying missiles when the train was in motion.

No. 168,359, October 5, 1875. Air Valve for Power Brakes. - An important improvement in the automatic brake, in which a slide valve and piston is substituted for poppet valves and diaphragms used in preceding structures. It was also the first triple valve with a normally open exhaust port.

No. 172,064, January 11, 1876. Air brake Valve. - An improvement in triple-valve construction in which a limited amount of lost motion between the valve stem and the slide valve is the important feature. This particular feature is an important element in all subsequent triple-valve constructions.

No. 214,602, April 22, 1879. Cocks for Fluid-Pressure Brake. - This invention was an important contribution to the improvement of air brakes, as it is the first engineers' valve arranged^ to store pressure in the main reservoir in excess of the brake-pipe pressure, to facilitate the release of brakes. It is of particular importance in trains of considerable length and the principle of excess pressure has ever since been employed in all operative airbrake systems.

No. 217,838, July 22, 1879. Automatic Brake Relief Valve. - The importance of this patent is that it contains suggestions subsequently embodied in the quick-action brake. In the form illustrated in the patent it was not a practically operative device.

No. 220,556, October 14, 1879. Regulating Valve for Automatic Brakes. - Illustrates the last important improvement in the plain triple valve, and its purpose is described in the specification as follows: "It is important in such device that the valve which governs the flow of air or other fluid shall move not only with great certainty to any desired position, but also shall move with slight variations of pressure on the piston, so that the application of the brakes with any desired power, and their ready release, may be quickly and easily effected at the pleasure of the engineer." With this improvement added to the then existing brake system the graduation of brake pressure was greatly improved.

No. 235,922, December 28, 1880. Fluid-Pressure Brake. - The first patent to describe the combination of the brake-cylinder auxiliary reservoir and triple valve in a single structure; created the general type of freight-car brake that has, since its invention, been employed almost exclusively in freight-car service.

No. 270,528, January 9, 1883. Air brake Pressure Regulator. - Describes what is technically termed a pressure-retaining valve, which is a device connected with the exhaust port of the triple valve, so arranged as to retain a predetermined pressure in the brake cylinder when the triple valve is in position for recharging auxiliary reservoirs in descending long and heavy grades. On level track it is caused to be inoperative by opening a direct passage from the exhaust port of the triple valve to the atmosphere. The addition of this device was necessary to make the automatic brake available for freight service. It, therefore, has a very important place in the patent record of the air brake art.

QUICK ACTION

No. 360,070, March 29, 1887, and No. 376,837, January 24, 1888. Fluid-Pressure Automatic-Brake Mechanism. - These patents disclose the invention of the quick-acting brake. The specification of Patent No. 360,070 clearly states the difficulties to be overcome and the general principles of the method employed to do it. The detailed construction shown in Patent No. 376,837 was embodied in the standard triple valve thereafter for both freight and passenger service. Next to the original invention of the automatic brake, the development and introduction of the quick-acting triple valve is the most important event in the history of power braking, for it resulted in the generalise of power brakes in freight service on long trains.

No. 448,827, March 24, 1891. Air Brake. - A quick-acting brake in which the train-pipe vent valve is not combined with the triple valve; a variation of the original quick-acting triple valve; not put into practical service.

No. 538,001, April 23, 1895. Quick-Action Valve for Air Brakes. - This patent describes a type of quick-acting triple valve in which the quick-acting feature is differentiated from previous patents in respect to the fact that its operation depended upon a relatively quick movement of the triple-valve piston, while in previous types the same result was obtained through a longer travel of the piston in emergency applications.

ELECTRO-PNEUMATIC

No. 243,417, June 28, 1881. Fluid-Pressure Brake. - This is believed to be the first patent issued for an air brake in which the air valves are electrically actuated. Improved and expanded by other additions, it is now largely used in some classes of railway service. The general principles revealed in this patent were largely used in electropneumatic switching and signaling.

ACCESSORIES

No. 117,841, August 8, 1871. Steam-Power Air brake Devices. - The purpose of this invention is described in the following quotation from the specification. "In applying car brakes it is desirable that the movement of the brake shoes at first be rapid, so that they shall engage the wheels as quickly as possible, and after they have engaged the wheels that they be pressed against them with great force. Before they touch the wheels they offer no great resistance. After they engage the wheels their motion is little, but the resistance is great." The form in which the invention was patented was used to a limited extent in the early days of the application of air brakes, but was abandoned as not satisfactorily accomplishing the desired result. In a modified and improved form it is now an essential feature of what is technically called the "empty and load brake," one of the latest air brake developments.

No. 134,178, December 24, 1872. Steam and Air Brakes. - In this patent means are proposed for automatically compensating for the wearing away of brake shoes, which must otherwise be done by hand adjustment. In improved forms, which embody the basic idea exhibited in this patent, many thousands of these devices are employed, and are practically standard in passenger service.

No. 136,631, March 11, 1873. Steam-Power Brake Couplings. - The purpose of this invention was to remove the necessity for a double line of pipes under the cars due to the type of coupling theretofore used. The following quotation from the specification describes the condition to be remedied and the method proposed in the patent for doing it: "In the patent granted to me, August 8, 1871, No. 117,841, provision is made for the reversal of a car without changing the relative arrangement of the couplings. This is done by branching the air brake pipe at or near each end of the car, and attaching a male coupling to one branch and a female coupling to the other, as therein described. In my present improvement I accomplish the same useful result by making a coupling wherein each half shall have a male and female part to couple into or with the female and male parts of the next coupling. With couplings so made there will be no occasion to branch the pipes, and the half coupling on either end of either car will couple on to any other half coupling on the train." Couplings of this form were experimentally used but did not become a part of standard apparatus.

No. 142,600, September 9, 1873. Railroad Car Brakes. - This is one of the earliest patents, in which the use of metal in brake beams is proposed, and it also includes improved methods of support and balancing. It was tried experimentally, and ultimately the principles embodied in this patent became general in practice.

No. 144,005, October 28, 1873. Locomotive Air Brakes. - This is the first of Westinghouse's inventions describing the application of power brakes to driving wheels of locomotives. The form here shown was applied to a limited extent.

No. 147,212, February 3, 1874. Car Brakes. - An important improvement in details of construction on Patent No. 144,005, for limited space between driving wheels.

No. 149,902, April 21, 1874. Car Brakes. - This patent covers important improvements in brake-beam construction, whereby wooden brake beams were sufficiently reinforced with metal truss rods so that they were capable of meeting the stresses due to the application of power brakes. Used to a very considerable extent in passenger service.

No. 157,951, December 22, 1874. Pipe Couplings. - A very important invention, and an improvement on Patent No. 136,631, by means of which the practical necessity for double lines of pipe and double hose couplings was avoided. It was immediately placed in service and has remained the standard hose-coupling device for air brake purposes.

No. 159,533, February 9, 1875. Pneumatic Pump. - This invention describes a steam-driven air compressor in which air is compressed serially or in stages, thereby effecting a substantial economy in the cost of compression. The application of this principle was delayed for many years, but it is now practically standard for steam-driven air brake compressors.

No. 180,179, July 25, 1876. Air Brake and Signal. - This is for a system of train signals employing compressed air as the medium of communication, and the specification states that the object of the invention is to enable the conductor to employ compressed air in communicating signals to the engineer. In a somewhat modified form it has come into general use on passenger service in America.

No. 214,336, April 15, 1879. Coupling Valve. - This patent is the first to describe the combination of a hose coupling with a valve arrangement controlling the flow of air through the train pipe in which the valves are automatically opened when the couplings are united, and closed when they are manually separated by partially rotating the two halves of the coupling with reference to each other. The valves, however, remain open if the couplings are separated by pulling them apart, as in the case of a parted train, thus providing for the escape of the air from the train pipe, causing the automatic application of the brakes. The successful employment of this device would dispense with the train pipe cocks that are otherwise required at each end of the car. Many variations embodying the basic idea have been proposed, but no satisfactory substitute for a train-pipe cock has been found.

No. 214,337, April 15, 1879. Automatic Brake Regulator. - This patent is of importance as showing one form of the appliance that was used in the Galton-Westinghouse tests, described in the Air brake chapter. The following quotation from the specification describes the object of the invention: "To ascertain if possible the laws governing the action of the various forces brought into play by the use of brakes, I had made a special brake-vehicle fitted with self-recording apparatus to register at each instant, first, the force with which the wheels were pressed by the brake shoe; second, the amount of resistance or drag between the shoes and wheels; third, the weight with which the wheels pressed the rails; fourth, the exact rate of speed of the vehicle; fifth, the rate of rotation of the braked wheels." The remarkable results obtained are set forth in the text.

No. 240,062, April 12, 1881. Fluid-Pressure Regulator for Automatic Brakes. - This patent is for automatically regulating the air pressure by controlling the flow of steam to the air compressor, resulting in the automatic maintenance of any desired air pressure. This device was at once put into practical operation, and in one form or another it forms a part of the existing brake system.

No. 401,916, April 23, 1889. Engineer's Brake Valve. - This patent describes a very important improvement in the engineer's operating brake valve set forth in the following quotation from the specification. "The object of our invention is, primarily, to provide for such gradual opening and closure of the valve which controls the discharge of air from the brake pipe as to cause a substantial equalization of pressure in the brake pipe and uniform application of the brakes throughout the length of the train, and obviate the liability to release the brakes on the forward cars, in long trains, which has heretofore been found to be induced by an inequality of pressure in the brake pipe occasioned by the quick release of a considerable quantity of air and the sudden closure of the discharge valve thereafter, and from which the breaking of the train into two or more sections has sometimes resulted." The gradual increase in length of trains rendered some mechanism of this general character necessary for satisfactory brake operation.

No. 415,595, November 19, 1889. Brake Apparatus for Six-Wheeled Trucks. - The first patent to describe a method of applying brakes to all of the wheels of a six-wheeled truck. A practical solution of the problem was reached with great difficulty, owing to the contracted space available for the application of the brakeshoes to the center pair of wheels. It was, however, accomplished substantially in accordance with the method proposed in this patent, and it is now in universal use.

No. 441,209, November 25, 1890. Compound Pumping Engine. - This is a patent for a compound direct-acting air compressor, in which both the steam and air elements are compounded. A substantial economy in steam consumption was effected by this invention, and compressors of the general design shown in the patent are in general use.

FRICTION DRAFT GEAR

No. 391,997, October 30, 1888. Buffing Apparatus. - This is the basic friction draft-gear patent, and the following quotation from the specification clearly states its object and the method of accomplishment. "My present invention relates to certain improvements in buffing apparatus designed to be interposed between a stationary and movable body, or between two bodies approaching each other either from opposite directions or between two bodies moving in the same direction, but at different rates of speed; and the invention has for its object a construction of buffing apparatus, whether applied to the draw bars or buffers of cars, or for other purposes, wherein a frictional resistance is employed, either in combination with a spring resistance or alone, for the purpose of modifying the momentum and impact of the meeting or separating bodies." Several succeeding patents (which included the generic invention) for improvements and modifications were issued to Westinghouse covering the various forms experimented with, leading to a successful commercial product.

It is an interesting fact that in the latest commercial development of the friction draft gear by the Westinghouse Air Brake Company, in which much greater frictional resistance is provided than is found in previous constructions, the detailed construction is substantially the same as that shown in the original patent, the principal difference being an increased thickness of the friction plates in the later construction.

HYDRAULIC DRAFT GEAR

No. 649,187, May 8, 1900, and No. 672,117, April 16, 1901. Draw Gear and Buffing Apparatus. - These patents are for draft gear devices in which hydraulic resistance is substituted for friction resistance, but these constructions did not prove to be an operative improvement upon the friction type and were not put into practical service.

No. 708,747, September 9, 1902. Car Coupling. - This patent covers an invention of great practical value in the operation of electrically propelled railway trains. The invention was important, and it has gone into large use. It is described in the text.

ELECTRICAL

ELECTRICAL DISTRIBUTION

No. 373,035, November 8, 1887. System of Electrical Distribution. - An alternating-current distribution system in which direct currents are locally derived from alternating for charging storage batteries to be held in reserve against emergencies. An alternating-current motor driven from the main circuit is provided with a commutator through which direct currents are delivered to local storage batteries, which in turn may at will be connected with the supply circuit when required.

No. 373,036, November 8, 1887. Automatic Circuit-Controlling Apparatus for Systems of Electrical Distribution. - Means are provided for interchanging the connections of the supply circuit, so that in case of interruption of one of the main lines, the apparatus being supplied is automatically connected with another main line.

No. 524,749, August 21, 1894. System of Electrical Distribution. - The organization of circuits is such as to enable the central stations to connect line transformers as required, and thus avoid unnecessary leakage through the primary coils. Fluid-pressure devices operated from the central stations are provided for controlling the connections of the primary coils of the various transformers.

TRANSFORMERS

No. 342,553, May 25, 1886. Induction Coil. - The patent, the application for which was filed February 16, 1886, was the forerunner of the modern type of transformer, in which the coils are essentially enclosed by a laminated iron core. The patent lays stress upon the importance of bringing a large amount of laminated iron into close proximity to the primary and secondary coils without undue heating of the core. In one form H-shaped plates, insulated from each other, are arranged in a pile and bolted together. The coils are then wound upon the central portion, partly filling the spaces between the projecting arms, which are afterward closed outside the coils by iron plates or laminae, thus completely enclosing the main body of the coils. The construction described in this patent led up to the modern form devised by Stanley and later improved by Albert Schmid, in which E-shaped plates are employed, permitting the separate winding and insulation of the coils, the enclosing core thereafter being built upon the coils.

No. 366,362, July 12, 1887. Electrical Converter. - This patent is well known to the art as the Westinghouse Oil-Cooled Transformer patent. It has been the subject of long-continued litigation, having been repeatedly sustained as covering the modern oil-cooled transformer. From the opinion of the Court of Appeals of the Second Circuit, in what is known as the "Union Carbide Suit" the following is quoted: "The practical result of the invention in suit, as testified to by complainant's experts, was to so increase the capacity of converters that, while a dry converter cooled by the natural circulation of air is limited to 10 kilowatts, the oil-insulated converters of the patent in suit are commercially serviceable up to 500 kilowatts." This early invention proved to be of great utility and has been extensively used in large transformers.

GENERATORS AND MOTORS

No. 582,494, May 11, 1897. Core for Electrical Machines. - In the early construction of laminated cores for electric machines the laminae were clamped together by end plates secured by transverse bolts. To lessen the labor and expense and other disadvantages of this construction, Westinghouse provided a cylindrical support having a flange or plate at one end. The core plates are built up about the central support and pressed together between the permanent flange or plate and a detachable plate surrounding the other end of the support, the second plate being then secured in position by an annular fastening ring, or key, located partially in a groove in the casting and partially in a groove in the plate. It is proposed to form the fastening ring of soft metal which could be poured through openings into the grooves. This may be melted out in case it is desired to disassemble the parts. The fundamental idea was improved upon by Albert Schmid, who devised an ingenious plan for inserting an annular soring-ring in the registering grooves.

METERS

No. 383,678, May 29, 1888. Electric Meter. - The invention of this patent was designed to supply the then pressing need for an alternating-current meter. Upon a disk driven at a constant speed there rests a spheroidical roller adapted to be tipped in proportion to the amount of current to be measured. With no current flowing the greatest diameter of the roller is coincident with the center of rotation of the disk, so that no rolling movement is communicated to it. When current to be measured flows it acts to tip the roller so as to bring its point of bearing upon the disk away from the center a distance dependent upon the amount of current flow. As the point of contact between the disk and the roller is thus changed the roller is revolved upon its axis at a rate proportional to the current flowing, and a clock train records the revolutions. This device, improved, as shown in a joint patent of Westinghouse and Lange No. 383,680, gave great promise of meeting the serious needs of the art at the time, and would have doubtless gone into extensive use but for the appearance of the Shallenberger meter referred to in the text.

ARC LAMPS

No. 428,435, May 20, 1890. Alternating-Current Arc Lamp. - In the development of alternating-current arc lamps it was found advantageous in many instances to use flat carbons. This patent sets forth the advantage of making the uer carbon thicker than the lower one for the purpose of more effectively projecting the light downwardly.

ELECTRIC RAILWAYS AND LOCOMOTIVES

No. 404,139, May 28, 1889. System of Electrical Distribution. - The object of the invention is to utilize the advantage of high-potential alternating currents for transmitting energy to a locomotive operated by low-potential continuous currents. The locomotive carries a current rectifier, such as a synchronous alternating-current motor, provided with a rectifying commutator. The energy derived from the alternating source is delivered as continuous current to direct-current propelling motors. | Potential-reducing transformers arranged along the railway serve to transform the transmitted high-potential alternating current to such low-potential current as may be conveniently delivered to the locomotive and then changed to direct current. This patent appears to have been a pioneer in the art of driving direct-current locomotives with energy transmitted from a distance in the form of alternating currents, as is indicated by the following sample claims: "The combination of an alternate-current electric generator, a converter reducing the potential of the currents delivered thereby, a rectifying commutator rendering continuous such reduced currents, and an electric railway supplied by such continuous currents. The combination of an electric locomotor, a current-rectifier upon said locomotor, a source of alternating electric currents, and means for connecting said source with said rectifier."

No. 450,652, April 21, 1891. Electric Locomotor. - The object of this invention is to increase the tractive effort of an electric locomotive truck. One end of the motor frame is sleeved upon the axle of one pair of wheels of a four-wheel truck to which the motor is geared; the other end of the frame is supported upon an axle carrying friction wheels serving to couple the driven truck wheels with the remaining pair of truck wheels. As the torque of the motor increases, the friction wheels bear down more heavily upon the driving and driven wheels, thereby insuring greater driving effort to be exerted by the wheels not directly driven by the motor.

No. 550,467, November 26, 1895. Electric Fluid Locomotor. - This is a fluid variable-speed and reversing gear for transmitting the power of a constant-speed driving electric motor to the driving wheels of a locomotor, and permitting the electric motor to be driven always in a given direction and at a constant speed. For this purpose a rotary eccentric-piston fluid pump, driven by a constant-speed electric motor, is included in a closed fluid circuit, containing similar eccentric-piston fluid motors, which, in turn, are connected with the driving wheels of the locomotor. By varying the eccentricity of the fluid pumps and fluid motors any speed and direction is readily obtainable. Other than electric motors may be used as the source of power, and the applications of the invention extend to other uses than driving locomotors, as evidenced, for instance, by the following sample claim: "The combination of a rotary pump driven by any source of power and a hydraulic motor connected to the pump by a liquid circuit and a means for altering the eccentricity of both pump and motor, substantially as described." A system of this general character was employed for running a freight elevator installed in the electric company's works at East Pittsburgh, where it operated successfully for a number of years.

No. 579,526, March 23, 1897. Electropneumatic Locomotive. - This invention was designed to relieve a driving motor from undue strain when starting a load from a state of rest. It provides a reserve source of energy in the form of compressed air, which may be availed of through a compressed-air motor to deliver power to the driving wheels. The compressed-air reservoir may be charged while the train is running by reverse action of the compressed-air motors.

No. 624,277, May 2, 1899. Electropneumatic Controlling System. No. 773,832, November 1, 1904. Controlling System for Electric Motors. No. 773,833, November 1, 1904. Westinghouse and Aspinwall. Controlling System for Electric Motors. - These patents cover the electropneumatic multiple-unit controlling system commonly known as the "drum control," which, with minor changes, is still largely used in electric railway service. The following quotation from the specification of Patent No. 624,277 well serves as a general description of the field of the invention: "My present invention also embodies mechanism actuated by fluid pressure for operating the controller, or each of the controllers, if several are in use; but instead of employing special train pipes and manually operated valves, I propose to supply the fluid pressure from either the brake train pipe or from a main reservoir on the same car with the controller, and to actuate and control the necessary valves by means of an electromagnetic system, the arrangement being such that the corresponding valves of each controller-operating mechanism in service may be simultaneously operated from any selected point on any car in the train, the combination and arrangement being such, moreover, that a single car may be operated with the same facility, the only couplings necessary in addition to those employed in trains controlled by air brakes and heretofore in use being those for the electric conductors, which carry the necessary current for energizing the electromagnets of the system." This patent contains twelve sheets of drawings, illustrating with remarkable care the details of the various mechanical parts of the apparatus; in fact, they are essentially working drawings. The patent is replete with ingenious devices and affords an excellent illustration of the fertility of mind of Westinghouse in devising simple mechanisms for accomplishing complicated interrelated mechanical movements.

No. 645,612, March 20, 1900. Method of Distributing Electrical Energy. - This patent sets forth a comprehensive plan for distributing power for electric railways over considerable distances, the power being supplied from widely separated power plants. To lessen the considerable losses of energy from various causes, it is proposed to supply different portions of the circuit only during the times they are called upon to deliver current. Gas engines are located at numerous sub-stations, these being arranged to be started quickly when required to supplement the power. The gas may be distributed through a main gas-supply line.

STEAM ENGINES

No. 50,759, October 31, 1865. Rotary Steam Engine. - Interesting as the first patent issued to Westinghouse, which was followed by many others related to the same subject. It was a phase of the engineering art that interested him throughout his entire life.

No. 131,380, September 17, 1872. Improvement in Balanced Slide Valves. - Those familiar with the development of steam engine practice are aware of the great interest that has always been taken in counterbalancing the pressure on the distributing valves of the slide type. This is an early contribution by Westinghouse to the subject.

No. 162,782, May 4, 1875. Governor for Steam Engine. - This patent describes a governor for regulating the speed of steam engines in which the valve mechanism for controlling the flow of steam to the engine is actuated by fluid pressure that is controlled by a centrifugal governor. By this method of construction a small amount of centrifugal force, operating through limited motion, is caused to actuate the large valve necessary to control the flow of steam from the boiler to the engine. In a modified form this device was applied to many of the ships of the United States Navy as well as to a large number of merchant vessels, for the purpose of preventing the racing of the engines when the screw propeller was thrown out of water in heavy seas.

No. 455,028, June 30, 1891. Rotary Engine. - This patent is of interest, as containing in the specification a clear statement of the difficulties theretofore encountered in attempting to produce an economical and serviceable rotary engine of the type described, and a proposed remedy. Following the general lines laid down in this patent, but with important variations of detail, Westinghouse produced many working examples of rotary engines with results that would probably have satisfied many less exacting inventors. There is good reason to believe that some of the forms produced could have been commercialized to advantage, but it was only after he became interested in the steam turbine that he felt satisfied with the solution of the rotary-engine problem.

No. 712,626, November 4, 1902. Rotary Engine. - This is one of the early examples, probably the first, of Westinghouse's contribution to the steam-turbine art, although in the patent it is called a rotary engine.

No. 807,003, December 12, 1905. No. 807,145, December 12, 1905. No. 807,146, December 12, 1905. No. 866,171, September 17, 1907. Elastic Fluid Turbine. - This group of patents relates to improvement in steam turbines to correct a difficulty inherent in their construction, particularly in the larger sizes. The following quotation from specification of Patent No. 807,003 sets forth the problem presented for solution. "The stationary elements or stators of elastic-fluid turbines it has been found under certain conditions encountered during operation distort, and in turbines where the clearances between the free ends of the blades and vanes and the stator and rotor are small these distortions are liable to cause trouble. To overcome the troubles incident to stator or rotor distortions has been an object of this invention. The steam, when it reaches the low-pressure end of steam turbines, is more or less saturated with water, and the throwing out of said water radially by the blades, due to centrifugal force, it has been found when using unshrouded blades, causes a pitting or eating away of the stationary element or stator in line with the rows of rotor blades; and a further object of this invention has been to provide in combination with the means for overcoming the troubles due to distortion means for overcoming this pitting or eating away of the stator." The importance of establishing the smallest possible clearance at the ends of the blading, without destructive mechanical contact, is recognized by all turbine engineers as of highest importance in the production of highly efficient machines. This was the purpose sought to be attained by the methods proposed in these patents.

No. 787,485, April 18, 1905. Fluid Pressure Turbine. No. 816,516, March 27, 1906. Fluid Pressure Turbine. No. 935,569, September 28, 1909. Elastic Fluid Turbine. No. 995,508, June 20, 1911. Elastic Fluid Turbine. - This group of patents describes the most important contributions of Westinghouse to the advancement of the turbine art, covering the features of single-double flow and reaction-impulse construction, by means of which the size and speed limits of turbine construction were greatly extended. The specifications of these several patents clearly state the purpose to be accomplished and the methods of doing it.

SIGNALING AND INTERLOCKING

No. 237,149, February 1, 1881. Railway Switch Movement. - Westinghouse's first patent in this art. It is "a part of a pneumatic or hydraulic apparatus," preferably compressed air. Two pistons of different area are connected by a motion plate. There is constant pressure on the smaller piston, which acts to hold the switch "normal," that is, set for the main track. The larger piston, when brought into action, overcomes the smaller and moves the switch to the turnout position. There is provision for locking the switch in either position. This device was modified to use one double-acting piston and cylinder, with means for using power on one side or the other of the piston, and in that form is now much used, notably in the New York subways.

No. 240,628, April 26, 1881. Block-Signaling Apparatus. - A fluid-pressure signal movement, automatically controlled by a track instrument. This combination was never installed in actual service. The patent has historical interest, as showing the general attitude at the time against the use of electric track circuits and electric apparatus for the control of signals, although the Robinson closed track circuit was known. Track conditions were unfavorable and the electric apparatus was not robust. Westinghouse sought simple and rugged means, using a track instrument, or treadle, actuated by passing wheels and, in turn, actuating valves and so setting in motion compressed air and liquid columns. Others used treadles to close contacts and send an electric impulse to the signal mechanism. Both systems were fundamentally unsafe, as a train in block was not acting constantly on the signal control. The closed track circuit eventually came into general use and corrected this defect.

No. 240,629, April 26, 1881. Switch and Signal Apparatus. - An interlocking system commonly known as the "hydropneumatic" system. The first system patent, showing fluid-pressure motors for moving switches and signals, closed hydraulic columns for controlling the motors, compressed-air apparatus for setting in motion the hydraulic columns, and an interlocking machine for manipulating the combination. The basis of a system that was much used between 1882 and 1890; replaced by the electropneumatic system.

No. 245,108, August 2, 1881. Fluid-Pressure Switch and Signal Apparatus. - A fluid-pressure switch motor controlled by an electromagnetic valve. The first appearance of the electromagnetic valve in this art an important step. The valve exactly as shown was never used in practice, but fundamentally the arrangement of valve, . magnet, and control circuits is that used today in electropneumatic switch operation. The provision of contacts for establishing indicating circuits to get indication of operation back to the operator is another feature of modern practice that originated in this patent.

No. 245,592, August 9, 1881. Combined Electric and Fluid Pressure Mechanism. - Possibly the most important patent granted to Westinghouse for a single signal mechanism, as its elements remain substantially unaltered and but little modified in detail in the many devices to which they have been applied during the past thirty-five years. It comprises an electromagnet, a double seated pin valve operated thereby, and a single-acting piston operated by pressure (against gravity) admitted and discharged by the valve. Not alone to signals has this combination been extensively applied, but to automatic train-stopping devices, drawbridge locks, contacting devices of various designs and for various purposes. It is used in the modern electropneumatic train brake and in the thermostatic control of ventilators, heaters, etc. In fact, it is an ideal means for the control of compressed air in almost any service where quick action is demanded of large volumes from remote points by an almost insignificant electrical impulse in diminutive conductors. To this device the E. P. block-signaling and interlocking systems owe their final success.

No. 246,053, August 23, 1881. Interlocking Switch and Signal Apparatus. - An interlocking machine. Supplements No. 240,629, which shows a system in combination. This patent covers specially the interlocking machine used in that system, which is hydropneumatic and soon gave way to the electropneumatic system.

No. 270,867, January 16, 1883. Electric Circuit for Railway Signaling. - An electric track circuit (closed) for single-track working. Controls both opposing and following movements. This patent marked a new era in the method of arranging and controlling automatic signals. Previous to the introduction of this method in practice (at Mingo Junction, Ohio, P. C. C. & St. L. R. R. in about 1883) the custom was to use a single signal at the entrance of each block section and to extend its control over the whole or a part of the next succeeding block section, thus insuring always two signals at "stop" in the rear of trams. This involved delay of trains. The system here shown eliminates this "overlapping" control and uses a separate auxiliary (cautionary or distant) signal located beneath the usual block signal. Thus the "home" or block signal proper governs to the end of its block only, while the "distant" or cautionary signal is controlled from the second block ahead. Separate indications are given the engineman as to conditions of two blocks at all times, and he may "proceed at caution" when only one block immediately ahead is clear.

No. 357,109, February 1, 1887. Electric Interlocking Mechanism for Switches and Signals. - Title misleading as "electric interlocking" has come to mean a system in which the switch and signal motors as well as the control are electric. The title was probably chosen as describing the interlocking machine. This is a fluid-pressure system using hydraulic motors and liquid columns to convey the control from interlocking machine to motors. Compressed-air valves and devices are used to set in motion the liquid columns. The air valves are controlled amongst themselves and from the switches and signals by electric circuits. Much the most comprehensive system of interlocking developed up to that time and it anticipates much in the further development of the art. As modified and improved in detail, it was used for a few years and then abandoned for the electropneumatic system, but disclosed many principles of control which were embodied in the electropneumatic development.

No. 358,519, March 1, 1887. Electropneumatic Interlocking Apparatus. - The first system patent in the electropneumatic art. Certain elements had already been designed and patented, and a system was disclosed in No. 357,109, hydropneumatic. No. 358,519 was never installed, as the hydropneumatic system filled the limited field until another electropneumatic system, simplified and improved, was brought out, four years later.

No. 358,520, March 1, 1887. Electric Fluid-Pressure Engine. - A piston engine to move switches and signals using fluid pressure, preferably compressed air operated by a fluid-pressure slide valve, controlled in turn by an electromagnetic valve. An element in an interlocking system permitting movement of a function from any distance, as power is stored at the place of operation and put in action by an electric impulse from an interlocking machine or track circuit. Fluid pressure is used for the distributing valve, as the stroke is too long to be economically made by an armature, but the control of the valve is within the range of motion of an armature. This patent further discloses the principle of "selection," by which two or more movements are controlled by one lever very important in the art.

No. 358,521, March 1, 1887. Electrically Actuated Fluid-Pressure Motor. - Differs from No. 358,520 in being designed for signals only and the piston is moved one way by gravity. The movement of the valve is, therefore, so short that it can be actuated directly by electricity, eliminating the fluid-pressure valve of No. 358,520. A signal-operating device of great simplicity, durability and efficiency, which has remained substantially unaltered for thirty-five years; possibly the best original adaptation of a conception to existing and future demands and requirements that can be found in any of Westinghouse's signal patents.

No. 358,713, March 1, 1887. Electrically Actuated Fluid Pressure Motor and Circuits Therefor. - An improvement on earlier designs to get greater safety. The movement of a lock in an interlocking machine or of a signal is made to follow the movement of a switch by means of an electric circuit. In this invention the circuit is made or broken not only by the movement of the piston of the switch motor but also by the movement of the valve. Thus the movement of the dependent function (lock or signal) cannot begin until the movement of the switch is begun and also completed. This principle of preliminary locking was familiar in mechanical locking, but was not so thoroughly used before in power interlocking.

No. 360,638, April 5, 1887. Railway Electric Signal Apparatus. - An improvement on No. 270,867, being track-circuit control particularly designed for double track. No. 270,867 was for single track. As here shown, this system was extensively applied on the Pennsylvania Railroad and other important trunk lines of this country. The control shown has also been extensively used on American railways with other types of automatic signals than those shown in the drawings of the patent.

No. 446,159, February 10, 1891. (Jens G. Schreuder, co-inventor.) Switch and Signal Apparatus. - Discloses what is practically the final form of the electropneumatic interlocking machine which Westinghouse had been working at for ten years, in combination with elements that he had developed and patented from time to time. It is his most important patent in this art, being the simplification and synthesis of all that had gone before. It is unusually elegant in detail and is an interesting example of evolution.

No. 1,284,006, November 5, 1918. Automatic Train Control. - This application was filed five months after the death of Westinghouse and the patent was issued to his executors. It was his last patent. The" automatic control of railway trains, to reduce speed or stop a train without the act of the engineer, has long been the subject of invention, but this is the only invention of Westinghouse in that field. The elements of his electropneumatic system had been very successfully combined into automatic train control, in important special cases, by the Union Switch and Signal Company. In this invention Westinghouse undertook a general solution of the problem, and he gave to it deep study and long and costly experimentation with apparatus so designed and built as to be fit for road service. He aimed to stop a train by setting the brakes; to limit its speed; to permit the engineer to throw the automatic apparatus out of service; to record every such manipulation, and to make a continuous record of the speed of the train. The brake application may be either service or emergency, and apparatus may be added to shut off power as well as to apply the brakes.

NATURAL GAS AND FUEL GAS

No. 301,191, July 1, 1884. System for Conveying and Utilizing Gas under Pressure. The first of a series of patents taken out during the development of the natural-gas distribution in the vicinity of Pittsburgh. - The objects of this first invention are: Protection against accidents due to leakage of gas at high pressure; to retain and utilize gas that may leak in transit; and to provide for the delivery of gas at desired points in the line and at determined pressure below that of the gas in the main conducting pipe. The conducting pipe is enclosed in a protecting casing. In this way compartments are formed, and these are charged with gas at low pressure. They receive and retain any leakage from the conducting pipe and have vent pipes and safety valves. A pressure-regulating valve covers the normal delivery of gas from the conducting pipe to the safety compartment. Gas is taken off for consumption by service pipes connecting with this low-pressure compartment.

No. 307,606, November 4, 1884. Well-Drilling Apparatus. - The object is to "facilitate and expedite drilling of wells" by avoiding the delays occasioned by the necessity of intermitting the drilling operation to remove the cuttings and other solid matters from the bore of the well. The invention combines rotary cutting apparatus and a fluid-pressure motor actuating it and means for sustaining and feeding said cutting apparatus and motor. In other words, the motor and pumping apparatus are kept well down in the boring, and the material to be cleared is forced out.

No. 306,566, October 14, 1884. Reissue No. 10,561, February 17, 1885. No. 312,541, February 17, 1885. No. 312,542, February 17, 1885. No. 312,777, February 24, 1885. No. 314,089, March 17, 1885. No. 315,363, April 7, 1885. No. 318,840, May 26, 1885. No. 318,841, May 26, 1885. No. 319,364, June 2, 1885. No. 319,365, June 2, 1885. No. 319,765, June 9, 1885. No. 323,246, July 28, 1885. No. 331,595, December 1, 1885. No. 331,596, December 1, 1885. No. 333,800, January 5, 1886. No. 340,266, April 20, 1886. No. 340,267, April 20, 1886. No. 342,659, May 25, 1886. No. 344,701, June 29, 1886. Detecting and Preventing Leakage. - The importance of preventing and detecting leakage of natural gas as it appeared to the mind of Westinghouse will be indicated by these twenty patents taken out in quick succession. Many serious and alarming accidents occurred in the Pittsburgh district from leakage which, owing to the fact that natural gas is comparatively without odor, was not always detected, and some very serious explosions took place. Westinghouse dwelt upon the fact that economical conveyance of gas over long distances demanded high pressures and large mains, hence unusual difficulties in controlling leaks. One method, shown in the patents, is to enclose the gas main proper in a second pipe, the space between the two being constantly filled with gas at low pressure. (See the first patent of July 1, 1884.) This prevented the entrance of atmospheric air and formation of an explosive mixture. This space was filled by occasional leakage from the high-pressure main, and by gas intentionally admitted into the space through regulating valves. The service pipes were tapped off from this low-pressure gas. Another method that proved effective was to surround the main with broken stone or other loose material, and carry to the surface pipes through which gas, leaking from the main, into this loose material, would be conveyed to the air and its presence easily tested by application of a light. Another precaution shown in a number of these patents had to do with expedients for making effective joints in the gas main and in the connections to the service pipes.

No. 312,543, February 17, 1885. No. 324,905, August 25, 1885. No. 341,295, May 4, 1886. No. 352,382, November 9, 1886. No. 389,032, September 4, 1888. Pressure Regulators and Cut-Off. - A small group of important patents is here shown. The necessity of stepping down the pressure from the main to the point of use is obvious. Another matter, not so obvious, was the necessity of automatically cutting off the flow of gas in case, for any reason, the pressure should fall below a certain fixed point. This is explained in the text. It was also found necessary to regulate the pressure to a degree workable in a proportional meter for measuring the consumption of gas.

No. 318,839, May 26, 1885. Regulator for Gas and Air Supply to Furnaces. - The object is "to obtain a higher degree of effectiveness and economy in the use of gas as a fuel for generating steam by provision of means for automatically regulating the supply of gas and air to a steam-boiler furnace, in accordance with and proportionately to variations in the pressure of steam therein." This device is designed to give automatic regulation.

No. 347,673, August 17, 1886. Proportional Meter. - The object is to measure the quantity of gas as well as the rate of flow. This is done by the combination of two operating valves covering the proportionate delivery of gas from the supply pipe to a meter, the capacity of which is a determined fraction of the total volume, and to a direct delivery outlet, a regulator acting to maintain uniform pressure in the meter and in the direct-delivery passages.

No. 365,454, June 28, 1887. Long-Distance Gas Distribution. - The essential feature of this patent is the use of a main of constantly increasing diameter. "It was the practice before this invention to lay lines of uniform diameter, and when it was desired to increase the quantity of gas to lay an additional line. The pipe used varied from 5 inches to 8 inches in diameter." This necessitates a high pressure throughout. In this invention the size and capacity of the main are increased at successive intervals. The advantage of enlarging the pipe is not only to lessen the average general pressure but also to provide a considerable reservoir capacity and at the same time to greatly accelerate the flow of the gas from the well to points of distribution.

No. 680,827, August 20, 1901. No. 680,828, August 20, 1901. No. 739,367, September 22, 1903. No. 890,951, June 16, 1908. Gas Producers. - These patents have especially to do with the production and use of fuel gas, a matter which for L long time occupied much of the attention of Westinghouse. The first patent is more directly calculated to use in connection with gas engines in order that the products of combustion from the engine itself should supply heat to the producer for the generation of additional gas. The other patents, while embodying the same idea, are devoted mainly to the improvement of the producer.

MISCELLANEOUS PATENTS

No. 61,967, February 12, 1867. Improved Railroad Switch. - The second of Westinghouse's recorded patents and, with No. 76,365, the foundation of his business. This is not properly a switch, but a re-railing frog designed to replace on the rail the wheels of a car or locomotive. A very early example, and possibly the first.

No. 76,365, April 7, 1868, and reissue No. 3,584, August 3, 1869. Improved Railway Frog. - The improvement consists chiefly in the arrangement of a chair under each end of the frog. A feature not claimed in the patent was the reversibility of the frog; that is to say, there were practically two frogs in one structure, so that after it was worn out on one side it could be turned over and used on the other. It was also probably the first steel casting used in railway work, as they were all made of crucible cast steel, and some thousands of them were sold. It was for the purpose of exploiting this particular device that Westinghouse went to Pittsburgh.

No. 223,201, December 30, 1879. No. 223,202, December 30, 1879. No. 224,565, February 17, 1880. Auxiliary Telephone Exchanges. - A very early example of what is now known as "Automatic Telephone Switching" or "Machine Switching." Designed primarily to automatically connect any one of a group of country subscribers through an automatic local exchange to a central exchange, thus saving wire as compared with direct connection from the subscriber to the central exchange. Never put into practical use.

No. 400,420, March 26, 1889. Fluid Meter. - This is a water meter, the object of the invention being to provide a meter in which only a comparatively small percentage of the pressure of the fluid to be measured is required to actuate the measuring devices and in which the movement of the measuring receptacles is continuous and progressive, avoiding the loss of power due to stopping and change of direction. This patent is taken in collaboration with Mr. C. N. Dutton, and is a particularly ingenious device, and has been largely used.

No. 493,881, March 21, 1893. Rotary Water Meter. - This patent is taken in collaboration with Mr. E. Ruud. The purpose is to provide a simpler and cheaper meter than that shown in the patent of Westinghouse and Dutton, No. 400,420.

No. 550,359, November 26, 1895. Exhaust Pumps. - This is for a pump particularly designed to exhaust bulbs of incandescent electric lamps It was made during the development of a lighting system for the Chicago World's Fair of 1893, the patent application having been filed November 26, 1892. It was a part of the general development which enabled the Westinghouse Electric Company to take and perform the contract for the lighting of the Fair.

No. 550,466, November 26, 1895. Rotary Pumping and Motor Apparatus. No. 550,467, November 26, 1895. Electric and Fluid Locomotor. No. 595,007, December 7, 1897. Elevator. - This group of patents is interesting, as they directly resulted from Westinghouse's experimentation in the rotary-engine field. The primary purpose of the invention was to devise a method and mechanism for translating uniform rotative speed into variable speeds. At 'the date of the issue of these patents alternating current motors were not capable of economical speed variation, and it was to overcome this limitation that the inventor developed the inventions shown therein. As already stated, in each case the devices proposed to accomplish the purpose of the invention contained the chief mechanical characteristics of the rotary engine.

No. 708,107, September 2, 1902. Furnace. - In 1895 Mr. James Douglas, an eminent mining engineer, in a paper on the Metallurgy of Copper, said: "A real improvement would be devising an air-jacketed furnace which would not buckle and in which the blast could be raised to a much higher degree than could be done by simply air-jacketing the crucible." This invention of Westinghouse is designed for an air-jacketed smelting furnace that should be robust enough not to be deformed under use, and that should have such large radiating surface as to make air-cooling effective.

No. 1,050,186, January 14, 1913. Dynamometer. - This is a very ingenious dynamometer designed for use in elaborate tests of the efficiency of propellers, which tests were carried on for a considerable time and on an elaborate scale. The object is to measure the power delivered to the propeller, together with which are measured and recorded the longitudinal thrust and the speed of the propeller, and the velocity of the water leaving the propeller.

No. 1,031,759, July 9, 1912. Vehicle-Supporting Device. No. 1,036,043, August 20, 1912. Fluid-Pressure Device. - These patents are for the inventions embodied in the Westinghouse air spring for motor cars, the characteristics of which are widely known.